Nihil Evadere

Nihil Evadere:

*How We Are Created
is How We Create*

*An Empirical Journey to the End of Marxist, Anarchist,
and Ultra-leftist Millenarianism*

Mickey Moosenhauer

Copyright ©Mickey Moosenhauer 2022

All rights reserved.

ISBN: 9798804971428
Imprint: Independently published

All monies received on the sale of this book go to farm animal sanctuaries.

Originally published as
Le Coin de la Carrière,
by Hugo Jacques Jaubert, 1862,
© Éditions Oie Galante.

It is as impossible to build Jerusalem as it is to escape Babylon.

The *flabulbert* is the only actually existing matter. Discovered in 1998 by French physicist, Guy Flabulbert, it is a quadrihexahedral mass in the center of an electron. It is impossible to utilize this matter because not only are electrons without reality, we are too.

Foreword

The writing of books may give one some enjoyment, and after they are done one may, or may not, feel proud of them. But their acceptance, or not, with a readership, is not a source of happiness. I have self-published this through Amazon because I cannot be bothered to crawl to publishers and I just want to see it in book form, as a kind of final written statement. I wrote *The Freedom of Things*, after being asked by *TSI Press* if I'd like to write a book for them, so I did. The main reason I was offered a book contract with them was because I had co-authored the book *Nihilist Communism* which was first produced at a photo-copying shop, at my own expense, in 2003, and then later, the main author, with no participation from myself, was involved in getting it reproduced professionally by *Ardent Press* in 2009. While I am still fond of almost all that is written in *The Freedom of Things*, I am now aware of the stupid millenarian phantasms that underpin the book *Nihilist Communism* (and *where they have led*), and I recommend that anyone who owns a copy immediately throw it away. The pieces in this current book can be read in any order, but I suggest starting with Chapter 7, followed by Chapter 10, then 3, after that, 12, then move to Chapter 6, then 5, followed by 14, 1, and 15, from 15 move to Chapter 4, then 2, then, 16, 9, 8, and 17, then 13, followed by 11. If this is not a suitable arrangement try the ordering of the contents as laid out in the Table of Contents.

Mickey Moosenhauer, April 2022.

Table of Contents

Foreword 6

INTRODUCTION 9

1 Prophecy in the Revolutionary Tradition (including *How Clothes Made Capitalism*) 14

2 Misunderstanding Agamben and Camatte 76

3 Wandering: Camatte, Millenarian Confusion, and the Humans who Escaped his Notice 120

4 Translating and understanding "die *wirkliche* Bewegung" 149

5 What is so Special about Relative Surplus Value? 151

6 The Society of Self-Realization 157

7 The Language and Discourse Trap 172

8 Adani and The Purpose of Education 179

9 From Goodall to Pinker to Bolsonaro 183

10 The Last Humans 192

11 Can We Halt the Complete Colonization of all Humans? 196

12 The Tyranny of The Consciousness-Raisers: Leninism, Anarchism, and Jesus 205

13 Fascism is not a Pathology 212

14 We Dream the Dreams of Capital 220

15 Threskiornis People, Canis People, Diptera People, Bos People… 232

16 Ultra-Left, Post-Left, Anti-Left Marxists… A Twitter Appendix 238

17 Just One More Thing… 277

INTRODUCTION

You can ignore this introduction, or maybe read it later, or last. This is a collection of essays written since the beginning of 2020. They have all been revised and amended. Some of the shorter pieces first appeared in crude form in the journal *CounterPunch*. A couple first appeared on the site *Ill Will Editions*. I was surprised *Ill Will Editions* published these pieces, I think my 'provenance' as a co-author of the book *Nihilist Communism* (which I now disown, amusedly, *in its entirety*) was the key factor, since what I wrote in both articles was actually *against* their core project (some kind of destituent-partisan-insurrectionary-communist-revolution, explicated in a literary fashion following the style of the group *Tiqqun* or *The Invisible Committee*, phrased in the terminology of Giorgio Agamben and Martin Heidegger).

My understanding of things in terms of my own perceptions of the world and our part within it has been an evolving one since the early 1980s, markers along the way have been the book *Nihilist Communism*, then the book *The Freedom of Things* (written under another name), and now this one. I have travelled an arc from youthful alignment with the 'social justice' imperatives of 'the left' through anarchism and ultra-leftism (though my particular ultra-leftism contained harsh critiques of the Leninism at the core of all ultra-leftism), and back to somewhere closer to where I started, but with what I feel to be a clarity of vision that is informed by my experiences and research. I have worked out why 'communist revolution' is impossible and why it 'fails' or is 'counter-productive;' and why it is a millenarian response to life in a State first manifested, or rather recorded, in the phenomenon of Zoroaster. That is, I think I have worked out why we cannot escape or 'overturn' the society we are born into. These are bold claims, and I am sure many will just stop reading now (bad luck if you *bought* the book, but at least your money goes to good causes), but I think, of course, that my insights and observations, especially since they are the result of traveling that specific arc, are worth consideration.

Although I started on this particular leg of my inconsequential journey in 2020 with an early version of the piece *Wandering: Camatte, Millenarian Confusion, and the Humans who Escaped his Notice* (originally titled, *The Gemeinwesen Has Always*

Been Here: An Engagement with the ideas of Jacques Camatte), it was the *Misunderstanding Agamben and Camatte* essay that proved pivotal.

This long essay was essentially written as a response, firstly, to the widely shared belief among, for want of a better word, the 'ultra-left' (but I mean specifically *Ill Will Editions*, the academic, Kieran Aarons, whose perspective forms the bulk of my criticism in the piece, and *Tiqqun/The Invisible Committee*) that Giorgio Agamben's concept of 'destituent potential' or 'power' is somehow a call to 'insurrectionary violence,' and secondly to the 'reverence' for Jacques Camatte that exists alongside the failure to understand what Jacques Camatte actually means by 'leaving this world.' The essay, apart from this, offers insights into various limits and contradictions within the work of both these thinkers, as well as containing a section that explores, in greater depth than was originally done in *The Freedom of Things*, the interpretations around Walter Benjamin's notion of 'divine violence.'

Through this investigation I also concluded that both Agamben and Camatte's *politics* were 'traditionalist' (though Camatte would, no doubt, object to this label for himself, see below) and that their philosophies opened a space for reactionary thinkers to use (the essay is bookended by this claim, but it is not properly explained in the essay, this has been rectified since, but elsewhere, and can be found in other parts of this book). The influence of Martin Heidegger, who stressed that we apparently live in 'destituent times,' is crucial here. The strand within 'Continental Philosophy' that connects in varying degrees to Heidegger is the complaint against 'modernity,' which always, ultimately, I argue, expresses itself as *traditionalism.* Indeed, this traditionalist trait extends back to Nietzsche, includes Jakob Bachofen and his admirer, Walter Benjamin, as well as Ferdinand Tönnies. It is also to be found in Marx, and, alarmingly or not, dependent upon one's investment in Marx, it is possible to equate Marx's 'species-being' with Heidegger's 'being-with.' The elaboration of these interesting connections however, which can be developed through an analysis of 'anti-modernism' and millenarianism, is for another time and another writer.

The 'space' for reactionary support that both Agamben and Camatte have made possible for themselves and within the 'ultra-left' or the 'anti-political' 'left' (please excuse these cumbersome labels) has been demonstrated or revealed by two small events. The first is Agamben's position on the pandemic, which has turned him into the philosopher of the 'anti-vaxxers' and those on the far-right who mobilize and monetize them.[1] The second is Camatte's long association with extreme-right publishers. With his full cooperation Camatte had key texts of his published in the early 1970s by the extreme-right Catholic publisher, *Jaca Book*. And presently his texts are being compiled and translated by the website *Il Covile*, which is a far-right traditionalist and Catholic phenomenon. He has also given a friendly interview to the group *Cercle Marx*,[2] who can be described as reactionary 'red-brown confusionists.'

I had a brief, accidental, involvement with Jacques Camatte and *Il Covile* in 2020, after having been introduced to *Il Covile* by an ultra-leftist acquaintance who had no idea the site was far-right. What ensued was, on the whole, fairly hilarious in its own small way. I did some translating of Camatte's work into English, this was an interesting and enlightening task, and hugely enjoyable, despite the fact that, eventually, Camatte neither liked my translations (he has historically been very harsh on all his translators) nor the article I wrote concerning his notion of *Gemeinwesen* (see *Wandering*). I then heard, from *Ill Will Editions* funnily enough, that *Il Covile* was a far-right site (despite its former connection with *Lotta Continua*, which was all I had been aware of). I investigated, and it was true. I contacted Camatte and he was, of course, fully aware, and told me about his former association with *Jaca Book*, beginning in the early 1970s. It is important to understand, here, that Camatte has absolutely no problem with this, since he views the 'left' and the 'right' as being equally in error (this is the basis of the 'anti-political' stance, but it is interesting that it *does seem to* facilitate, here and elsewhere, strong connections with the right *against* the left) and he does not in any manner try to hide his associations. I also communicated with *Il Covile* concerning my 'discovery' of their 'politics.' After a brief exchange, with both Camatte and *Il Covile*, centering mainly around 'gay marriage' and movements for equality (although the association of *Il Covile* with fascists was enough for me in regard to them) I ceased all communication with both parties, requesting that my name and translations be removed from *Il Covile* (though I think some of my original phrasing, due to the translations becoming part of a group effort after I had ceased helping, still exists in places. Oh well).

---

[1] One of Agamben's strongest American supporters, and a major (and now former) translator of and collaborator with Agamben, Adam Kotsko, has finally (February 2022) attempted to distance himself from Agamben's pandemic writings, and believes that Agamben's stance on the pandemic is the logical outcome of his earlier work, which Kotsko indicates he is now beginning to reassess. See Kotsko's piece "What Happened to Giorgio Agamben?" in *The Slate*, Feb 20, 2022.

[2] See 'Interview with Jacques Camatte (2019)' on the site, *Libcom*.

One of the things that connects Camatte and *Il Covile* is a tendency toward 'traditionalism,' though Camatte would no doubt angrily refute this term and describe his own stance as something like 'an opposition to artificiality.' One of Camatte's key texts in this regard is *Amour ou combinatoire sexuelle*. If one reads this, along with other instances where Camatte writes about 'artificiality' and the role of 'woman' it becomes clear that one of the reasons a far-right Catholic group would like Camatte is because he is against things like gay marriage since it leads to things like artificial insemination and surrogacy. He insists, however, that he is not homophobic by any means ("It's complicated," he says), and one must take him at his word... but what this means in practise, or in the eyes of others who wish to achieve greater equality in our society, is another matter.[3]

Both Camatte and the far-right, then, wish to slow down or reverse certain tendencies within modern society. Camatte's insistence that we should resist all artificiality and begin to, as it were, 'find our place in the world' (or begin to stop "wandering") folds in perfectly with Heidegger's vision[4] (who was disappointed that the Nazi's didn't go far enough) and the traditionalist yearnings of the far-right. But it is important to remind oneself that the complaint against 'modernity' is made by the whole of the Frankfurt school and Michel Foucault, thus feeding into the phenomenon of *Continental Philosophy* as well as into the tendency of the 'ultraleft' that began after WWII with *Socialisme ou Barbarie*, going to Debord and beyond. As I indicate elsewhere in this book, it is now apparent to me that the complaint against 'modernity,' from wherever it emerges, tends to become fodder for ideologues of reaction. Perhaps the contemporary case of Aleksandr Dugin, who has drawn much of his thinking from continental philosophy as well as from Jean Baudrillard and Guy Debord, is a case in point.

> For Guy Debord, 'revolutionary theory' was like an imaginary, but conflicted, friend, always there beside him, but always 'against itself.' He wrote, "Revolutionary theory is now the enemy of all revolutionary theory, and knows it." Eventually, Debord shot himself.

What this means is that we should perhaps reassess our relationship to 'modernity' and the 'revolutionary' or 'traditionalist' impulse. If we want to engage with the world politically then it might be better to follow the Rousseau

---

[3] Like many on the 'anti-political' spectrum, Camatte is effectively against any movement for equality, and this is another way such ideology feeds into far-right discourse.
[4] Of Heidegger, Camatte says: "It's complicated. To see what there is of interest, of importance in Heidegger, you have to really mine his thought to the end, it's complicated." From Interview with Jacques Camatte (2019).

Nihil Evadere

who said that we are stuck in civilization and there is no going back, and the Camus who said that we should rebel but not try to make a revolution.

The title of this book, *Nihil Evadere*, means 'no escape' or 'nothing escapes.' We have, while we live, a hill to climb, always and forever, over, and over

> In later life, philosopher Martin Heidegger regularly entered annual pumpkin competitions in his hometown of Meßkirch. In a 1966 *Der Spiegel* interview, when asked about his Nazi affiliations, he stated that those days were over and now "Only a gourd can save us."

1 Prophecy in the Revolutionary Tradition (including *How Clothes Made Capitalism*)

PART I

The Emergence of Prophecy

We tend to assume that humans began their existence in a state of ignorance of the world, unable to understand what was happening around them, in fear of their lives from predatory animals and natural disasters. These early humans, we are led to imagine, found refuge in caves, and struggled to simply survive. In order to make sense of all these difficult things, we are led to believe, early humans invented a supernatural world, filled with gods and spirits. This cosmology enabled them to put everything in order. Their narratives made sense of what they could not understand. But we are also led to believe that these humans had a desire to escape the misery and poverty of their existence. They were curious, they left their caves, they travelled the world. They invented fire, they invented agriculture, the wheel, and other amazing things that prove to us, we who are apparently more developed and wiser humans, that they had *potential*. Over time, chiefs took control, despots flourished, they turned their primitive spirit world into organized religion, they created temples to worship at, and the priests became all-powerful. But the rise of organized religion was also the rise of rationality, the next step was to go beyond religious ways of organizing the populace and base the organization of people on sound rational, economic, and humanist principles (Aristotle, for example, reportedly wrote 158 State constitutions). And so, *politics* emerged, and the new leaders of society, or its critics, were now more secular than sacred, that is, their 'belief' in a God or Gods became an awareness of how such 'belief' could be used.

But maybe this trope of the ignorant cave-dweller and the long march through superstition to enlightenment and reason is mistaken, and maybe it was *politics* that gave birth to religion? We should always remember that for the vast majority their existence all humans lived on the planet without being organized in a State, or in a hierarchical chiefdom, or in civilization. And we should always remember that today there still exist many peoples around the world who have no contact with whichever State exists around their remote regions.[1] If we believe the trope of the ignorant cave-dweller existing in a fearful world of superstition then we are forced to wonder a few very *imperialist* and racist things about these peoples who still live outside civilization, and who, as Yanomami spokesperson, Davi Kopenawa says, "did not become white people."[2]

Firstly, we should ask ourselves how it is that these peoples have not set up States[3] and become civilized? Are they just *stupid*, or are they just *incredibly* slow? Next, we must ask ourselves how it is that they have not established religion as we know it? Where are their temples, where are their high priests? (And do not confuse the shamanic world of these peoples with *religion*.[4]) Once again, are they just *stupid*, or are they just *slow*?

Secondly, we should question the apperception that *politics* comes after *religion*. For example, one can view Jesus Christ as an expression of political discontent within a Roman occupation, no matter how much he was influenced by Judaic teachings. His rebellion was a response to the objectionable aspects of a particular State power. He was doing politics. In fact, all religions that we know of began as a response to the misery, or dissatisfaction, of living in a State, starting with Zoroastrianism, and ending, most recently, with Marxism. Religion is the offspring of a predictable social discontent — caused by exploitation, poverty, and ennui — *first organized as politics*.

It is no coincidence that the story of the Garden of Eden is about the loss of 'innocence' — 'Adam and Eve' being the peoples who lived prior to their tragic immersion in a State. When States first appeared, as the archaeological evidence

---

[1] See the 'Uncontacted Tribes' section of the *Survival International* website.
[2] Kopenawa, D., *The Falling Sky: Words of a Yanomami Shaman*, by Davi Kopenawa and Bruce Albert, HUP, 2013, p25.
[3] I capitalize the word 'State' following the tradition in political and philosophical writing, now gone, that uses this device to ensure readers know that the word is in reference to a specific political structure, no matter how varied it is/was.
[4] For an extensive exploration of genuine shamanism see Kopenawa, *The Falling Sky*; also, *Cannibal Metaphysics*, by Eduardo Viveiros de Castro, Peter Skafish (trans.), Univocal, 2009/2014. Viveiros de Castro writes: "The shaman I term the 'sacrificer-victim' is the horizontal kind; this particular specialist, as [Stephen] Hugh-Jones observes, is typical of those Amazonian societies having an egalitarian, bellicose ethos. The vertical shaman, on the other hand, is present only in hierarchical, pacific societies, and verges on being a priest figure" p154. Whether it is assumed that a peaceful, hierarchical society, with shamans 'on the verge' of becoming priest figures, is a sign that such societies are becoming 'civilized,' is another matter, but if this is so then they still lag behind 'us' by at least 7000 years.

shows, people became hungrier, they were exploited, they were subject to hierarchy and terror. No wonder they looked back to a receding golden age. The story of the Garden of Eden was based on a real folk memory, but it was taken up and developed by those in power, *by Statist politics*, to warn people that they were in new, inescapable territory, it was their fault, and that if they didn't follow a sound moral code then everything would become much worse. A transcendental rather than immanent supernatural force — God — was now said to be presiding over the house, and he wasn't often pleased. But radicals, who hung onto the *promise* of the Garden of Eden rather than the *threat*, claimed, *for their own political purposes* (freedom and equality), that God didn't like these conditions, which were even being pursued in God's name, and what he really demanded was that all this corruption should be swept away. Thus, they began a political movement that appealed not to true democracy, or communism — as might occur today — but to the true God.

The utopian or millenarian radicals believed, like Jesus did, that heaven was to be established, or re-established, on Earth at some appointed time, and that if people wanted to get there then they should break with their old traditions, their old family-life, and join the prophets of a new future.[5]

Life in an exploitative and hierarchical society naturally generates opposition. We can see it every single day in our personal resentments and observations, even if we suppress these personal aggravations because they make us unhappy, we can see they exist by watching the global news networks. Life in civilization therefore generates thinkers — philosophers, politicians, radicals, political and religious extremists — who try to work out, and write down, how best to endure in such conditions. Some of them decide that we cannot endure and need to change the whole order of things, root and branch, as quickly, and often as ruthlessly, as possible.

A prophet in the strict etymological sense is a person who has the gift of interpreting the will of God. A prophecy, then, is a message from God that is relayed to others by a prophet, it can be a warning that if things don't change then consequences will ensue, or it can be a call to take up arms against the present conditions. In a secular society the label of prophet can be given to anyone who interprets events or signs in such a way that an outcome can be articulated. Therefore, someone who has looked at, for example, the scientific data regarding the current ecological state of the planet and then forecasts a

---

[5] For a thorough exposition, which finds the millenarianism of the distant past repeated in Bolshevism, see Yuri Slezkine, *The House of Government*, PUP, 2017.

possible doomsday scenario, can be called a prophet. Equally, a financial expert who analyses the markets and predicts a boom in the economy could also be called a prophet. It could be said that, for the secular prophet, the 'deity' that is being interpreted and used to justify their predictions is the data of empirical science, or material events. Of course, in order to believe such a prophet one has to also believe that the empirical science referred to, or the actual events, are real and true, just like one had to believe in the particular God referred to by prophets who claimed that He spoke to them. If one listened to the prophet of those who believed in a different God then one would presume, naturally, that it was all just bunkum. Similarly, if a radical of the left listens to a prophet of the right, or vice versa, then each will scoff at the predictions and lamentations of the other. But these 'prophets' of the economy or the climate are not real prophets they are merely people making predictions. A true prophet works out prophecy from a central and sacred authority.[6]

Perhaps the first prophet known to history is Zoroaster from Iran, who lived anywhere between 8000 and 2500 years ago. Despite the vast timespan of when he *might* have been alive Karl Jaspers places him within the narrower timespan of what he has termed the Axial, or pivotal, Age. This was a period of several centuries, after the first civilizations had been established, when there was, as history informs us, a great blossoming of thought that emerged simultaneously from China to the West. It was the era within which scholarly philosophy began, and when the world's religions emerged. Jaspers describes this time as one of flux, when old certainties were being questioned, and when new ones were just coming into being. This pivotal age forms part of his narrative of the purpose of history, and it was introduced to the world in his book of 1949, *The Origin and Goal of History*. It is likely, however, that this was less a time of all-round pleasant philosophical advance across the Middle East, India, China, and the West, and more, as Jaspers' himself indicates, one of serious tumult and revolt.

Zoroaster, for example, was not proposing changes in the way society was organized, he was, as Yuri Slezkine writes, "prophesying the absolute end of the world. There was going to be one final battle between the forces of light and darkness and one last judgement of all human beings who had ever lived — and

---

[6] If one thinks of Marxism, or the theory of the proletariat, as something of a central and sacred authority, then one could claim prophet status. As Jacques Camatte writes: "it is through me that a certain humanity establishes itself. I want to bear witness to this. I am, if you want, like a prophet" 'Extrait de lettre,' 1978, appendix: Origine et fonction de la forme parti (R.I.).

then there would be nothing but an all-encompassing, everlasting perfection: no hunger, no thirst, no disagreement, no childbirth, and no death."[7]

The Christian bible is suffused with prophecy, both in the Hebrew, or Old Testament, of 2500 to 3000 years ago, and in the New Testament. Particularly, there is reference in both to 'the end times.' For the Hebrew bible the end of days will be marked by a regathering of the Jewish diaspora, the coming of a Messiah, and the saving of the righteous. For the New Testament, the end times consist of the second arrival of Christ who, after much earthly turmoil, will defeat the Anti-Christ, and then proclaim the Kingdom of God. For Islam the end times consist of the arrival of the true Messiah (Jesus was only a prophet), the judgement of all, and the resurrection of the righteous. In Hinduism (and Sikhism), the period of strife, discord, and corruption, known as the *Kali Yugi*, that began 3000 years ago, will end in the distant future when Vishnu will arrive on earth to eliminate all the unrighteous.

In Buddhism, there are long cycles of birth and rebirth, good and bad social organization, finally ending simply in the planet's destruction. In Daoism and Confucianism, the universe is viewed as constantly recreating itself and there is no liturgical apocalypse.

The emphasis in these last three schools of thought is on personal redemption through being at one with the world, with Confucianism placing great stress on the need for 'good,' humanist government and social organization.

Buddhism, Daoism, and Confucianism, therefore, sit outside the prophetic millenarian tradition in which all will be judged, and the righteous will be saved, expressed, for example, in Zoroastrianism, Judaism, Christianity, Islam, and Hinduism. *All* these religions and schools of thought reveal, however, that around 3000 years ago, a very great many people decided that they lived in a corrupt and evil world from which they needed either *to escape*, via the intervention of God, or *to correct* as best they could. In Buddhism, Daoism, and Confucianism there is, however, no presence comparable to the *God* (or Hindu/Sikh *Gods*) of the other religions and there is no divine retribution — there is only advice as to how to live well and harmoniously in the world.

We can surmise, then, that the first irruptions of prophecy on a world scale occurred within States and civilizations that had existed for some time. We can also surmise that the prophecies reflected a general, and powerful, discontent

---

[7] Slezkine, ibid., p76.

with things as they were, and we can see that the role of prophecy was intimately linked to millenarianism: the desire for a complete purging of sin in the world and the establishment of peace and harmony.

But perhaps the appearance of prophecy comes right at the beginning of the formation of a State, that is, as soon as people begin to feel that things are not as they should be, or that things could be different? This is the suggestion of the ethnographer Pierre Clastres in his description of the *karai* prophets of the Amazonian *Tupi-Guarani* — who emerged in the middle of the 15th Century, that is, *before* the arrival of the whites. Clastres argues that the phenomenon of the *karai* prophets differs to all other known instances of prophetic movements amongst Indigenous peoples — for example, cargo cults — because it occurred without the pressure of European invasion, which is the sudden arrival of a State. Clastres writes:

> "The combined effect of demographic factors (a strong increase in population), sociological factors (the tendency of the population to concentrate in large villages, rather than to disperse, as is the usual process[8]), political factors (the emergence of powerful chieftains), brought the deadliest of innovations to light in this primitive society: that of social division, that of inequality. Profound malaise, the sign of a serious crisis, stirred these tribes, and it is this malaise that the *karai* became conscious of. They recognized and declared it as the presence of evil and sorrow in society, as the world's ugliness and deception. One might say the prophets, more sensitive than others to the slow transformations taking place around them, were the first to become aware of and to articulate what everyone was feeling more or less confusedly but strongly enough so that the discourse of the *karai* hardly seemed the aberrations of madmen. There was thus profound agreement between the Indians and the prophets who told them: we must find another world."[9]

At the beginning of the 16th Century, according to Clastres, after years of proselytising in the region, the *karai* took more than ten thousand people with them eastwards, towards where the sun rose, to where the Land Without Evil was prophesied to be, and ten years later, unable to traverse the obstacle of the

---

[8] Apart from his own works, for a detailed discussion of Clastres' concept of 'centrifugal society' see *The Freedom of Things: An Ethnology of Control*, P. Harrison, TSI Press, NJ, 2017.
[9] Pierre Clastres, 'Myths and Rites of South American Indians,' in *Archeology of Violence*, P. Clastres, trans. Jeanine Herman, Semiotext(e), LA, 2010, p160.

sea, only three hundred were left alive to limp into recently Spanish occupied Peru.[10]

PART II

Prophecy in The English Revolution

We now jump from early State forms and the beginnings of history to the 17th Century in England, where prophecy came back to the forefront of politics and was democratized.

The historian Christopher Hill informs us that during the early years of the English Revolution, or Civil War (1642-49), "Astrological almanacs sold even better than the Bible."[11] There was a great deal of prophecy going on in 17th Century England: "The English, wrote [Thomas] Fuller [*Church History of Great Britain*, 1655] in the mid-17th Century are said always to carry 'an old prophecy about with them in their pockets, which they can produce at pleasure to promote their designs.'"[12]

> To escape the debts that plagued him most of his life, the philosopher Sir Francis Bacon attempted to acquire patents for various types of cutlery. He was unsuccessful except for the ladle, which he patented in 1613. Unfortunately, it failed to resolve his financial woes.

Hill warns the reader, however, to be wary of judging these people of the 17th with condescension since early scientists such as Francis Bacon, Robert Boyle, and Isaac Newton, all shared this attachment to prophecy. Indeed, across Europe people such as Tycho Brahe, Johannes Kepler, and Galileo were all important astrologers and magi. The Protestant ascendancy, which emerged from the Reformation of the 16th Century, in its study of "the prophetical books of the

---

[10] It is perhaps worthwhile noting that Clastres' insists that his interpretation of "Tupi-Guarani prophecy" contradicts previous interpretations. As he writes: "It is a matter, then, of a native phenomenon which owes nothing to contact with the West, and which, for this very reason, was in no way directed against the whites; it is indeed a matter of native prophecy, for which ethnology has not found a single equivalent anywhere else," ibid., p156.

[11] Hill, C., *The World Turned Upside Down: Radical Ideas During the English Revolution*, Penguin, London, 1975, p89.

[12] Ibid., 90.

Bible" aimed at putting "the science of prophecy on a rational basis." Hill continues by explaining one of the purposes of abandoning what were perceived as the superstitious attributes of Catholicism:

> "The Bible, if properly understood, really would liberate men [sic, et al] from their destiny, from predestination. By understanding and cooperating with God's purposes men believed they could escape from the blind forces which seemed to rule their world, from time itself; they could become free. [...] It was in a *scientific* spirit that scholars approached Biblical prophecy. It was the job of mathematicians and chronologers, like Napier, Brightman, Mede, Ussher and Newton. Such men believed in the possibility of establishing a science of prophecy..."[13]

Indeed, as Bernard Capp writes:

> "As early as 1597 one writer had fixed on 1666 as the date when Antichristian Rome would fall, a prophecy which later found widespread support, and there was general agreement that Christ's coming was imminent. The most important of these writers was John Napier of Merchistoun, the Scottish laird who invented logarithms, who reconciled for the first time all the prophetic numbers and identified all the seals, trumpets, woes and vials [various calculations and signs of God's wrath and imminence]. Napier concluded that Rome and her allies would fall by 1639, and that the world would end about 1688."[14]

Alongside this scientific endeavor was a democratization in interpretations of the Bible, aided by the wide distribution, via the printing press revolution, of the vernacular Bible. In mid-17th Century England there was a proliferation of 'mechanik preachers' — untrained intellectuals who interpreted the Bible in their own way. Indeed, as Hill explains, "The Bible was the accepted source of all true knowledge. Everybody cited its texts to prove an argument, including men like Hobbes and [Gerrard] Winstanley, who *illustrated* from the Bible conclusions at which they had arrived by rational means."[15]

All these people — from astrologer scientists, philosophers, and celebrated theologians to itinerant lay preachers, to Levellers, Ranters, and Diggers — were

---

[13] Ibid., 92. Original emphasis.
[14] Capp, B., *The Fifth Monarchy Men: A Study in 17th Century English Millenarianism*, Faber, 1971, p15 (this is a digital copy and the pages may not be aligned to the print version properly, so page numbers are approximate).
[15] Ibid., 94. Original emphasis.

grappling intellectually with the momentous events that were affecting the whole of society, by which I mean, the establishment of a new economy amidst the precarity of the old order. Winstanley observed that "the old world... is running up like parchment in the fire."[16] They sought answers and solutions to what was strongly felt as an apocalyptic[17] crisis, and they perceived that in this chaos there was the opportunity to achieve a better world.

Prophecy, based on the direct word of God, or the interpretation of the Bible, was their way of pointing to a way forward, but with *authority*.

It is worth reading Capp's condensed history of what might appear to us as either the liveliness or craziness of those times, but which should also be considered as an expression of the wide dissemination of revolutionary ideas:

> "One development in the civil war period was the emergence of a large number of prophets in the tradition of Hacket (a malt-maker who declared in 1591 that Christ had returned in him, and that he was to become the king of Europe, and then led a multitude through London supporting his cause, before being detained and executed). In 1644, for example, a laborer named Rowland Bateman claimed to be both the Son of God and Abraham, and said that the king was his son Isaac. He announced that he must be hanged, and would rise again on the third day, and that the millennium would begin in nine years' time. Despite the confusion of his ideas, there were fears about the 'many severall sorts of People that hourly flocke unto him.' Nicholas Nelson was sent to the Gatehouse in 1647, after saying 'he is the Lord's Anointed for this Kingdom, to lead them that are the Lord's as Moses led the Israelites out of Egypt; and that the King is a murderer.' Rhys or 'Arise' Evans, a Welsh tailor who had been a self-appointed prophet since the 1630s, stood up in St. Botolph's, Bishopgate, in 1647 and proclaimed that he was Christ. For a time he belonged to Chamberlen's Fifth Monarchist congregation, but later became a royalist propagandist. Several women claimed to be with child by the Holy Ghost, and that their child would be the Messiah. John Robins, a Ranter, claimed to be God the Father, and found a number of disciples. A sect arose at Andover in 1649 led by a rope-maker named William Franklin, who had deserted his wife to live with Mary Gadbury, who sold pins and

---

[16] Ibid., 14.

[17] It is worth remembering that the word 'apocalypse' comes from the Greek, *apokálupsis*, meaning 'revelation,' or 'uncovering.' An apocalypse, therefore, is not just an ending of things in a great tumult, it is the opening of peoples' eyes, and an instauration of peace and harmony for the elect. *The Book of Revelation* in the Bible is an apocalyptic work and is also known as *The Apocalypse of John*.

laces and was accused of keeping a brothel. They moved to Hampshire (the land of Ham, Psalm cv.23), and Franklin announced that he was Christ and about to establish the millennium. His 'very plausible' tongue won many converts, including a local minister. His followers also claimed to have visions, and ascribed to themselves such roles as John the Baptist, the two witnesses and the angels who were to destroy God's enemies, among whom were listed several unpopular local figures. Franklin was arrested and recanted in 1650, when his sect already numbered five or six hundred. George Foster, claiming to be the voice of God, declared that the chosen people of all lands would gather in Jerusalem to inaugurate the millennium. Lodowick Muggleton, claiming that he and his friend John Reeve were the two witnesses, founded a sect which lasted for several centuries. The London goldsmith, Thomas Tany, claimed descent from Henry VII and Aaron, High Priest of the Jews, demanded the crowns of England, France, Naples, Rome and Jerusalem, and proclaimed that he was to lead the Jews back to Israel. In 1655, inspired by a vision to kill all members of Parliament, he attacked the house single-handedly, wearing an ancient costume and armed with a rusty sword. The doorkeeper was wounded and Tany was sent to prison."[18]

We should remember that however these aspirations were expressed, they were aspirations to create a world without evil. They were millenarian aspirations. They also received widespread support, and were regarded as rational, even if the most extreme actions were punished by the authorities. Remember that the culmination of all this was the beheading of King Charles I, who claimed to the end, following the notion of 'the divine right of kings,' that he was appointed by God.

Tabor and Münster

To understand how these millenarian aspirations might play out if they achieved certain degrees of success it is worth looking, for example, at the Taborite revolution, in Bohemia, which lasted for perhaps three decades from 1420, or the Münster rebellion of 1534-35. The events in and around Tabor are detailed by Norman Cohn (*The Pursuit of the Millennium*),[19] which when compared to the complex twists and turns of the Russian Revolution appear remarkably similar. It is also possible that Tabor, at certain points, may have gone further than Russia did in facilitating a flowering of egalitarianism, indicating that, in

---

[18] Ibid., 26.
[19] Norman Cohn, *The Pursuit of the Millennium*, OUP, 1970. See Chapter 11.

certain respects, and at certain times, there was to be found there more anarchism than 'Leninism.'[20]

But here I focus on Münster. In early 1534, the Anabaptists — a movement emerging with the radical and apocalyptic preaching of the Zwickau Prophets and Thomas Müntzer — seized control of the German city of Münster. Most of the Lutherans, who were seen as appeasers of the old order, fled the city, and messages were sent out for supporters of the Anabaptists to come to Münster, the New Jerusalem; and they were encouraged to bring weapons. When the Dutch prophet, Jan Matthys, arrived in the city he soon gained authority. He argued that the remaining Lutherans and Roman Catholics who would not submit to rebaptism should be executed, but after it was observed that this might bring down an immediate retribution from external forces, they were only driven out. The city was now solely occupied by the elect, the Children of God, and, as Cohn writes: "These people, who addressed one another as 'Brother' and 'Sister,' believed that they would be able to live without sin, in a community bound by love alone."

Matthys had a clear vision of how to redistribute the wealth and forge social equality. First, he took all the properties of those who had left the city and put it into stores to be available to the poor. Then he ordered that there must be no private ownership of money or anything that could be used as money. Artisans were paid for their services in kind, and most probably by Matthys' government. Property ownership was deemed immoral and all houses had to leave their doors open so that they could be used communally. Food was a communal resource, in fact, all goods were held in common, under the watchful eyes of Matthys and his seven deacons.[21]

---

[20] See Murray Bookchin, *The Ecology of Freedom*, Cheshire Books, Palo Alto, 1982. The anarchist Bookchin, quotes Kenneth Rexroth, anarchist and poet: "Tabor was never able to balance its popular communism of consumption with an organized and planned communism of production, nor the exchange of goods between city communes and peasant communes," p203. Of course, the Bolsheviks solved the problem of exchange between city and countryside by forced collectivisation and the starvation of the peasantry. The Bolsheviks could be seen, in this context, to have erred, as it were, on the side of 'planned communism of production.'

[21] These reforms took place while Munster was under siege but, as Cohn insists: "it is certainly mistaken to suggest — as has sometimes been done — that 'communism' at Munster amounted to no more than requisitioning to meet the needs of war." Page 323. Also note, most of the historical information presented here is from Cohn.

Nihil Evadere

A pamphlet was sent out to other Anabaptist towns in the region holding up Münster as a model:

> "Everything which has served the purposes of self-seeking and private property, such as buying and selling, working for money, taking interest and practising usury — even at the expense of unbelievers — or eating and drinking the sweat of the poor (that is, making one's own people and fellow-creatures work so that one can grow fat) and indeed everything which offends against love — all such things are abolished amongst us by the power of love and community."[22]

After Matthys recklessly went out of the city to attack the opposition and was killed, it was left to the prophet Jan Bockelson to continue the good work. He introduced polygamy, which was first resisted by an armed uprising that failed, leading to the execution of fifty persons. Anyone who criticized anything done or said by the leaders of the rebellion was now executed. Eventually, after another successful repulsion of an enemy attack, directed by Bockelson, he was declared King of the New Jerusalem. Bockelson now proceeded to ennoble himself completely and dressed and behaved like an actual King. He explained that the luxury he surrounded himself with, which was denied to those outside his inner circle, and which appeared to contradict the communism he had espoused, was *nothing* to him and, indeed, they too would soon find themselves languishing in such ornate luxury.

We are all products of our era and our environment. 'Extraordinary' people, like the rest of us, do not come to us as if from another planet, they are socially constructed. Some people might reduce the characters of Matthys and Bockelson to images of 'fanaticism' or simple power-hungry greed, but such reductions — all honest historians will caution — serve only to distort a wider reality. In fact, the progress of the Terror that they inflicted upon the populace that allowed them to assume control can easily be compared to the rational Terrors initiated by Robespierre and then the Bolsheviks (persons constructed in a similar way, in not dissimilar environments). And one may be tempted, perhaps not wrongly, to see Lenin as a return of Matthys, and Bockelson as a prefiguring of Stalin.[23]

---

[22] Ibid., 323-24.
[23] For a compelling character analysis of Lenin as a person in no way betrayed by Stalin, see chapters 22-24 in *Everything Flows*, Vasily Grossman, Vintage Books, 2011.

Dividing Lines

In remembering that these extraordinary people, these prophets, did not come from another planet and were products of their time and social environment we are forced to consider the actual circumstances of their appearance. The first wave of prophets I have discussed emerged in what has been described by Karl Jaspers as the axial, or pivotal, age — a time well after the establishment of the first States and civilizations. One may, as Jaspers tends to, see this period as one of a flourishing of human thought in line with notions of the spiritual and intellectual evolution of Homo sapiens. He writes:

> "An axis of world history, if such a thing exists, [...] would be situated at the point in history which gave birth to everything which, since then, man [sic, et al] has been able to be, the point most overwhelmingly fruitful in fashioning humanity; its character would have to be, if not empirically cogent and evident, yet so convincing to empirical insight as to give rise to a common frame of historical self-comprehension of all peoples — for the West, for Asia, and for all men on earth, without regard to particular articles of faith. It would seem that this axis of history is to be found in the period around 500 B.C., in the spiritual process that occurred between 800 and 200 B.C. It is there that we meet with the most deep-cut dividing line in history. Man, as we know him today, came into being. For short we may style this the Axial Period."[24]

While the pinpointing of this 'event' as being around 2500 years ago may now be viewed as perhaps a little too specific, or even late, it does still resonate with a generally accepted view of history — there was indeed a span of relatively short time in which the religions and philosophies we know today came into existence. Jaspers was especially intrigued by the phenomenon of this dividing line because it seemed to occur simultaneously *and* independently across three separate civilizations. But perhaps these civilizations were not as separate as he thought. More recent histories of the ancient past, even for during medieval European times, tend to reveal much greater interaction between peoples over vast geographical areas than has been documented previously. While, for example, fifty years ago it was taken for granted in Western discourse that there was not that much movement between peoples across the world, today there is a growing recognition that there was. And while Jaspers does tend to see the Axial Period more as something of an event in human evolution, or

---

[24] Karl Jaspers, *The Origin and Goal of History*, Michael Bullock (trans.), Yale University Press, 1965 (1949), p1.

consciousness, he does also note that the period was also one of historical flux. He writes:

> "Corresponding to this new *spiritual* world, we find a sociological situation showing analogies in all three regions. There were a multitude of small States and cities, a struggle of all against all, which to begin with nevertheless permitted an astonishing prosperity, an unfolding of vigor and wealth. [But] what began as freedom of motion soon became anarchy. When the age lost its creativeness, a process of dogmatic fixation and levelling-down took place in all these cultural realms. Out of a disorder that was growing intolerable arose a striving after new ties, through the re-establishment of enduring conditions... Mighty empires, made great by conquest, arose almost simultaneously in China (Tsin Shi hwang-ti), in India (Maurya dynasty) and in the West (the Hellenistic empires and the *Imperium Romanum*)."[25]

How similar is the upheaval outlined above to the circumstances that generated the English Civil War, the colonization of the Americas, the Industrial Revolution, and the rise of the modern empires? I would argue that they are very similar indeed.

The Watershed of The Industrial Revolution and How Clothes Made Capitalism

Whatever the possible limitations of Jaspers' definition of an Axial Age are, I think that there was a definitive 'dividing line' in the history of civilization in this period. This dividing line can be compared to the line that divided what is known as *pre-history* from *history*, that is the emergence of the State, first identified in the emergence of the civilization known as Mesopotamia. It can also be compared to the dividing line that is dramatically represented by the Industrial Revolution.

Yet these dividing lines are often obscured by historians. Jaspers may have helped facilitate this with his emphasis on the notion that the Axial Age was a phenomenon located in the development of human consciousness, or spirituality, thereby making it seem like part of an almost inevitable evolutionary process. But we should be wary of any narrative tending to indicate that 'history' expresses some kind of progress or growth in *the qualities* of the human being. We have only to consider the continued, precarious existence of peoples who

---

[25] Ibid., 4-5.

have avoided the State and civilization right up until this moment, to discover a destabilization of this idea. (Indeed, the neglect of any serious consideration of these peoples in any history of civilization amounts, perhaps unconsciously, to what might now be regarded as a colonial and racist ethos.)

The historian Kenneth Pomeranz, writing in 1998, warns us of this tendency in perspectives concerning the Industrial Revolution: "In some recent treatments, industrialization itself disappears as a turning point, subsumed into centuries of undifferentiated [European] 'growth.'"[26]

So, if the Industrial Revolution was not imported to earth by aliens, and it was not the culmination of millennia of human biological development, what were the factors that generated this explosion of technology?

Ellen Meiksins Wood, in *The Origin of Capitalism: A Longer View*, offers a version of the background to this explosion that is based on detailed study of what is often referred to as 'the transition from Feudalism to Capitalism.' This is a topic that once produced mountains of complex literature, particularly from Marxist or Marxist-influenced perspectives, because it sought to understand the origins of the present global society we inhabit — a society that is clearly quite different to all previous hierarchical and exploitative societies, or economies, of the past. Wood writes:

> "The critical factor in the divergence of capitalism from all other forms of 'commercial society' was the development of certain social property relations that generated market imperatives and capitalist 'laws of motion,' which imposed themselves on production. The great non-capitalist commercial powers had producing classes and especially peasants who remained in possession of their means of subsistence, and land in particular. They were ruled and exploited by dominant classes and states that relied on 'extra-economic' appropriation or 'politically constituted property' of various kinds. The great civilizations were not systematically subjected to the pressures of competitive production and profit-maximisation, the compulsion to reinvest surpluses, and the relentless need to improve labor-productivity associated with capitalism."[27]

---

[26] Kenneth Pomeranz, *The Great Divergence: China, Europe, and the Making of the Modern World Economy*, PUP, NJ, 2000, p5.
[27] Ellen Meiksins Wood, *The Origin of Capitalism*, Verso, 2002, pp75-76.

Wood suggests that it was a combination of factors affecting the agrarian situation in England, which then led to particular developments there, that established the capitalist mode of production — that is, the particular economic system that introduced the 'relentless' and 'compulsive' practices of 'competitive production,' 'reinvesting surpluses' and 'improving labor-productivity.' What she is talking about, but doesn't name it, is what Marx referred to as the acquisition of *'relative* surplus value.'

The conscious generation of this value is the key underlying feature of the capitalist economic system.[28] The extraction of surplus value based on simply making people work harder and longer but for less remuneration, termed *'absolute* surplus value,' comes up against predictable limits. As does the continual expansion of one's landholdings. But development in social organization and technology — driven by the rational goal of increased profit via the introduction of mechanics and organizational techniques that increase productivity — is only constrained by a lack of imagination. The social organization and astonishing technology we see in the world around us is less the invention of particularly clever people who have been particularly well-trained, and more the product of the imperative to increase *relative surplus value*, the particularly capitalist way of increasing profits. By the time a figure such as James Watts appeared on the European landscape the new economic model, the acquisition of relative surplus value, had become the form and the motor of social life.

The sustained achievement of relative surplus value relies on an array of social and technological devices forming a cohesive social whole. These include the displacement of workers from their rural roots; their relative impoverishment; discipline; a new work ethic; enhanced social control; the assignment of workers to particular tasks in the creation of products (given perfect expression in the assembly line); the building of component-making machines that require increasingly less supervision as they are improved and refined; and the establishment of efficient supply and distribution chains. Everything in society now only achieves substance, and even reality, if it passes through the market. This includes people. People are now freed from all ties: the vast majority can only survive by purchasing essential items from a market and placing themselves within the market as labor to be hired, bought, or sold. But, as Wood stresses, the new economic model has a relentless and dizzying internal dynamic of

---

[28] See, for example, Karl Marx, *Capital, A Critique of Political Economy, Volume I*, Ben Fowkes (trans.), Penguin Books, London, 1976, pp431-432 and 975-978. Also, Ernest Mandel, *Introduction*, in the same volume, pp32-35.

competition in which the social organization and technology that assists or controls labor must be persistently improved upon, or revolutionized, if one wants to remain a serious player in the game.

What was particular to England around four hundred years ago, Wood argues, was the gradual transformation of rural labor from one in which that labor had traditional 'rights' to land, to one in which they had none. Entrepreneurs of the land, the big landholders, were concerned to 'improve' the land in a variety of ways, from improving farming techniques, to sequestering or 'enclosing' what were once common lands. The most famous and dramatic example of enclosure is the phenomenon of the Highland Clearances. A labor force being divorced from its subsistence-rights connection to the land was in the process of being established prior to the English Revolution. This was creating a large and mobile workforce that could be utilized in any entrepreneurial activity, it also created a population that relied on markets to survive, thereby further stimulating commodity production — where else would one obtain food and clothes?

Wood writes: "The first major wave of socially disruptive enclosure occurred in the sixteenth century, when larger landowners sought to drive commoners off lands that could be profitably put to use as pasture for increasingly lucrative sheep farming."

"Enclosure," Wood adds, "surfaced as a major grievance in the English Civil War."[29]

The Wolf in Sheep's Clothing

But there is something else missing (apart from the misrecognition of the importance of the extraction of relative surplus value) in Wood's account, even though it is mentioned: sheep farming. If we consider why sheep farming became such a driver of capitalist development in England, then we can perhaps discern an earlier point of divergence that ended with our present-day economy and society.

My contention is that the capitalism we know today, although forms of it existed in isolation in several historical periods (as Marx and others note), came about through innovations within the woollen-weaving industry of the Netherlands and Belgium. Due to flooding and overpopulation in Flanders in

---

[29] Ibid., 108-9.

the 12th Century a great number of Flemish weavers and other artisans migrated to England. So many, in fact, that King Henry I moved a large portion of them to Pembrokeshire in Wales, where these new Flemish/English migrants created an English cultural and language domain inside Wales that exists to this day. Meanwhile back in the Netherlands the industry of weaving was being transformed by the dynamics of a trading relationship between Antwerp and Lisbon, and the rise of Protestantism.

Historian Jairus Banaji writes:

> "The great centers of modern capitalism were Lisbon and Antwerp. [As Alberto da] Viega-Simoes wrote: "the whole of the new commercial life and even the capitalist system stem fundamentally from Portuguese economic policy at the end of the 14th and beginning of the 15th centuries."

Banaji continues:

> "By the time Dom João II ascended the throne in 1481, Portugal was Europe's first colonial power, the 'driving force of a capitalist revolution' [Manuel Nunes Dias] of far flung trading establishments (*feitorias*, 'factories') buttressed by military fortresses."[30]

The Portuguese transferred the focus of international wealth creation from the Mediterranean, where it was dominated by the Venetian republic and Islamic trade centers, to the African and South American coasts of the Atlantic, where gold, spices, sugar, and slaves could be resourced. And, in the first half of the 16th Century, Antwerp became the richest city in Europe because all international trade, from gold to pepper — and that significant item, cloth — was now processed through the city.

In the latter half of the 16th Century there was a second wave of Dutch migrants to England. These were predominantly Calvinists — radical Protestants — escaping persecution. They arrived mainly in the city of Norwich, where a short while previously Queen Elizabeth I had invited 30 skilled Dutch textile masters to set up homes and businesses in order to revive the flagging economy. In England, Calvinism became Puritanism. Oliver Cromwell was a Puritan.

---

[30] Jairus Banaji, *Theory as History: Essays on Modes of Production and Exploitation*, Haymarket Books, Chicago, 2011 pp253-4.

As one becomes more aware of the vast topology of the early history of capitalism it is easy to become overwhelmed. The interest of the investigation, however, lies not in an immense assembling of facts, but in the perspective one employs or develops as to *what it is to be 'human.'*

Max Weber's book, *The Protestant Ethic and The Spirit of Capitalism*, puts the notions of Calvinism/Puritanism at the heart of the capitalist ethos and enables us to begin to understand our own inner drives and impulses (we are socially constructed persons; our society is capitalist). But the temptation to think that capitalism was the result of a Calvinist work ethic is, however, to abandon a materialist view of history. It is to begin to deny that humans are socially constructed beings, or that history is the product of chance combinations and oppositions, and to affirm that history is the narrative of human spiritual progression — a tale in which, though there may be some horrible setbacks along the way — humans are advancing in their consciousness. This is where the progressivist and civilizational advocacies and presumptions of thinkers as various as Hobbes, Hegel, Jaspers, Pinker, and even Marx, meet. (Recently, of course, the 'elephant in the room' of technological progress and 'human advance' — ecological collapse — has suddenly made itself very evident.)

So, we can, in broad terms, and for example, decide to think that capitalism was the result of a philosophy of work and life developed by Protestants, or we can decide that the 'Protestant Work Ethic' came into being because of how people were already living. Remember that Wood defines capitalism as a relentless competition in which the imperative to improve production is paramount. Did the Calvinists, *et al*, come to the view that their labors should be like this, or did they *justify* why their labors were like this after the event? Their philosophy, remember, was that labor, for both the entrepreneur and the workers they supervized, was 'a calling.' They gave a rational and religious framework to the acquisition of relative surplus value, and they let the workers beneath them know that this was just what God wanted? Or, did they have all these ideas and then create an economic system to accommodate and promote them?

To resolve this one must choose one's historical perspective and one must choose how one views human beings. Are we products of our environment, even though that environment is built by humans who do not know what they do in ultimate or 'historical' terms — Marx said: 'people make history, but not of their own choosing'[31] — or does our soul, our spirit, our mind, our consciousness — collectively and individually — mean that we are, as *consciousnesses*, effectively, from another planet, and therefore able to import ideas that have no earthly cause? Or perhaps we are like little gods with a plan all worked out, even if that plan resides only in the 'unconscious' 'spirit' of our species? It is because of this question, and how our answers to this question shape our actions and perspectives, that research into how capitalism began is interesting.

Another reason capitalism is often hard to define is because it is physically expressed in so many ways: capitalism is alienation from one's own labor; it is private, corporate, or State, ownership of the means of production; it is waged-labor; a money economy; general alienation; consumer society; commodity production; supply and demand; and so on. But these factors can all be found in exploitative — economic — societies of the past that are not quite the same as ours. The difference with our society is that it is driven by the continual *re-investment in economic processes* in order to make them more efficient.

Whenever we say the word 'capitalism' we should think of it as 'capital-*ism*' — that is, not as a noun or adjective but as a verb — or as 'capital-*ising*.' Having, or owning, capital means one intentionally builds funds for making investments in the development of industry. Capital is not just money under the bed, it is profit that is specifically to be used to go back into the further production of wealth. Capital-ism is the process whereby profits are used to generate even greater profits by investing in improved production methods, it is a conscious process in which *money is not left idle*.

The Calvinists and the Puritans, those formulators of the work ethic that dominates us — which is *written into us* — were so eloquent and so 'correct' because not only was their new ethos about the 'proper' use a human should make of their life, it also encompassed all material objects, the entire universe — it told us what we already knew about the world, because we lived it every moment. Money is nothing unless it is made to work; the forests are nothing unless they are made to work; the seas and the air and space are nothing unless they are made to work. All those people who lived outside civilization, enjoying the adventures of living, were *nothing* until they were made to work by their colonial saviors. (There are a few, of course, still holding out against civilization around the world, but their existences are perilously threatened.)

---

[31] The full quote is this: "People make their own history, but they do not make it freely, and not in circumstances of their choosing, but under circumstances that are proximate, pre-existing, and handed-down" from Der achtzehnte Brumaire des Louis Bonaparte I, 1852 (*The 18th Brumaire of Louis Bonaparte*) at *mlwerke* online. My translation.

But to return to my own assembly of facts... Before the Portuguese set sail there was the woollen-weaving industry. It was in this industry — which began with entrepreneurs and merchants buying cloth woven by individual rural weavers to sell at a market — that capitalism took hold on our reality. The merchants began to realize that they could increase their profits by supplying the weavers with more wool than the weavers could procure themselves from their own livestock. This became known as the 'putting-out system,' whereby entrepreneurs 'put out' material to weavers. It soon became apparent that the entrepreneurs could improve things for themselves further by ensuring that the handlooms were efficient, or more efficient. Successful handloom weavers were then inspired to engage other artisans in a hierarchical relationship.

These entrepreneurs began to see that the whole process — from original resource to sale at a market — was *one* process and that the more control of it one had the better, but the problem was that all the parts of the process were disconnected and the entrepreneurs could not simply buy *everything*: they couldn't buy all the lands the sheep were on, all the sheep that were on the lands, the weavers and their machines, the means of conveying materials to workers and then to markets, etc. They had to operate, negotiate, make deals, in all sorts of different environments and locations. Therefore, people of all sorts began to be drawn into one system, in which the role of each became increasingly essential to the 'success' of all.

Perhaps at first, as Max Weber indicates, the capitalist process of 'putting-out' — which was marked by a continual re-investment of resources to be sold on or hired out — was originally fairly 'leisurely.' But then dramatic changes, as Weber writes, began to occur:

> "What happened was [...] often no more than this: some young man from one of the putting-out families went out into the country, carefully chose weavers for his employ, greatly increased the rigor of his supervision of their work, and thus turned them from peasants into laborers. On the other hand, he would begin to change his marketing methods by, so far as possible, going directly to the final consumer, would take the details into his own hands, would personally solicit customers, visiting them every year, and above all would adapt the quality of the product directly to their needs and wishes. At the same time he began to introduce the principle of low prices and large turnover. There was repeated what everywhere and always is the result of

such a process of rationalization: those who would not follow suit had to go out of business."[32]

Such a change in how things were done — in which smarter working and clever thinking gave greater rewards — encouraged the rise of an ethos such as Calvinism, and particularly Puritanism: in which work was to be viewed as a holy calling.

And now the game was afoot. The new wealth of these industrious families enabled their children to study the sciences and this pursuit of knowledge was repaid handsomely in the refining of processes and the invention of new machinery. The young of the newly affluent class had time on their hands, but more than this, they had grown up in the atmosphere of 'improvement,' they were brought up to believe that work was a blessing and that profits had to be re-invested in order to maintain wealth, and so they directed their efforts in this way. The families of the old noble classes saw that the new fashion for work and invention was unstoppable, and those that were clever made sure they got onto the right side of history. In England — the place that became 'the workshop of the world' — they evicted the peasants and covered the rolling landscape with sheep.

And so, the captains who sailed from Portugal were already of a capitalist mindset, and there was now to be a maelstrom of factors leading inexorably to space travel and the silicon chip. Woollen weaving was improved with the flying shuttle, then spinning machines. Wool, though still very important, as the woollen industry in Australia proved, was now superseded by cotton produced by African slaves in America. The wealth of England, which was directed (reinvested) into the emergence of what became known as the Industrial Revolution, was built on wool, then slaves, sugar, and cotton.

These commodities were the key components in the creation of what we refer to as the modern world. But at their base, at their origin — that is, what made these commodities so historically powerful — was the principle of acquiring 'relative surplus value,' which can only be acquired by the clever and ruthless use of human beings. And since wool, and then cotton, are so key to this narrative one could say that it was clothing that made capitalism, and that it is the historical development of the production of clothing that shapes the way we think.

---

[32] Max Weber, *The Protestant Ethic and The Spirit of Capitalism*, (1905), Talcott Parsons (trans.), Dover, NY, 2003. Pages 67-68.

PART III

Prophecy Reborn

Now we must take leave of this digression (because I am in charge here) and return to the question of prophecy. The momentous events of the French Revolution of 1789, the first time non-religious revolutionaries had seized State power, led many to consider that a total revolution, based entirely on rational, *Radical Enlightenment*,[33] principles and without reference or obeisance to God, was now a possibility for the future.

The new materialist universe of *thinking*, generated by the new economic situation of capitalism, originally, perhaps, set out by Baruch Spinoza, gained ground across the world of philosophy and was epitomized and completed in the works of Karl Marx.

Industrial capitalism in Europe created great oppositions and great misery along with great wealth and 'progress.' People realized, a little too late, as must always be the case (since our consciousness of the world cannot precede the world), that they were at the culmination of the kind of flux that Jaspers had described for another period as *the Axial Age*. For they now lived just past the Axial Age and in the era of the new "mighty empires." But still, apocalyptic sentiments and prophecies were again being forged amidst the increasingly rapid pace of change, revealed by iron, steam power, and William Blake's 'dark Satanic mills.'

As I have described above, the prophets of a new world at the time of the Axial Age or at the time of the English Revolution lent authority to their predictions and warnings by an interpretation of the word of God, whether it was through the Bible, or by direct communication. It is also useful to recall that the notions of apocalypse and final redemption are especially particular to those societies that had established a religion with one God, that is, the Abrahamic religions. Hinduism and Sikhism do have apocalyptic prophecy in their liturgy, but they have several deities and, for example, many avatars for Vishnu, and an emphasis on time as cyclical. The Abrahamic religions posit a linear time that leads to a

---

[33] For an exploration of the radical wing of the Enlightenment, and how Spinoza is connected to Marx, see Jonathan Israel, *Radical Enlightenment: Philosophy and the Making of Modernity 1650-1750*, Oxford University Press, 2001.

definite and socially cataclysmic end — this endpoint resulting in a heavenly timelessness for those who will be saved.

After the establishment of the empirical method in science and the resistance to all things that relied for their existence on faith alone — that is, all things supernatural — a strange new God was ironically born to the descendants of the Abrahamic religions in Europe: materialism. And for Marx the sacred center of his theory became materialism *and* the proletariat.

In the broad spectrum of the Left there is a much-misunderstood phrase from Marx: "Philosophers have hitherto only *interpreted* the world in various ways; the point is to *change* it." This was never meant to be a simple urging of philosophers to get off their backsides and do something useful for the cause. After his engagement with Feuerbach's work Marx decided that philosophers should abandon the world of 'universal absolutes' and 'Idealism' and work within the social and environmental processes that were *actually in existence*. If they did this, Marx believed, they would no longer be 'idle philosophers,' they would become *scientists*. This is why Isaiah Berlin considered him "the true father of modern economic history and, indeed, of modern sociology," while noting that "his achievements in this sphere are necessarily ignored in proportion as their effects have become part of the permanent background of civilized thought."[34] In Marx's era it was the scientists who were seen to be changing the world, and, according to Marx and Engels, proletarians and philosophers would be able to do likewise if they became 'scientists' too or, more precisely, dialecticians of the materialist conception of history (historical materialists).[35]

But, according to David Harvey, Marx also wanted science itself to develop a keener edge through scientists being aware of their own historical context. "Marx," Harvey stresses, "considered himself a scientist... but his materialism is different from that of the natural scientists. It is historical." He quotes Marx: "The weaknesses of the abstract materialism of natural science, a materialism

---

[34] Isaiah Berlin, *Karl Marx*, PUP, 1978. Pages 147-8. Berlin himself interprets Marx's phrase in the standard, erroneous way. He writes that it means that "Theory and practice are, or should be, one and the same thing" (p136). This interpretation ignores the revolutionary potential that Marx saw in the scientific method itself and falls back into an appeal to individual subjectivities to try to align thought and action. Darwin's work, for example, was revolutionary — it changed the world — not because Darwin was a 'revolutionary,' but because it exposed genuine, empirically proven, truths.

[35] For a clear explanation of the scientific method favored by Marx and Engels see *Ludwig Feuerbach and the End of Classical German Philosophy*, Part 4, at MIA, from the paragraph beginning: "But what is true of nature…"

which excludes the historical process, are immediately evident from the abstract and ideological conceptions expressed by its spokesmen whenever they venture beyond the bounds of their own speciality."[36] What this means, as Harvey explains, is that someone like Darwin was considered by Marx to be great in his own field and speciality, but lost in a fog of traditional biases outside of it.

Prophecy now relied for authority on material events, the struggle between classes, the dialectic, and the proletariat, rather than God. It was only through a scientific examination of real events and the 'movement' of the proletariat that one could make predictions. Just as the physical sciences were uncovering the truth about the world and thereby enabling human progress, so too the 'material conception of history' — later called historical materialism — allowed philosophers, sociologists and historians to analyze events scientifically, and therefore to make predictions based on apparently empirical observations.

The Communist Manifesto of 1848, by Karl Marx and Friedrich Engels, begins: "A specter is haunting Europe — the specter of Communism... [and] it is high time that Communists should openly, in the face of the whole world, publish their views, their aims, their tendencies, and meet this nursery tale of the Specter of Communism with a Manifesto of the party itself."

After a few pages, the contradictions of the modern economy are unraveled, the evils of the system are noted, and the prophecy is made:

> "The essential condition for the existence, and for the sway of the bourgeois class, is the formation and augmentation of capital; the condition for capital is wage labor. Wage labor rests exclusively on competition between the laborers. The advance of industry, whose involuntary promoter is the bourgeoisie, replaces the isolation of the laborers, due to competition, by their revolutionary combination, due to association. The development of Modern Industry, therefore, cuts from under its feet the very foundation on which the bourgeoisie produces and appropriates products. What the bourgeoisie, therefore, produces, above all, is its own grave-diggers. Its fall and the victory of the proletariat are equally inevitable."

The prophecy, of course, is written into the last sentence, the justification for the prophecy is written above it. Marx and Engels have reviewed the facts of the modern economy and society — not the 'desires' of people (including Marx and

---

[36] David Harvey, *A Companion to Marx's* Capital, Verso, 2010, p197. The quote from Marx comes from footnote 4, p494, of *Capital* (see footnote 28 for bibliographic details).

Engels themselves), their hopes and dreams, or what they think about themselves — and they are therefore able to make scientific predictions. (They did not begin their book in this way: *We think the present society is rotten and harmful and we know a lot of you do too, so let's get rid of things as they are!*)

Albert Einstein explains this predictive process well when he describes the nature of his scientific method (in reference to theories of relativity):

> "But in addition to this most weighty group of theories, there is another group consisting of what I call theories of principle. These employ the analytic, not the synthetic method. Their starting-point and foundation are not hypothetical constituents, but empirically observed general properties of phenomena, principles from which mathematical formula are deduced of such a kind that they apply to every case which presents itself. Thermodynamics, for instance, starting from the fact that perpetual motion never occurs in ordinary experience, attempts to deduce from this, by analytic processes, a theory which will apply in every case. The merit of constructive theories is their comprehensiveness, adaptability, and clarity, that of the theories of principle, their logical perfection, and the security of their foundation. The theory of relativity is a theory of principle. To understand it, the principles on which it rests must be grasped."[37]

Of course, we are aware that Einstein's theories/predictions/principles have actually been proven correct: the splitting of the atom proved that mass was super-condensed energy, and that this energy can be released, or transformed, and used. What Marx was arguing, half a century before Einstein's theories appeared, was that by using a particular kind of materialist method in all disciplines, including history, economics, and the social sciences, scientists (or all *thinkers*) could literally change the world by sending it into a new direction... just as knowledge of 'Boyle's Law' (the relationship between pressure and volume of a gas) was crucial in the development of the steam engine. Marx hoped that a 'materialist conception of history' (historical materialism) would do the

---

[37] Albert Einstein, 'Time, Space and Gravitation,' in *The London Times*, Nov. 28, 1919, can be found on the Internet. By referring to the analytic/synthetic distinction Einstein is affirming his empiricism. In semantics the distinction is portrayed by these kinds of sentences: 'dentists are doctors' (analytical) vs 'dentists are wealthy' (synthetic). In the same way, for example, Marx might say that the overthrow of capitalism is inevitable due to certain contradictions in its dynamic, but would not say that that capitalism needs to be abolished because it is evil — even if he points out that aspects of it are terrible and inhumane.

same thing for the social sciences (and it did to a certain extent, in that it is the basis of sociology at least, but he envisaged it would do more).

There is another interesting thing to note here. Einstein writes: "The theory of relativity is a theory of principle. To understand it, the principles on which it rests must be grasped." Marx and Engels first laid out the principles of communist revolution in *The Communist Manifesto*, which were based on their social and economic theories. Of course, they both had a passion for equality and freedom for humankind but what they claimed to discover was that this hope could be physically extrapolated from the data of human experience and turned into a law: it wasn't, they decided, just a utopian ideal. So, after the Manifesto was published Marx set about writing down the principles on which the theory rested, and the work on *Capital* was begun. The volumes of *Capital* were intended to lay out the facts of modern society necessary to grasp the inevitability of communism.[38] Marx shifted his philosophical (and economic, historical, and social) enquiries from the traditional arenas of Platonic absolutes and German Idealism to the burgeoning domain of the scientific method, and he urged other thinkers to follow his lead.

An Idealist Apologia

There has, of course, been much debate over just how Marx and Engels used the term 'inevitable' amongst those who have tried to protect their legacy, arguing that Marx and Engels do not mean 'inevitable' in the way we might initially think it is meant. Put simply, there is the recurring 'problem' in their work of using the word 'inevitable' but then also encouraging political action and education, that is, if it is inevitable, what point is there in doing anything to bring it about? G. A. Cohen resolves this dilemma in this way:

> "Marx and Engels believed that the advent of a socialist society was inevitable. How was that belief compatible with their advocacy of political activity to bring about socialism? I reply that Marx and Engels thought

---

[38] See Ernest Mandel, 'Introduction', in Karl Marx, *Capital Volume 3*, David Fernbach (trans.), Penguin, 1991: "While these volumes contain a tremendous amount of intellectual and moral dynamite aimed at bourgeois society and its prevailing ideology — with all that these entail for human beings, above all for workers — they give no precise indication of the way in which the system's inner contradictions prepare the ground for its final and inevitable downfall" (pp9-10). Mandel was a leading Trotskyist, and it is significant to note that both Lenin and Trotsky abandoned Marx's thesis of inevitability, while thinkers such as Luxemburg and Pannekoek did not.

socialism was inevitable, not whatever people might do, but because of what people, being rational, were bound, predictably, to do. It is therefore no more irrational for Marxists to struggle for the goal they regard as inevitable than it is for an army of overwhelming strength to fight and thereby achieve its inevitable victory."[39]

Later, Cohen adds that, in Marxian terms, to ask a socialist why they are bothering to fight for socialism when it is inevitable anyway "would be like asking why an army of overwhelming strength bothers to fight when its victory is inevitable. For its victory, although inevitable, is not inevitable whether or not the army fights. Its victory is inevitable only if and because it will fight."[40]

But this is not entirely clear. To follow it properly one must make further guesses at meaning. For example, are people rational? Or is the making of people rational the task of the revolutionary? If they are already rational then, surely, they are all consciously fighting for socialism already? If their rationality relies on the intervention of socialist propagandists then, surely, these people have a lot of work to do and the inevitability of socialism becomes ever more uncertain. But maybe people will become rational in the moments when the veils of irrationality are lifted by actual events and the class struggle that workers are inevitably and regularly forced into? But then the need for socialist propagandists prior to such events again becomes unnecessary to the inevitability. (Stay with me on this, the torturous semantics here are only my in-good-faith response to the torturous semantics of G. A. Cohen in his article.)

Then there is the question of the 'army of overwhelming strength.' In this formula Cohen is transferring the inevitability of socialism itself to the inevitability of its success *if rational people are prepared to fight for it*. Marx would never write this because he was a scientist of the materialist conception of history, he was not an idealist who pinned his hopes on the good will and innate or transhistorical 'rationality' of the people. He always argued that the veils of mysticism and irrationality would fall from peoples' eyes through the process of historical — material — events, not on account of some kind of spiritual awakening. In fact, Cohen is even further off the mark here on the question of 'rationality' because Marx stressed that the veil of 'irrationality' could not disappear completely for humans until they had put the production of their

---

[39] Cohen, G. A., et al. "Historical Inevitability and Human Agency in Marxism [and Discussion]." *Proceedings of the Royal Society of London. Series A, Mathematical and Physical Sciences*, vol. 407, no. 1832, 1986, pp. 65–87. Can be found online at jstor. Page 65.
[40] Ibid., 68.

material life "under their conscious and planned control."[41] That is, *after* the victory of the revolution.

Like many followers of Marx, Cohen does not give anywhere near enough credit to the fact that Marx claimed first and foremost for his theory of communist revolution *not* that it was a beautiful ideal, or the result of a sudden mass 'rationality,' but that it would be the result of an inevitable, material, *dialectical process*. His conclusions, he claimed, were not 'idealistic,' but based on scientific investigations into history and the economy.

Marx writes: "communism is humanism as a perfect naturalism and naturalism as a perfect humanism."[42] In using the term 'humanism' here Marx is referring to the notion that all concepts and events should be explained in terms of human social relations within particular material circumstances, or eras, not as eternal absolutes. In using the term 'naturalism' here Marx is referring to the Enlightenment tenet that all beings and events in the universe are natural, that is, not 'supernatural,' and are therefore knowable and understandable through science, or the scientific method. In writing this sentence Marx, being a person of his time, is nailing his colors to the mast of the newly sailed ship of science. If this driving feature of his work is ignored, many of his themes, as Cohen unintentionally demonstrates, end up as vague and confusing mantras.

Friedrich Engels elaborates on how the empirical method, or materialism, that was central to their theories, came about:

> "The old metaphysics, which accepted things as finished objects, arose from a natural science which investigated dead and living things as finished objects. But when this investigation had progressed so far that it became possible to take the decisive step forward, that is, to pass on the systematic investigation of the changes which these things undergo in nature itself, then the last hour of the old metaphysic struck in the realm of philosophy also. And in fact, while natural science up to the end of the last century was predominantly a *collecting* science, a science of finished things, in our century it is essentially a systematizing science, a science of the processes, of the

---

[41] Karl Marx, *Capital Volume 1*, (as above), p173.
[42] Marx, Point 3, 'Private Property and Communism,' in *Economic and Philosophical Manuscripts*, 1844, at the *Marxists Internet Archive* (MIA). See also, Marx, 'First Premises of Materialist Method,' in *The German Ideology, Part 1*, 1845, also at MIA.

origin and development of these things and of the interconnection which binds all these natural processes into one great whole."[43]

No doubt Marx would be appalled if the scientific predictions (or "theories of principle" as Einstein might term them) he formulated concerning society and the way it should behave were considered as *mere prophecies*. But Marx did not have our vantage point in history, he did not see how the "empirically observed general properties of phenomena" played out over the century after his death. His prediction of an inevitable victory of the proletariat and the establishment of a production of material life based on the free association of the producers themselves has not come true. It is reasonable now to cast his predictions in a frame of idealistic hope (or perhaps 'necessity,' or moral imperative) rather than a frame of science, but to do so without reference to the fact that this is *opposite* to his modus operandi is to betray his methodology and his perspective. Indeed, by not recognizing the scientific method at the heart of Marx's predictions, this is exactly what thinkers such as Cohen effectively do. It is also reasonable to perceive a connection with the tradition of prophecy in viewing the *authority* for his predictions as empiricism and the material circumstances of the proletariat rather than God or the Bible. It is no longer the direct word of God or passages in the Bible that give authority to particular — millenarian — prophecies but the proper interpretation of data and events based on a theory of the proletariat.

It should be noted that not all revolutionaries of Marx's time, by any means, were swept up in the mechanisms of the scientific method. Mikhail Bakunin, for example — while considering *Capital Volume 1* as unique in containing "an analysis so profound, so luminous, so scientific, so decisive, and if I can express it thus, so merciless an expose of the formation of bourgeois capital and the systematic and cruel exploitation that capital continues exercising over the work of the proletariat"[44] — objected to the scientific certainty of Marx's attitude.

Bakunin wrote: "As soon as an *official truth is* pronounced — having been scientifically discovered by this great brainy head laboring all alone — a truth proclaimed and imposed on the whole world from the summit of the Marxist Sinai, why discuss anything?"[45] Where Marx had scientific prediction based on the empirical data, Bakunin only had hope and, equally importantly, doubt. For this reason, Bakunin's hope, as ruthless, authoritarian, and nihilistic as it might

---

[43] Friedrich Engels, 'Part 4: Marx,' in *Ludwig Feuerbach and the End of Classical German Philosophy*, 1886, MIA.
[44] Mikhail Bakunin, *The Capitalist System*, (no date), MIA. Footnote 2.
[45] Bakunin, *On the International Workingmen's Association and Karl Marx*, 1872, MIA.

be,[46] could never be translated into prophecy, or written as a prophetic certainty. The *hope* that Bakunin had in the lower classes' potential to overthrow tyranny and exploitation was just that, it was not a prediction of a certain endpoint that was relayed to humanity either through an interpretation of the word of God or via an interpretation of historical forces.

Before I explore how latter-day Marxian, or Marxist, thinkers who have tried to stay true to Marx's prophecy in an environment where they are, perhaps uncomfortably, aware that the inevitability of communism is a receding vision, it is worth picking out some other prophetic remarks and their justifications, and also noting the amendments of Trotsky and Lenin.

Luxemburg

In objecting to Eduard Bernstein's 'revisionism' of Marx and his pointing to the possibility of achieving socialism through gradual reformist, rather than revolutionary (millenarian), means Rosa Luxemburg, at the beginning of the last century, reaffirms the authority of science that Marx and Engels first set out:

> "The scientific basis of socialism rests, as is well known, on three principal results of capitalist development. First on the growing anarchy of capitalist economy, leading inevitably to its ruin. Second on the progressive socialization of the process of production, which creates the germs of the future social order. And third, on the increased organization and consciousness of the proletarian class, which constitutes the active factor in the coming revolution."

Luxemburg argues that Bernstein, by discounting the scientific inevitability of communism as proclaimed by Marx, reduces "the explanation of the socialist program" to one of "pure reason." "We have here, to use simpler language, an idealist explanation of socialism. The objective necessity of socialism, the explanation of socialism as the result of the material development of society, [in Bernstein's conception, therefore,] falls to the ground."[47]

---

[46] See *The Rebel*, by Albert Camus, 1951, for the genealogy of Bakunin's nihilism. Camus: "Bakunin contributed a germ of political cynicism which will congeal, with Nechayev [despite their falling out with each other], into a doctrine, and will drive the revolutionary movement to extremes... Bakunin contributed as much as his enemy Marx to Leninist doctrine." Lenin idolized Nechayev, referring to him as the "Titan of the revolution."

[47] Rosa Luxemburg, 'Reform or Revolution' (1898, 1899, and 1908), in *The Essential Rosa Luxemburg*, Helen Scott (ed.), Haymarket Books, 2008. Pages 45 and 47.

In the piece from which the quote above is taken Luxemburg frequently and clearly insists on the *inevitability* of the collapse of capitalism and the *inevitability* of the victory of the workers. The authority for this prophetic certainty is not God or the Bible but, as she states, *science*: "our dialectical system."[48]

Trotsky

In 1938, Leon Trotsky reiterated Luxemburg's objection to reformism, but there is a twist here: "We must give a scientific explanation of society, and clearly explain it to the masses. That is the difference between Marxism and reformism."[49] In 1925, he wrote:

> "Marxism rejected super-historical essences, just as physiology has renounced the vital force, or chemistry [has renounced] phlogiston. The essence of Marxism consists in this, that it approaches society concretely, as a subject for objective research, and analyses human history as one would a colossal laboratory record. Marxism appraises ideology as a subordinate integral element of the material social structure. Marxism examines the class structure of society as an historically conditioned form of the development of the productive forces; Marxism deduces from the productive forces of society the inter-relations between human society and surrounding nature, and these, in turn are determined at each historical stage by man's [sic] technology, his instruments and weapons, his capacities and methods for struggle with nature. Precisely this objective approach arms Marxism with the insuperable power of historical foresight."[50]

The twist is the notion that a scientific approach allows the "power of historical foresight." Trotsky, like Lenin (see below), had, unlike Luxemburg, actually departed from prophecy.

Historian Isaac Deutscher, a life-long admirer of Trotsky, wrote an extensive biography of Trotsky over three volumes in the 1950s and 1960s. He titled these works, *The Prophet Armed*, *The Prophet Unarmed*, and *The Prophet Outcast*. The titles of the books were inspired by a passage from *The Prince* by Machiavelli that Deutscher reproduces at the beginning of the first book:

---

[48] Ibid., 99.
[49] Leon Trotsky, (Discussions) *On the Transitional Programme*, 1938, MIA.
[50] Trotsky, *Dialectical Materialism and Science*, 1925, MIA.

"...there is nothing more difficult to take in hand, more perilous to conduct, or more uncertain in its success, than to take the lead in the introduction of a new order of things. Because the innovator has for enemies all those who have done well under the old conditions, and lukewarm defenders in those who may do well under the new...

"It is necessary, therefore, if we desire to discuss this matter thoroughly, to inquire whether these innovators can rely on themselves or have to depend on others: that is to say, whether to consummate their enterprise, they have to use prayers or can they use force? In the first instance they always succeed badly, and never compass anything; but when they can rely on themselves and use force, then they are rarely endangered. Hence it is that all armed prophets have conquered, and the unarmed ones have been destroyed. Besides the reason mentioned, the nature of the people is variable, and whilst it is easy to persuade them, it is difficult to fix them in that persuasion. And thus it is necessary to take such measures that, when they believe no longer, it may be possible to make them believe by force.

"If Moses, Cyrus, Theseus, and Romulus had been unarmed they could not have enforced their constitutions for long — as happened in our time to Fra Girolamo Savonarola, who was ruined with his new order of things immediately the multitude believed in him no longer, and he had no means of keeping steadfast those who believed or of making the unbelievers to believe."[51]

While this piece from Machiavelli is pertinent in terms of how prophets can be effective, it does not quite fit with Trotsky, who had clearly abandoned prophecy by the time he formulated the concept of the 'permanent revolution' (see below). It may be then that the practical tasks of seizing control of a State tend to diminish the prophetic impulse in favour of getting on with things *that need to be done...* If Marx was a prophet, then his armed incarnations were Lenin and Trotsky. But, as with all human incarnations of *the practical*, the question of *belief* is set aside for those who have gained power — and belief itself becomes simply a tool to maintain loyalty (see Bockelson, above).

---

[51] Isaac Deutscher, *The Prophet Armed*, Verso, 2003. Page xii. Quote from *The Prince*, Chapter 6. Machiavelli is probably being a little unfair to the millenarian prophet Savonarola who gained political ascendency in Florence between 1495 and 1498 — his violent rhetoric was backed up, in fact, by gangs of youths who roamed the city enforcing his moral codes. Still, it could perhaps be argued that he was not armed enough.

Pannekoek

Renowned astronomer and council communist, Anton Pannekoek, a loyal prophet of the inevitable — though he would likely prefer to be described as a scientist or dialectician — wrote in 1946:

> "More powerful than before, capitalism will tower after the [Second World] war. But stronger also, the fight of the working masses, sooner or later, will arise over against it. It is inevitable that in this fight the workers will aim at mastery over the shops [workshops/ factories], mastery over production, dominance over society, over labor, over their own life. The idea of self-rule through workers' councils will take hold of their minds, the practice of self-rule and workers' councils will determine their actions. So from the abyss of weakness they will rise to a new unfolding of power. Thus a new world will be built up. A new era is coming after the war, not of tranquility and peace, but of constructive class fight."[52]

Remember that an apocalypse is a revelation in which good triumphs over evil. After reading this passage from Pannekoek — a man who has a crater on the moon named after him, as well as an asteroid, an honorary degree from Harvard awarded in 1936, and the Gold Medal of the Royal Astronomical Society (UK) awarded in 1951 — one almost wants to shout "Hallelujah!" ... for this is truly the word of the materialist dialectic.

Althusser

It is important, I think, to keep returning to how Marx perceived his methodology, and Louis Althusser defines it very neatly:

> "It is neither reliance on a particular philosophical system, nor a sort of intrinsic virtue, an absolute 'logical' necessity, that makes the dialectic indispensable to Marx and Engels. *The dialectic is validated only by its concrete [positif] utilisation, by its scientific fecundity.* This scientific use is the sole criterion of the dialectic. It alone makes it possible to speak of the dialectic as *method*. Marx, says Lenin, did not 'plaster' the dialectic onto reality:

---

[52] Anton Pannekoek, *Workers' Councils* (1946), Robert. F. Barsky (ed.), original Dutch translated by Pannekoek, AK Press, 2003, p187.

"Marx only studied and investigated the real process ... the sole criterion of theory recognized by him was its conformity to reality.... What Marx and Engels called the dialectical method — as against the metaphysical — is nothing else than the scientific method in sociology, which consists in regarding society as a living organism in a state of constant development," (Lenin, *What 'The Friends of the People' Are*, [see MIA])."

"And," Althusser continues, "Lenin cites the famous sentence from the second Preface to *Capital* in which Marx defines the dialectic: 'The whole matter thus amounts to a "positive understanding of the existing state of things and their inevitable development."[53]

Marx's methodology gave him the upper hand in debates with others because he could always refer to his empirical investigation of the constantly moving contradictions in society, which put everything he argued on a scientifically materialist basis, and therefore enabled him to be able to easily discount other peoples', as he insisted, simple, or naïve, conjectures.

PART IV

A Shaken Confidence

The Situationists did not properly wear the mantle of prophecy, even though they were Marxian-inspired millenarians in their politics. For this reason, though they were materialists who used the science of dialectic materialism to inform their philosophy, they were never fully Marxist, never proper historical materialists, even though they wrote: "Marx's thought is obviously the first

---

[53] Louis Althusser, 'On Marxism,' 1953, MIA, original emphasis. Lenin is here trying to establish that Marx was not applying a strict law of history but a correct *methodology* to use in understanding the world. In the Penguin, 1976, translation the quote Lenin refers to is written as: "In its rational [non-Hegelian] form [the dialectic] is a scandal and an abomination to the bourgeoisie and its doctrinaire spokesmen, because it includes in its positive understanding of what exists a simultaneous recognition of its negation, its inevitable destruction; because it regards every historically developed form as being in a fluid state, in motion, and therefore grasps its transient aspect as well; and because it does not let itself be impressed by anything, being in its very essence critical and revolutionary," *Capital*, p103.

Nihil Evadere

which must be rediscovered."[54] The 'proper' Marxists, of course, scorned what they perceived as their inchoate anarchism. But, having said this, Guy Debord did, following the Marx who followed Hegel, write, in *The Society of the Spectacle*, "The economy's triumph as an independent power inevitably also spells its doom." Maybe Debord's Marxism was also occasionally expressed in an impulse to prophesy?

In *The Revolution of Everyday Life*, 1967, Raoul Vaneigem writes: "To embrace revolution while abandoning oneself — as all militants do — is to work arse-backwards. Down with voluntarism — but down likewise with the mystique of revolution's historical inevitability!"[55] This would seem to separate Vaneigem from the notion of 'historical inevitability,' but there is a contradiction. Vaneigem also took up the phrase from Marx — "the *real* movement"[56] — that underpins the kernel of prophecy that still exists in groups of today who seek the authority of science and dialectics (what once was God) for their theory and *raison d'etre*. So maybe the Situationists prevaricated, or weren't so sure as to how to present themselves. If capitalism was dooming itself and communism is *a concrete becoming* (or 'real movement') in society, then Marx's beating heart of prophecy is still there.[57]

> A guest once, at the home of Michèle Bernstein and Guy Debord, noticed that, after dinner, Bernstein was doing all the washing up. Instead of offering to help, as one might, the guest shot a quizzical look at Debord, who explained, "She does the dishes, I do the revolution."

---

[54] 'The Bad Days Will End,' April 1962, in *Situationist International Anthology*, Ken Knabb (trans. and ed.), Berkeley, 1981. Page 84. Of course, the use of the word 'will' probably reveals a prophetic tendency in the S.I.

[55] Raoul Vaneigem, *The Revolution of Everyday Life*, Donald Nicholson-Smith (trans. revised), PM Press, 2012, p245.

[56] The full sentence from Marx in German from which this is taken is: "Wir nennen Kommunismus die *wirkliche* Bewegung, welche den jetzigen Zustand aufhebt." This is generally translated as something like: 'We call communism the real movement that abolishes the present state of things.' But in order to more exactly understand what Marx is trying to get at here it can equally justifiably be translated as: 'We call communism the *concrete* becoming that abolishes the current conditions.' The quote is from the first part of *The German Ideology*, 'The Contrast of Materialist and Idealist Perspectives,' and can be found in German at *MLwerke*.

[57] For Vaneigem's use of the term 'the real movement,' see 'Basic Banalities (II),' 1963, in *SI Anthology*, p122. Also, see 'Notes on the SIs Direction,' 1970, and 'Several Precise Points,' 1970, that can be found at the *NOT BORED!* website.

The Situationist International, and its precursors, existed within the same radical milieu as the ultra-left group *Socialisme ou Barbarie* (1948-1967), of which Guy Debord was a member during 1960-61.[58] It was perhaps in the theoretical work of *Socialisme ou Barbarie* that the prophecy of the inevitability of communism was reconfigured into a humbler version; a version in which the prophecy could not simply be *proclaimed*, as Marx had done, but had to be delivered through an articulation of the presumed actuality of the proletariat and the class struggle — that is, 'the real movement.'

Cornelius Castoriadis, of *Socialisme ou Barbarie*, wrote in 1959:

> "There is no 'proof' of the inevitable collapse of the system of exploitation. There is even less 'truth' in the possibility of socialism being established by a theoretical elaboration operating outside the concrete content created by the historic and everyday activity of the proletariat. The proletariat develops on its own toward socialism — otherwise there would be no prospect for socialism. The objective conditions for this development are given by capitalist society itself. But these conditions only establish the context and define the problems the proletariat will encounter in its struggle; they are a long way from determining the content of its answers to these problems. Its responses are a creation of the proletariat, for this class takes up the objective elements of the situation and at the same time transforms them, thereby opening up a previously unknown and unsuspected field of action and objective possibilities. The content of socialism is precisely this creative activity on the part of the masses that no theory ever could or ever will be able to anticipate. Marx could not have anticipated the Commune (not as an event but as a form of social organization) nor Lenin the Soviets, nor could either of them have anticipated workers' management."[59]

The vantage point of later history — which had witnessed the Russian Revolution, the events in Spain, and the European genocides, as well as the undermining of the promises of the Enlightenment already begun, for example,

---

[58] For the interesting relationship between SouB and Debord/IS see 'L'Internationale Situationniste, Socialisme ou Barbarie, and the Crisis of the Marxist Imaginary,' by Stephen Hastings-King, *SubStance*, Vol. 28, No. 3, Issue 90: Special Issue: Guy Debord (1999) – which can be found free online if one looks hard enough. Also see 'Now, The SI,' Guy Debord, 1964, in *Situationist International Anthology*, Ken Knabb (trans. and ed.), Berkeley, 1981, pages 135-142.

[59] Cornelius Castoriadis/Paul Cardan, 'Proletariat and Organization,' *Socialisme ou Barbarie*, 27 and 28, 1959, in *Socialisme ou Barbarie – an Anthology*, a translation of the French book (published by Acratie, 2007), available at NOT BORED! Pages 328-9.

Nihil Evadere

by Adorno and Horkheimer and later completed by Foucault — meant Castoriadis had to reject the simple repetition of Marx's prophecy that the fall of the bourgeoisie "and the victory of the proletariat are equally inevitable," and replace it with something that perhaps could be described as more nuanced, or subtle.

One can see in Castoriadis' formulation the seeds of a modern explication of Marx's 'real movement,' and it is reasonable to assume that this notion, or way of reconsidering the historic importance of the proletariat, naturally formed a basis for Situationist theory. Then after the events in France of 1968, Gilles Dauvé, the principal writer of the book, *Eclipse and Re-Emergence of the Communist Movement*, was able to develop Castoriadis' way of approaching the phenomenon of the proletariat and develop what became known as 'communization theory.' So now we move on to the latest prophetic strands in the revolutionary tradition, of which there are, essentially, three.

Lutteomancing

The prophecy of 'the real movement that will abolish existing conditions' has, therefore, been re-articulated by Castoriadis in the light of 'defeats' of the first half of the twentieth century, taken up by the Situationists, and then become the founding 'praxis' of groups and individuals since the 'defeat' of 1968.[60] These 'defeats' have forced radicals to tone down their prophetic impulses, but they are still there.

Communization, for those unfamiliar with the term, is the name for what might be termed *real movement-ism*, even though the founder of the theory of communization, Gilles Dauvé, no longer appears to believe (see below) in the inevitability of communism that is central to Marx's use of the term (real movement).

In its so-called insurrectionist variant, expressed by the group *Tiqqun*, communization is explained thus: "As we apprehend it, the process of instituting communism can only take the form of a collection of *acts of communization*, of making common such-and-such space, such-and-such machine, such-and-such knowledge. That is to say, the elaboration of the mode of sharing that attaches

---

[60] The Frankfurt School applied the same perspective to the German Revolution of 1918, thereby pre-empting the post-1968 thinkers by several decades.

to them. Insurrection itself is just an accelerator, a decisive moment in this process."[61]

In its more Marxist variant — which is critical of the 'voluntarist/insurgent' emphasis of *Tiqqunism* — communization is explained by the group *Théorie Communiste* by using the term "communizing measures": "the proletariat" contains within its logic the "dissolution of all existing conditions" and so "*communization* is nothing other than *communist measures* taken as simple *measures of struggle* by the proletariat against capital."[62]

Before I proceed, it is valuable to indicate the difference between 'acts of communization' and 'communizing measures.' The first (*Tiqqun*) reflects, as described above, a value in the spontaneous, appropriation of space and productive apparatus, so that it can be used collectively and shared. The second — *Théorie Communiste*'s 'communist measures' — reflects the necessary tasks needed to establish a social dictatorship and then to reconcile the differences between different sections of society. Although *Théorie Communiste* states that, "*communization* is nothing other than *communist measures* taken as simple *measures of struggle* by the proletariat against capital," they also, in the same text, unwittingly it would seem, spell out why leaders, experts, and 'parties' will definitely emerge, even in a 'communizing' revolution, in a passage (reminding one of Lenin) that calls for "the dictatorship [through "armed struggle" and "overcoming the conflicts" between different elements of society, for example, employed/unemployed, rural/city, etc] of the social movement of communization."[63]

Both these explanations of communization, however, appear to be essentially based upon the formula given below by Gilles Dauvé in 1972:

> "Communism is not an ideal to be realized: it already exists, not as a society, but as an effort, a task to prepare for. It is the movement which tries to abolish the conditions of life determined by wage-labor, and it will abolish them by revolution. The discussion of communism is not academic. It is not a debate about what will be done tomorrow. It is an integral part of a whole

---

[61] *Tiqqun* 2004, *Call*, available at Bloom0101 website, p66, original emphasis.
[62] Théorie Communiste, 2011, 'Communication in the Present Tense,' in *Communization and its Discontents: Contestation, Critique, and Contemporary Struggles*, Benjamin Noys (ed.), Minor Compositions, New York. Page 53, original emphases.
[63] TC, 'Communization in the Present Tense,' pp55-58.

series of immediate and distant tasks, among which discussion is only one aspect, an attempt to achieve theoretical understanding."[64]

The notion of 'the real movement' was referred to, but not referenced, in *Eclipse*. The term receives a similar presentation in *Situationist International* texts (by Raoul Vaneigem,[65] for example), which suggests it formed a clearly understood axiom in radical left French circles in the 1960s and 1970s. It was in Dauvé's essay in *Eclipse* that the notion of 'the real movement' — at least for many others — became the underpinning image, or assumption, for his newly articulated concept of communization.[66] In 2000, Dauvé indicated that communization theory emerged from within the perspectives of the Situationist International[67] but the real debt, as I see it, is to the perspectives developed by *Socialisme ou Barbarie* after WWII.

If we go back to the quote from Dauvé just above, it might seem that the prophesying has been eradicated. The word 'tries' is used, and when he writes that "it *will* abolish them by revolution" this is probably only intended to mean that it is *only* by revolution that "the conditions of life determined by wage-labor" *can* be abolished. But the reconfiguring of Marx's prophecy does not leave all the prophesying baggage behind. The correct interpretation of material events, the reading of signs in the struggles of the working class that point to ways forward have now replaced the historical materialism that itself replaced the Bible or the direct word of God.

Since its emergence in the 1970s, the group *Théorie Communiste* have also substituted the giddy euphoria of prophecy with a searching for *signs*.[68] They state that an aspect of the 'communizing current' consists of a recognition "that all permanent organization of the class, all organization prior to struggles and persisting beyond them, is nowadays confronted by failure" and that "Communization is not a program to be applied, nor even something that we

---

[64] Gilles Dauvé and François Martin, 2015 [1972], *Eclipse and Re-emergence of the Communist Movement,* PM Press, Oakland, p7.
[65] For Vaneigem's use of the term 'the real movement,' see 'Basic Banalities (II),' 1963, in *SI Anthology*, Page 122. Also, see 'Notes on the SIs Direction,' 1970, and 'Several Precise Points,' 1970, that can be found at the *NOT BORED!* website.
[66] Dauvé and Martin, p30, and page 23ff.
[67] See 'Back to the SI,' at the *Troploin* website.
[68] The group *Endnotes*, who might be considered as the inheritors of T.C., defined this sign seeking as 'rune reading' in 2020: "the task for a contemporary science of the species is to once more read the runes of our times," 'Onward Barbarians,' *Endnotes* website, p45 (PDF version).

can already describe, but the ways to it are to be explored and this exploration must be international."[69]

There are two things happening in these statements. The first is a kind of caution reflected in uncertainty and prevarication: they do not want to appear ridiculous, that is, *anarchist,* by coming across as naïve or 'idealistic,' while also wanting to separate themselves from any residue of the old workers' movement. The second is a stated commitment to theorize 'struggles' so that "ways to it [communization]" are revealed and elaborated. For them "theoretical production,"[70] of course, is itself part of the 'communizing current.' Since the old workers' movement is now deceased, they claim to seek new theory in the examination of 'international struggles,' and this new exploration is implicitly defined as *materialist and scientific,* rather than *idealist.* (Such a job, then, is only for an expert, or dialectician, truly sensitive to the historically 'positive' or 'real' aspects of every event, that is, a *Marx* rather than a *Bakunin.*)

And there is a deeper contradiction, or confusion: there is the problem that theory, even in their terms, always arrives after the event (*after* the experiment, *after* the review of the data; if it comes *before* then it is 'descending,' as Marx wrote, 'from heaven')… yet they insist that they must study struggles… but these studies are not written in an attempt to form 'theories of principle'… On the one hand they state that their written contributions explore "ways to" communization while on the other they insist that whatever they might come up with is "not a program to be applied." This leads one to think that perhaps *Théorie Communiste*'s written work is 'simply' journalism, or a way of trying to transmit 'inspiration' to readers. But journalism is always objectively encouraging or discouraging readers to follow particular lines of thought, all journalism is propaganda. And any political leaflet that connects viscerally, poetically, or intellectually to a cause is also attempting to inspire, that is, propagandize. So, what is it, exactly, that *Théorie Communiste* consider they are doing?

In Marx and Einstein's terms, and in the methodology of the scientific method, theory cannot be arrived at prior to empirical endeavor, but the theory formed can be used to predict future possibilities or phenomenon. Through mathematics Einstein worked out that there was immense power within matter, and this set others on a study of how to access that power (Marx worked out

---

[69] See 'Meeting: Revue Internationale pour la Communisation (2003–2008),' on the *Libcom* website.
[70] See 'Théorie Communiste,' 'an Introduction for the *young Lyonnaise*,' 2014, on the *Libcom* website.

that the historical contradictions within capitalism created a class of people that would fulfill the inevitable destiny of establishing communism by overcoming capitalism, and this set others on a study of how to nurture or access that power). Prediction has always been the backbone of empiricism, but *Théorie Communiste* have taken out that backbone and are seemingly just left with a confusing 'looking.' Any truly 'communizing' initiatives, even by their own logic (all organization prior to, or post, struggles, they write, is marked by failure), will never be helped by theory (any 'help' an existing theory could give would be deleterious), and so theorizing about the potentials of struggles is at best pointless[71] and at worst counter-productive. A theory is a permanence. To use theory to inform a practice, or strategy, is to rely on a *permanent organization of ideas*.[72] But what is the point of "theoretical production" if it is not to inform future practise? Theorists such as *Théorie Communiste* are therefore, in fact — in their own terms (and perhaps amusingly?) — *counterrevolutionary*.[73]

Théorie Communiste have not worked out the implications of what Castoriadis wrote above — "There is even less 'truth' in the possibility of socialism being established by a theoretical elaboration operating outside the concrete content created by the historic and everyday activity of the proletariat. The proletariat develops on its own toward socialism... The content of socialism is precisely this creative activity on the part of the masses that no theory ever could or ever will be able to anticipate" — and have instead, despite their differences, followed Gilles Dauvé into a kind of hobbyism in which they read the future from

---

[71] In *Eclipse*, p7, Dauvé wrote: "The communist revolution, like every other revolution, is the product of real needs and living conditions. The problem is to shed light on an existing historical movement." Why does light need to be shed upon this movement except for journalistic purposes? Why, indeed, is this a "problem"? On the other hand, won't any written intervention, if anyone involved actually reads it, only serve to hinder or thwart this "existing movement"?

[72] I do not refer here to the concept of 'praxis,' which requires another discussion. Henri Lefebvre writes: "All praxis is situated in history; it is a creator of history," *Metaphilosophy*, D. Fernbach (trans.), Verso, 2016 (2000), p7. In this sense we are all products and functions of our society, therefore whatever I or *T.C.* write is contained, trapped, within 'our world' — none of us can truly introduce an idea from another society (outside of capitalism), as if from another planet. In this way all our ideas 'serve' our society. Therefore, the question is: what do we *think* we are trying to achieve, or may achieve, by writing theory?

[73] The impossibility of their position was earlier, and equally unconsciously, defined poetically (and necessarily mystically) in the popular quote from Guy Debord in Thesis 124 of *Society of the Spectacle*: "Revolutionary theory is now the enemy of all revolutionary ideology and knows it."

'struggles' in the same way a tasseomancer[74] reads the future from the tea leaves in a cup.

But, to be fair to *Théorie Communiste*, not even Castoriadis had worked out the implications of what he had written. This, from 1964, sounds just like the project of *Théorie Communiste*:

> "But these ideas [of 'a socialist revolution'] run the risk of remaining empty abstractions, pretexts for sermons or for a blind and spasmodic activism, if we do not strive to understand how society's divisions are concretely being realized at the present hour, how this society functions, what forms of reaction and struggle laboring people adopt against the ruling strata and their system, what new kinds of revolutionary activity, related to people's concrete existence and struggle in society and to a coherent and lucid view of the world, are possible under these conditions."[75]

In 1959, Castoriadis — unwittingly one must presume — consigned the theorists of revolution to the dustbin, but in 1964 he put them firmly back in their desired place, the place *Théorie Communiste* has set aside for itself. Of course, there are other groups and tendencies that share this view of revolutionary theory and theorists. For example, *Endnotes*, *Riff-Raff*, *Blaumachen*, *Aufheben*, *Přátelé komunizace*, *Chuǎng*, *Kommunisierung*, *Research and Destroy*, *Il Lato Cattivo*, *Ill Will*, *Cured Quail*, *Echanges et Mouvement*, and, of course, *Troploin* (Dauvé), among others.

In these groups and individuals — who lean more toward Marx than Bakunin — the prophesying impulse, or the prophetic tradition that Marx rebirthed, has been suppressed, or hidden — or perhaps it is fairer to say it has just been forgotten about — but the science of observing and understanding in order to relay the parameters of possibility, or truth, to others has been maintained. 'Struggles' are the things to be observed, and theory is what is written about them, and the hope is that these writings will aid future struggle. But perhaps what is written 'after the event' — that which becomes theory or is viewed as a possible a route to theory — is a husk, a residue, a blight... which if fed back into future events — the future 'creative activity of the masses,' as Castoriadis wrote — would only have the effect of poisoning them?

---

[74] *Tasse* is 'cup' in French, and a *mancer* is someone who divines, or foretells, the future by magical, or supernatural, means.
[75] Castoriadis, 'Recommencing the Revolution,' 1964, in *Socialisme ou Barbarie: an Anthology*, page 400.

The authority for their conclusions, or pronouncements, is no longer the accurate interpretation of the word of God but the accurate interpretation of 'struggles' against things as they are, more specifically, the *movement* of the *proletariat* in what is its persistent natural resentment of its exploited condition. But, in their hands, this actual, recurrent and continuous phenomenon of writhing resentment in society is *reified* — perhaps *deified* would be more accurate — so as to serve the purposes of an aggrandizing, neo-Marxist, critique that is, significantly, dominated by and fed through *the University*. The theory created is then meant to be relayed back into future struggles,[76] just as the feedback of the word of God was meant as a call to action in the Reformation. To return to the tea-leaf-reading analogy, these theorists could be called *lutteomancers*: the diviners of *struggle*; the movement, or dynamic, of the proletariat. Like an old mole, the impulse to prophesy continues its work.

Invariance

Amadeo Bordiga and Antonio Gramsci were involved in a split in the Italian Socialist Party in 1921 that led to the formation of the Communist Party of Italy, with Bordiga as its secretary. It was soon clear, however, that Gramsci and Bordiga did not share the same approach to revolution, though they remained friends. Bordiga led the numerically strongest faction of the party but, through Gramsci's political maneuvering, the center and 'right-wing' of the party was able to assume control in 1926. This led to the leadership of Palmiro Togliatti and the eventual expulsion of Bordiga in 1930. Bordiga was never able to repeat the historical presence he had attained prior to 1926 but he was a major influence in the ever-numerically-diminishing left-communist circles in Italy and worldwide until his death, and beyond.

In 1952, Amadeo Bordiga argued, amidst the general uncertainty, that all those revolutionaries who now doubted Marx's prophecy of inevitable revolution — which he referred to as a 'system,' in the same way as Luxemburg above — were worse than wrong because they denied the "invariance" that informed all struggles, and indeed Marxism itself. He wrote:

---

[76] If it is not, then what is the point, beyond 'mere' curiosity — a noble endeavor of course — of examining past or current events? And, as explored above, such evaluations are always, necessarily, and logically, too late anyway in a situation where the creativity of the class is supposedly the driving factor.

"The materialist denial that a theoretical 'system' that had arisen at a particular moment in time (and, worse yet, one that had arisen in the mind and took shape in the works of a particular man, a thinker or historical leader, or both at the same time) could irrevocably apply to the whole course of the historical future, its rules and its principles, must not be understood in the sense that there are no stable systems of principles that are applicable to very long stretches of historical time. To the contrary, a system's stability and its powers of resistance against being mutilated and even against being 'improved,' constitute a primordial element of the power of the 'social class' to which that system pertains and whose historical mission and interests it reflects. The succession of such systems and bodies of doctrine and praxis is not connected with the advent of men who define the stages, but with the succession of 'modes of production,' that is, of the varieties of the material organization of life of human collectivities."[77]

What Bordiga is saying here is that revolutionaries have stepped back from Marx because they perceived their adherence to Marx as a kind of worship of an individual — but they are wrong to do this, he insists, because they have misunderstood the nature of the genius of Marx. Marx was the product of a 'mode pf production' — yes, he was 'a genius' but only because he was able to articulate the mode of production (society) he happened to be born into, and he was able to create (or perhaps one could think of it as *channel*) a 'system' or 'body of doctrine' based on that. The theoretical system he elaborated was not 'his' it was "an element of the power of the 'social class' to which that system pertains and whose historical mission and interests it reflects." Bordiga is correctly referring here to the fact that we are all products and functions of our era and our society (geniuses do not come from another planet), while also admonishing those who have forgotten this truth.

The prophecy of revolution, that Marx proclaimed, had to be correct, according to Bordiga, because it was a truth derived from the correct interpretation of material events, it was a result of the application of dialectical materialism — which exposed "the historical invariance of the doctrines that reflect the missions of the contending classes." Bordiga continues: "We maintain that all the great events of recent times are just so many categorical and integral confirmations of Marxist theory and its predictions."

---

[77] Amadeo Bordiga, 'The Historical *Invariance* of Marxism – Presentation to the International Communist Party,' 1952, *Libcom* website. Subsequent quotes from Bordiga are from the same piece.

Nihil Evadere

Bordiga identifies three opponents to Marxism, and he reserves his greatest ire not for the bourgeoisie (the "deniers") or the Stalinists (the "falsifiers") but those revolutionaries who have turned against the predictive power of Marxism (the "modernizers") — who he considers "to be the worst of the lot." He is, of course referring to those who are associated with, or agree with, the perspectives of *Socialisme ou Barbarie*, which was formed in 1948. He writes that these "self-declared advocates of the revolutionary doctrine and method... attribute its current abandonment by the majority of the proletariat to defects and initial gaps in the theory that must, therefore, be rectified and brought up to date." They are, in their denial of the central strength of Marxism, as he states, worse than the bourgeoisie itself... there is a comedy to be written here, but maybe *Monty Python* already did it with *The Life of Brian*.

The notion of an 'invariance' in the struggles of the proletariat has been retained to this day by the collaborator of Bordiga, Jacques Camatte. From 1968 he has produced a journal titled *Revue Invariance*, which can be found on the Internet. The events of 1968 had a huge impact on Marxist and revolutionary theory.[78] It was seen as an expression, or indication, of the final defeat of the old workers' movement. The first shock to the system of the revolutionary movement occurred from 1917 to 1945 — and resulted in the reconfiguring of the Marxist schema described above with such hostility by Bordiga. The second blow was 1968. It led many to become far more cautious in their pronouncements, and to become prepared for very slow progress. Jacques Camatte, echoing Bordiga's contempt for *Socialisme ou Barbarie*, saw this as an unhealthy despair. In 1983 he wrote:

> "It is magnificent that Dauvé/Barrot has entitled his magazine 'La Banquise' [Pack Ice],[79] which corresponds very well to what he and his companions are: the living dead. It also corresponds to the fact that his pupils called him an undertaker! Obviously the living-dead cannot 'create' another dynamic of life. But there is more, by reproaching me for 'my optimism' they resign from their position as representatives, as they conceive of themselves, of a class that must be revolutionary. Indeed, what are leaders who cry out for defeat, for asphyxiation, worth? It is certain that blissful optimism is ridiculous, but

---

[78] Their thinking was prefigured and influenced by *The Frankfurt School* understanding of the German Revolution of 1918.

[79] *La Banquise* ceased in 1986, and Dauvé started a new journal with a more positive title, *Le Brise-glace*, or Icebreaker, in 1986. His current magazine, on the Internet, is *Troploin* — which translates as 'too far' or 'too far away,' and may indicate that his pessimism has returned.

optimism determined by a certain prediction is an assurance of strength for a struggle or for staying alive."[80]

Camatte keeps the fire of prophecy firmly lit.[81] Indeed, since the 'defeat' of 1968 he has reconfigured, just as Bordiga did after the defeat evident at the end of WWII, the prophecy of communism. Whereas Bordiga placed the Marxian prophecy within the concept of 'invariance,' Camatte has reconfigured the concept of invariance itself, so that it still retains its kernel of prophecy.[82] The revised invariance, the revised prophecy, concerns the coming of a new *species* of human being:

> "From then on, an historical-theoretical investigation of the human phenomenon became necessary in order to situate the wandering of the species, to understand how the separation from nature and the dynamics that followed from it had come about. In particular, it was necessary to grasp how the development of the dynamic of value and then capital was set in motion, firstly in the West, and then elsewhere. At the same time, it was necessary to make an inventory of the contributions of other geosocial areas to the species' future. This led to an investigation into the various traumas of the species across different areas. From all this, the emergence of *Homo gemeinwesen* — the species that will succeed *Homo sapiens* — could be revealed. The new species will be in continuity with nature and the cosmos. Its consciousness will not possess a function for justifying its existence — the species will operate solely within the activities of enjoyment.
>
> "Initially we operated in a dynamic of struggle and opposition, which aimed at the negation of this world and its replacement with a society that affirmed the true *Gemeinwesen* of humanity (K. Marx). We abandoned the struggle and the opposition because it was ineffective, and we sought another dynamic of life. This led us to locating the starting point, the origin of Homo sapiens, and then to detecting the emergence of another species."[83]

---

[80] Jacques Camatte, 1980 (2001), 'La Mort Potentielle du Capital,' at the site *Revue Invariance*. Translations are my own.

[81] See footnote 6.

[82] For Bordiga the 'invariance' of Marxism was the theory of the proletariat, which necessitates, or generates, communism. Camatte amends this slightly: "the theory of which invariance was posited is communism," and explains just what he means by the invariance: "The invariance is that of the yearning to rediscover the lost community; this is achieved not by a re-actualisation of the past but through an act of creation," 'Affirmations et citations,' in *Invariance*, Series II, No. 3, April 1973, p121.

[83] Jacques Camatte, 'Point de Départ,' at R.I.

Michael Hardt and Antonio Negri appear to pursue a similar 'evolutionary' theme (though they still call for insurrection): "The primary decision made by the multitude is really the decision to create a new race [sic] or rather, a new humanity. When love is conceived politically, then, this creation of a new humanity is the ultimate act of love."[84]

The Mao of Badiou

French philosopher, Alain Badiou is also an adherent of the idea of 'the real movement.' But he associates his 'real movement' with Mao, who, he says, "thinks in an almost infinite way."

> "On the one hand, there is no doubt that two fundamental episodes of Mao's political struggle can be regarded as grave failures, which took a high toll in human lives: the Great Leap Forward and the Great Proletarian Cultural Revolution. And [one is] right in seeing in both of them a passion for the infinite real movement. But, on the other hand, these two episodes proved Mao's determination to find new ways to really move toward communism. Mao wanted a communist revolution in a socialist state. So he had to keep creating something new, keep forging ahead, keep trying, because communism is precisely the infinite that the finitude of the state, including with its brutality, is incapable of by itself."[85]

For Badiou, the Cultural Revolution of 1966-67, particularly the establishment of the Shanghai Commune, is at least as important for the restructuring of Marxism in the West as the events in France during 1968.

---

[84] Hardt and Negri, *Multitude: War and Democracy in the Age of Empire*, The Penguin Press, 2004, p356.

[85] Alain Badiou, interviewed in 2014. Transcript: 'Creative Nonfiction: A Lecture Performance by Alain Badiou,' 2015, at *leapleapleap* website. For Badiou, materialism is "an assault philosophy" (A. Badiou, *Theory of the Subject*, Bruno Bosteels (trans.), Continuum, 2009/1982, p185). And for there to be an 'event' there must be an 'intervention' which alters the situation or causes a 'rupture' — therefore, Badiou's claim to be a 'philosopher of this hidden progress' could also be regarded being a claim to be a philosopher of the 'intervention.' This fits well with his Maoism, and with his notorious invasions of Deleuze's lectures (he called Deleuze "an enemy of the people") in the late 1970s. See, François Dosse, *Intersecting Lives*, Deborah Glassman (trans.), CUP, 2010 (2007), pp365-8.

Yiching Wu's subaltern history of this period, *The Cultural Revolution at the Margins: Chinese Socialism in Crisis*, describes the Maoist Cultural Revolution as an event that demonstrated "Mao's inherently contradictory role as both the chief of China's Leninist party-state and the rebel leader"[86] and as something that ended with Mao needing to crush the "freewheeling mass politics" which had been "unleashed by Mao [himself]."[87]

Wu also notes the tremendous influence of Maoism and the Cultural Revolution on a generation of political activists, including Badiou and Fredric Jameson.[88] Hardt and Negri summarize the significance of the Cultural Revolution for leftist ideology in the West: "Mao himself had called upon the Chinese masses to attack the party-state apparatus and claim power for themselves. *The image of China thus served as an alternative to the Soviet model* and the various Communist parties that followed the Soviet line, but it also posed the notion of a full and free engagement of the masses with no centralized control. The external image of the Cultural Revolution was thus one of anti-authoritarianism and radical democracy."[89]

Around 2009, Badiou and Slavoj Žižek, and others, tried to reformulate communism to fit with unpromising times in order to bring the concept back to life. Alain Badiou defines the re-conceptualization of communism in these terms: "The decisive issue is the need to cling to the historical hypothesis of a world that has been freed from the law of profit and private interest — even while we are, at the level of intellectual representations, still prisoners of the conviction that we cannot do away with it, that this is the way of the world, and that no politics of emancipation is possible. That is what I propose to call the communist hypothesis. It is in fact mainly negative, as it is safer and more important to say that the existing world is not *necessary* than it is to say, when we have nothing to go on, that a different world is possible."[90]

---

[86] Yiching Wu, *The Cultural Revolution at the Margins: Chinese Socialism in Crisis*, Harvard University Press, 2014, pxv.

[87] Ibid., xvi.

[88] Ibid., 1-2.

[89] Hardt and Negri, *Multitude: War and Democracy in the Age of Empire*, The Penguin Press, 2004. Page 76, original emphasis.

[90] Badiou, *Theory of the Subject*, Bruno Bosteels (trans.), Continuum Publishing, London. Pages 63-4, original emphasis.

This apparent 'pessimism' converges with the cautiousness of the 'communizers,'[91] a cautiousness directly descended from the adaptation of Marxism expressed, for example by *Socialisme ou Barbarie*, and so ferociously condemned by Amadeo Bordiga. But other elements of it converge with Jacques Camatte. Badiou writes that it is "more important to say that the existing world is not *necessary*." Badiou describes himself (see below) as a philosopher of a "hidden progress" that is altogether *actual*. Such positions are reflected in Camatte, who writes:

> "Each one of us starts from their own position, in order to reach and meet others, to walk with them, undertaking the necessary inversion to the best of our abilities. This divergence, this other path, will lead to the later and full affirmation of liberation/emergence — which is begun in the first perception of the need for it."[92]

Camatte's concept of 'inversion' — the process by which the new human species will emerge — begins as a personal journey that finds fulfillment when it becomes part of a communal awakening.[93] As he writes above, this new species is already emerging, and the liberation of humanity — which is simultaneous with the emergence of the new species — will occur at some point in the distant future… but only if Homo sapiens, the current species, doesn't allow itself to become extinct before then.[94]

In his definition of 'inversion' Camatte writes that it "refers to the establishment of a future contrary to that effectuated until today, including in particular: the exit from nature, repression, refusal, abstraction, riots (uprisings, revolutions), but also wars and peace… [It is a question of] accessing something in germ within us, in this case: the deep naturalness that has always been

---

[91] See, for example, 'We Unhappy Few,' *Endnotes* 5, online, 2019. In this article the writers demonstrate a change in the attitude of Endnotes to the concept of 'the real movement' — it is as if the ghost of Bakunin has gently taken hold of them. In 2011, Endnotes wrote: "Communization is a movement at the level of the totality, through which that totality is abolished." (Endnotes, 'What Are We To Do?' in *Noys*, p28, see fn 62). But in 2019, in 'We Unhappy Few' they write: "A notion of the real movement can, it seems, mean (and justify) anything, everything and nothing," p29. It is uncertain whether Bakunin would smile at this glacially slow abandonment of the mysticism he observed in Marxian thought or whether he would wring his hands.

[92] Camatte, 'Deroullement,' on the *Revue Invariance* website, behind the photo of the tree.

[93] Camatte, 'Deroullement,' as above.

[94] Camatte, 'Instauration du risque d'extinction,' 2020, *Revue Invariance*.

repressed and largely obscured, and a continuity with all living beings and the cosmos."[95]

Camatte would, therefore, perhaps also agree that a good starting point for people who want to live differently is to become aware that 'the existing world is not necessary.' Camatte retains his optimism, or his belief — his loyalty to the prophecy of Marx — that this concrete becoming (the real movement), is an inevitable aspect of a developing human future, even if it might take a long time, and may be thwarted by human extinction.

And Badiou, though he may appear more cautious in proclaiming the future, because he suspects that this in itself will hinder its progress, does *still believe*:

> "Let me tell you this: capitalism is a totally artificial social system. We're still faced with the alternative established by Marx: communism or barbarism. Currently, barbarism is very dominant. But awareness of its pathological aspect is also making progress. The progress is slow and invisible, but entirely real. I am one of the philosophers of this hidden progress."[96]

But Badiou does not want us to think that his method is simply one of belief or is simply an idea of "a utopia for beautiful souls."[97] He does not want to be associated with *the anarchists*. In 2010, Badiou wrote: "We know today that all emancipatory politics must put an end to the model of the party, or of multiple parties, in order to affirm a politics 'without party,' and yet at the same time without lapsing into the figure of anarchism, which has never been anything else than the vain critique, or the double, or the shadow, of the communist parties, just as the black flag is only the double or the shadow of the red flag."[98]

> In the 1970s, philosopher Alain Badiou led several student disruptions of lectures by fellow philosopher, Gilles Deleuze, and referred to Deleuze's concept of the 'rhizome' as 'The Fascism of the Potato'. After Deleuze's death Badiou insisted that they had always been good friends.

---

[95] Camatte, 'Inversion,' in the *Glossaire* on *Revue Invariance*.
[96] Badiou, interviewed in 2014. See fn 85.
[97] Bruno Bosteels, *The Actuality of Communism*, Verso, 2011, p19.
[98] Badiou, A. 2010, *The Communist Hypothesis*, David Macey and Steve Corcoran (trans.), Verso, p155.

Badiou, then, clearly sees the opposition to capitalism as a "progress." One can usefully substitute the word progress with 'becoming.' He is not saying that there is an interminable, repeating, struggle against the conditions of our lives, he is saying that there is an actual process happening in society that will lead to the overcoming of these conditions, and he regards himself as a reporter and helper of this process.

In a similar maneuver, Gilles Dauvé and the group *Théorie Communiste* have transformed the concept of 'the real movement' into the theory of 'communization.' Essentially, these theorists maintain that if there is going to be a revolution that obliterates capitalism then it has to happen 'at once,' through practical daily-life measures, with no 'transitional programme' (notwithstanding T.C.s contradictory affirmation of "The dictatorship of the social movement of communization," see above), and it must not be mediated by leaders or 'parties.' The term 'the real movement,' then, should be understood in our time as 'becoming,' or an immanence.

Scholar of Badiou, and major participant in the project to reformulate the idea of communism begun in 2009, Bruno Bosteels, notes that "the central passage which is repeated like a mantra not only in the present book [his own, *The Actuality of Communism*] but also in almost every contribution to the volumes that have resulted from 'The Idea of Communism' conferences so far" are the lines from Marx concerning "the *real* movement which abolishes the present state of things."[99] Bosteels works through the problem of the dissonance between the prophecy of scientific (dialectical) inevitability in this passage and the indication that "a subjective political intervention is needed to actualize the moving contradiction of capital's economic tendencies," but his hermeneutics do not take into account the fact that Marx insisted he was doing science (cf. Cohen), and this leads Bosteels to conclude that:

> "Communism must not only be rehistoricized outside all suppositions of historical necessity and stageism, it must also be actualized and organized as the real movement that abolishes the present state of things. In other words, communism must again find inscription in a concrete body, the collective flesh and thought of an internationalist political subjectivity — even if it may no longer be necessary for such an act of subjectivization to pass through the traditional form of the party for its embodiment."[100]

---

[99] Bruno Bosteels, 'Preface to the Korean Translation of *The Actuality of Communism*,' 2014, can be found on the *Academia* website, individuals can join for free access to papers uploaded.
[100] Bosteels, *The Actuality of Communism*, 2011, p239.

Here we can see that Bosteels actually dismisses the dialectical, materialist, processes that Marx told us would create the intellectual and physical gravediggers of capitalism, in favour of a return to the voluntarism and evangelism of an organization of utopian thinkers — "an internationalist political subjectivity." But I don't think Bosteels realizes that he has done this. And I am sure that the Marx of the 19th Century would object to this reformulation and intellectual retreat in similar terms to those issued to the 'modernizers' by Amadeo Bordiga in 1952.

So, what we have here is a *belief* in the notion of 'the real movement' — which Bosteels refers to as a "mantra" — that sits side by side with the idea that communism as 'the real movement' must be "actualized and organized [through] an internationalist political subjectivity." Are we talking science here, or moralism? That is, 'science,' or just 'good idea'? The balance of Bosteels' analysis reveals that he has, unlike Badiou, drifted into the realm of the 'beautiful souls' and 'vain critique' — but, even worse, in a case of 'having one's cake *and* eating it,' Bosteels has, like a true *lutteomancer*, held onto the mystical scientific prophecy as a marker of materialist credibility.

Dauvé vs The *Real* Movement

Although Gilles Dauvé is central to an examination of 'the *real* movement' as an indicator of the prophecy of Marx, it is necessary to note that his position has changed. Dauvé long ago abandoned the determinism and prophecy in Marx's formulation. If one reads through the debate between *Théorie Communiste* and Dauvé (*Troploin*), reproduced in the first issue of the *Endnotes* Journal (2008, available online), it becomes apparent that Dauvé does not insert the Marxian conceptualization of 'the *real* movement' — *inevitability* — into communization, whereas *Théorie Communiste*, however weakly or surreptitiously, continue to do so.

Endnotes summarize the differences between the two presentations of communization:

> "Thus for Troploin, communism as communization is an ever-present (if at times submerged) possibility, one which, even if there is no guarantee that it will be realized, is an invariant in the capitalist epoch. By contrast, for TC communization is the specific form which the communist revolution must take in the current cycle of struggle. In distinction from Troploin, then, TC

are able to self-reflexively ground their conception of communization in an understanding of capitalist history as cycles of struggle." ('Afterword.')

So, to explain: if Dauvé views communization as a "possibility," then communism itself is only a possibility. *Théorie Communiste*, in contrast, are arguing that communization is the form communist revolution will ("must") take in every different capitalist era.[101] They write:

> "Does that mean that the revolution and communization are now the only future? Again this is a question without meaning, without reality. The only inevitability is the class struggle though which we can only conceive of the revolution of *this* cycle of struggle, and not as a collapse of capital leaving a space open, but as an historically specific practice of the proletariat in the crisis of this period of capital... The outcome of the struggle is never given beforehand. It is self-evident that revolution cannot be reduced to a sum of its conditions, because it is an overcoming and not a fulfilment." ('Much Ado About Nothing.')

In this almost opaque passage, *Théorie Communiste* are keeping their empirical predictive powder dry. They refuse to answer in simple and honest terms, like good politicians, the question put by Dauvé:

> "Who could argue that communism is bound to happen? The communist revolution is not the ultimate stage of capitalism." ('Love of Labor? Love of Labor Lost...'- written with Karl Nesic.)

So, it is now clear that the only people who uphold the empirically predictive power of the notion of 'the *real* movement,' are *Théorie Communiste* (who rarely use the term itself), *Endnotes* (who use the term frequently) and Alain Badiou.[102] Of those others who use the term, including those *around* Badiou, as well as *Endnotes* and *Théorie Communiste*, it is reasonable to say that their interpretation is contrary to Marx's — which is fine, of course, as it doesn't matter, even though it demonstrates a critical lacuna in historical and philosophical understanding.

---

[101] Readers may object that I am neglecting to mention the different ways Dauvé and *TC* theoretically approach past revolts, but they are not needed for my argument here.

[102] Jacques Camatte's adherence to the predictive power within Marx's theory is different of course, as explained. For the record, however, it should be stated that, as through the 1970s, in the current resurgence of interest in his work Camatte remains significantly *unread* and therefore misunderstood.

It seems likely, based on the readings (and perhaps the ages of the participants?), that the arc of prophecy that runs through the work of Badiou, *Théorie Communiste* and *Endnotes* will end either in disappearance or in the anarchism they resist — a political tendency, we should recall, that, despite its millenarianism and cultism, does *not* do Marxian certainty. Bakunin must be spinning in his grave. As for Camatte, like Bordiga, he seems adamant in retaining the Marxian prophecy of a new world, and there seems little chance of him reversing his 'anti-enmity' position (see his definition of *inversion* above) and slipping into an advocacy for the confrontational political styles — riots etc. — affirmed by anarchism or by those recently inspired by the revolts in the USA (2020).

A Strangeness

I have examined the trajectory of revolutionary prophecy in three significant instances of its historical expression. Prophecy still exists in the Abrahamic religions, and in the three revolutionary strands identified above. Strangely, perhaps, it does not exist in Trotskyism or the modern-day oppositional Communist Parties. The eminent Trotskyist, Ernest Mandel, wrote in 1988:

> "If there is no coherent anti-capitalist theory, no systematic anti-capitalist education, and no anti-capitalist activity by revolutionary organizations, then no victorious proletarian victory is possible in the imperialist countries and therefore there will be no solution to humanity's crisis, no future."[103]

This is a clear backing away from any prophecy of the inevitable arrival of communism (unlike the Badiou-ian and part of the *lutteomancing* tendencies).

Then there is the *International Communist Current*, a group formed in 1975 not in 'despair' at the glacial slowness of the approach of revolution (see Dauvé, above), but as a consequence of what they saw as the hopeful upsurge of struggles from 1968 onwards. The ICC does not prophesy a revolution through the real movement, they, more moderately, while regarding revolution as a moral imperative, only view it as a genuine *possibility*: "The present resurgence of the proletarian struggle indicates that once again the perspective of communism is not only an historic necessity, but a real possibility."[104]

---

[103] Ernest Mandel, 'The Reasons for Founding the Fourth International, And Why They Remain Valid Today,' 1988, MIA.
[104] *Platform of the ICC*, 2004, see their website.

But Hardt and Negri in their 2004 book, *Multitude, do* allow prophecy into their analysis, the very last lines of the book are:

> "We can already recognize that today time is split between a present that is already dead and a future that is already living — and the yawning abyss between them is becoming enormous. In time, an event will thrust us like an arrow into that living future. This will be the real political act of love."[105]

This certainty of a coming event is not so apparent in Negri's analysis in the 1970s. Negri, like the Situationists, also uses the term 'the real movement' without any reference to its source — as if it is 'a given' in continental Europe — in *Marx Beyond Marx*, but his use of it is highly ambiguous, and confers upon modern revolutionaries the task of 'materializing communism' as "an historical force."[106]

The more orthodox, or mainstream oppositional Marxist organizations, such as the *Fourth International*, have long since abandoned prophecy. Ironically, these are the organizations that pin their allegiances most closely to a simplified Marx (they wear hammer-and-sickle tee-shirts, etc), while those who have thought most hard and deep about the legacy of Marx's philosophy, beginning with the left-communists of the early 1920s, and through the analysis of groups such as *Socialisme ou Barbarie* — and who now even hesitate to call themselves Marxist — are the ones who have retained the prophetic — or mystical — element of his discourse.

It was Lenin himself who began the process of divorcing the bulk of revolutionary Marxists from the paroxysm of prophecy (Trotsky extended the process with his notion of the 'permanent revolution'). By properly formulating a strategy for a transitional phase between capitalism and communism (electrification and education), and by also separating the term 'revolution' from the establishment of an 'immediate communism' — making it a phenomenon that would come after revolutions of national liberation — Lenin, like Trotsky, was able to retain the science of the Marxist dialectic without having to establish peace and happiness on earth immediately. One can sense this approach when Lenin writes, in 1918: "We are banking on the inevitability of the world

---

[105] Hardt and Negri, *Multitude*, p358.
[106] Antonio Negri, *Marx Beyond Marx*, (1978), Harry Cleaver, et al (trans.), Autonomedia/Pluto, 1991, p184. This earlier interpretation, of course, is entirely in line with the strategy Bosteels suggests above to re-ignite the idea of communism.

revolution, but this does not mean that we are such fools as to bank on the revolution inevitably coming on a *definite* and early date."[107]

We *Writhe*; we do not *Become*

Historically, the practice of prophecy is particular to elements within a State formation. By 'State formation' I mean a society that is exploitative and hierarchical — that is, a civilization, or proto-civilization, or an emergent civilization (as Clastres points out, above, it is also triggered at the very moment that a mass society — State/Chiefdom — begins). Prophecy is part of a critique of society that calls upon a supposed higher authority for validation of its radical, revolutionary, and apocalyptic theses. Without this higher authority the prophecy loses its world-significance and remains merely an idea, an ideal, or *an idealism*. Prophecy became established as an intellectual tradition in the Abrahamic religions. Christianity was the motor that enabled prophecy to become embedded in the scientific revolution in Europe. Early European scientists were all magi of some kind and the dramatically changing times — the transition from feudalism to capitalism — meant they also expressed a general feeling that the end times were approaching. In the first great capitalist revolution, in the British Isles, the radicals who observed the increasing misery of the times sought authority for their warnings and hopes (prophecies) from God or the Bible.

As the Enlightenment became more established the notion of God was diminished, and so radicals no longer used the methods of prophecy to proclaim their views. It was Marx who brought prophecy back into the revolutionary tradition: by replacing God, as the authority for his views and observations, with *the scientific method*, empiricism, or dialectical materialism. In so doing, Marx, turned all academic investigation of social matters into empirical sciences, which is why they later became known as the social *sciences*. As Lenin wrote in 1894: "[The] idea of materialism in sociology was in-itself a stroke of genius."[108]

Part of the great debate between Marx and Bakunin at the time of the First International was over the empirical validity of Marx's theories, or how Marx was able to impart a scientific authority to his theories and views. Through science Marx was able to make prophecies for society in the same way that emergent chemistry, for example, was able to make predictions about the

---

[107] V.I Lenin, 'Letter to American Workers,' 1918, original emphasis, MIA.
[108] V.I. Lenin, 'What *The Friends of the People* Are, Part 1,' 1894, MIA.

Nihil Evadere

behavior of matter in all cases. His methodology did indeed reveal the historical forces that shaped social phenomena or, at least, the truth that social phenomena are shaped by historical forces. But Marx let this insight go to his head and this allowed him not only to prophesy, but to claim that all his views were the result of a careful empiricism rather than wishful thinking. Bakunin, unlike Marx, did not reshape his utopian visions through a rubric of science and his argument could therefore be discounted by Marx as 'unscientific.' Many of Bakunin's objections — such as the one that questioned the proposed Marxian relationship between town and country — could therefore be written off by Marx as 'schoolboy drivel.' Forced collectivization and the extermination of the 'kulaks,' of course, proved that Bakunin was right.

The irony for those revolutionaries who still refer to 'the real movement' or 'invariance' is that their apparent materialism is built upon mystical grounds. Marx considered himself to be a *scientist*, and any interpretation of Marx that does not properly recognize this fact becomes a betrayal of his work. But Marx rediscovered the power of prophecy *through science* — in a way that mirrors the work of people like John Napier and Isaac Newton — and he made science the religion, or dogma, at the basis of what became Marxism. Marx laid the groundwork for a system of *belief*, one that had a sacred, central authority, and which re-imagined God as the materialist dialectic. (And his methodology became, as Isaiah Berlin observed, "the permanent background of civilized thought.") Marx, therefore, is perhaps the last great prophet of Abrahamic religion.[109]

The *lutteomancers*, those who search for signs of the future revolution in the 'struggles' of today are divided into two camps: those who insist that the signs they see are evidence of the truth of the prophecy; and those who merely see the signs as evidence of a possibility. The first group would these days appear only to consist of *Théorie Communiste*, *Endnotes* and Badiou. I have not gone through the texts of those other Marxist-leaning groups listed above (in reference to the exaltation of theory) to see if they retain the prophetic element or not. Certainly the 'group' *Ill Will Editions* define 'the real movement' in terms that deny inevitability, recently they wrote: "we use the term "real movement" as a shorthand to name all those features of rebellion that bypass representation, discourse, and dialogue, and instead pursue the antagonism with the state and

---

[109] "Marx is simultaneously a bourgeois and revolutionary prophet. The latter is better known than the former. But the former explains many things in the career of the latter. A messianism of Christian and bourgeois origin, which was both historic and scientific, influenced his revolutionary messianism, which sprang from German ideology and the French rebellions." Albert Camus, *The Rebel*, 1951.

capital directly, even *physically*, if you will."[110] This formulation of the term abandons the prediction of the inevitability of communism in favor of an affirmation of the radical potential of social resistances that are not immediately co-opted by political organizations or individuals. (They make a distinction between a 'mediated' *social* movement and an 'unmediated' *real* movement.) They do not use the phrase in the properly Marxian conceptualization, by which the inevitability and prophecy is essential to the phrase. They are, in this sense, closer to Dauvé's conception of communization/communism (as possibility) than *Théorie Communiste*'s.

Lutteomancy, whether it is performed by those who prophesy communism or those who simply *want* communism is, therefore, another word for 'theory.' And those who make theory (which means writing things down) are generally quite unreflexive in their reasons for making it. If theory is not meant to inform future practise and show us the truth that should be revealed in the future — if it is not in the form of a 'theory of principle' — then it is locked into a perpetual past, it is a form of journalism, or propaganda.

Events always race ahead of our consciousness of them. If a theory on an event is written it is out of date as soon as the first letter on the keyboard is struck. One can write down what one perceives an event to mean, but it has no other use than as a way of trying to get readers to think about things in the way the writer does. The analysis is already formed in the writer's mind and is therefore already dated. Revolutionary theory never keeps up with what is happening in the world simply because none of us ever keep up with anything that is happening in the world, which means we never even keep up with ourselves. We can only *begin* to understand what is happening after it has already happened — this means not only that we are 'late' in understanding, it also means that we think things are happening when they are, in fact, already finished, already happened, already established, already superseded.

---

[110] *Ill Will Editions*, 'The Shifting Ground: A Conversation on the George Floyd Rebellion,' 20th September 2020. Online. Much of their perspective has been developed in conjunction with their witnessing of the 'yellow-vest movement' in France, a phenomenon that has morphed into the 'anti-vax' movement. Indeed, if one reads what they say above again, one can see that they could easily end up supporting all kinds of 'spontaneous' revolts against 'the State' from whatever quarter, and *Ill Will* have regularly demonstrated support for far-right inspired actions across the world in the last year or so. But, despite their popularity, they are by no means great theoreticians, and one suspects that their trajectory is informed more by naivety and immaturity than a logical joining of (even their own) dots, or an understanding that there are many layers to an 'event.'

Theory, then, in the sense that revolutionaries use it, is not what it claims to be. It is 'just' writing, and all writing is an expression of money or power, or potential oppression — it is most probable that writing itself emerged from accountancy in trade and the organization of people within States.[111] As Claude Lévi-Strauss observes:

> "If my hypothesis is correct, the primary function of writing, as a means of communication, is to facilitate the enslavement of other human beings. The use of writing for disinterested ends, and with a view to satisfactions of the mind in the fields either of science or the arts, is a secondary result of its invention – and may even be no more than a way of reinforcing, justifying, or dissimulating its primary function."[112]

Why am I writing this essay then? Well, firstly, if I really knew why I was writing this — or doing anything at all — then I would be in possession of some kind of impossible consciousness, far above anything that a brain and nervous system is capable of. But, no, that is wrong. Humans believe in the possibility of a higher consciousness, or are at least tempted by the idea, because their consciousness, as Schopenhauer and Nietzsche suggested, is a "superficial and falsifying"[113] consciousness, consisting of categorizing and classifying the world, a process that requires a focus that excludes other truths. This is why humans *can* build cities and colonize the planet, and it is why those outside of civilization refuse this 'ability' — which they regard as a curse. Humans in civilization, then, look for a future of hope for humanity at other levels, whether it be transcendent or immanent, that is, in a higher consciousness, or a deeper consciousness. Either way, they are predictable hopes and intellectual strategies for an animal that embraces the tendency to classify and objectify, to judge, to organize, and omit — this animal being the civilized animal.

---

[111] See, Denise Schmandt-Besserat, 2006, *How Writing Came About*, University of Texas Press; James Scott, 2009, *The Art of Not Being Governed: An Anarchist History of Upland Southeast Asia*, Yale University Press, p 228, 388n23; Elman Service, 1975, *Origins of the State and Civilization: The Process of Cultural Evolution*, Norton, New York, p7; Thomas Suddendorf, 2013, *The Gap: The Science Of What Separates Us From Other Animals*, Basic Books, New York, p270-1.
[112] Claude Lévi-Strauss, 1961 (1955), *Tristes Tropiques*, John Russell (trans.), Criterion, p292.
[113] See Paul Katsafanas, 2018 (2016), *The Nietzschean Self*, Chapter 3. Also, Virginia Woolf, *The Waves*, 1931: "Louis, wild-eyed but severe, in his attic, in his office, has formed unalterable conclusions upon the true nature of what is to be known," and, "Let a man get up and say, 'Behold, this is the truth,' and I instantly perceive a sandy cat filching a piece of fish in the background. Look, you have forgotten the cat, I say." (Vintage Classics edition, pages 156 and 133, respectively.)

I am writing this... because I can...; because I am interested in it; because the process of writing things like this is very enlightening for me (I research intently); and because I want to get readers to think about what I am writing, and then to make up their own minds... which means that I want them to agree with me (*oh, how base my motives are...*) — even though I suspect that hardly anyone will agree, and I have become perfectly happy for them not to.

> Maurice Merleau-Ponty saw human activity as based not upon a Descartian 'cogito' but upon 'perceptions' received by parts of the body, therefore beyond the control of one's 'mind'. Indeed, *The Visible and the Invisible* was written, against his wishes, entirely by his left knee.

I want to answer my question of why I am writing this with: *It is, in the end, just writing*. But is this true? Is Lévi-Strauss correct? Am I unsuspectingly attempting, dear reader, to enslave you? Yes, of course. All writing, all *recording*, is oppressive, and a mark of the tyranny we accept and inflict. But why I write is also an expression of that writhing movement we all make under the condition of existing within a State and civilization. Instead of actually living, something eternally denied in civilization,[114] I am, like you, trying to work something out that on every level cannot be worked out (even though this effort may help build new tyrannies and put new masters in place). I, we, continue to writhe — we can do nothing else. Anyway, in my opinion, the only *value* in writing is if it destabilizes the thoughts, or assumptions, of readers.

The production of theoretical or revolutionary texts points to a religious hope, cloaked in materialist conceptions. To maintain the veneer of credibility 'struggles' must be examined, as Castoriadis argued, under what might be termed a 'real movement' lens: one looks for signs, in the endless cycle of revolts, for the germ of world revolution, and then one tries to participate, or tries to demonstrate one's usefulness to the cause of the higher goal by writing about these apparent signs. In this way, whether one understands what Marx meant by 'the *real* movement' or not, one becomes a *lutteomancer*: a searcher for sacred signs of the promise of a new world in '*struggles*' — just as tasseomancers make predictions from the tea leaves in a cup. And in so doing one enters a mystical realm in which one's revolutionary, communist, conviction — the one thing shared by Marx and Bakunin — orbits the planet like a Russell's Teapot.

---

[114] Those against 'lockdowns' and proofs of vaccination appear to believe that we had freedom and autonomy *before* the pandemic.

Nihil Evadere

There is indeed a *real movement* in civilized society, but it is just that, a *movement*, or a reflex — a resentful individual and social *writhing* — not a becoming. It is a *built-in* persistent, natural, and eminently noble *resentment* — a constant, or recurring, emotional, physical and intellectual discourse between the exploited and the terms of their exploitation. As such, it is inherent to individuals of all classes. It is not a *becoming* that is leading toward the opposite of how we live and who we are. It is not an evolution towards a better world where hierarchy and exploitation no longer exist. It is the abiding condition of those, us, who exist in civilization — a form of society from which, once established, as with all societies and any society, there is no escape. No one can, by the power of their will or imagination escape, genuinely transform or transcend the society that has constructed them.

2 Misunderstanding Agamben and Camatte

Nowhere since the 1980s does Agamben call for armed revolt, yet his interpreters often use him to validate armed insurrection. Part of the reason is a literal reading of Tiqqun, *combined with a tendency to regard their work as mirroring Agamben's. But Agamben views* Tiqqun *as a phenomenon just beginning, for him, to ask the right questions. Camatte, in contrast, is highly regarded because of his early formulations on the domestication of humanity and capital's hegemony, yet his core thesis, that humans must abandon enmity, remains unrecognized. Moreover, due to their insistence on revolution – a stance of 'all or nothing' even though it lacks a violent aspect — these tendencies ultimately, because of the* abstentionism *that their revolutionism entails, strengthen the politics of reaction.*

I

If one picks carefully over the millenarian and revolutionary events of the last 500 years, and in particular since 1789, it may be that one begins to concur with Albert Camus who, after living through the absurdities of the aftermath of the Russian Revolution, the Holocaust, and WWII, changed his mind about his own 'revolutionary' commitment, he wrote:

> The revolutionary is simultaneously a rebel or he is not a revolutionary, but a policeman, or a bureaucrat, who turns against rebellion. But there is absolutely no progress from one attitude to the other, but co-existence and endlessly increasing contradiction. Every revolutionary ends by becoming either an oppressor or a heretic. In the [...] universe that they have chosen, rebellion and revolution end in the same dilemma: either police rule or insanity. (Camus: 218: 1951)

Certainly, this was the fate in Russia of the Kronstadt rebels in 1921, as well as individuals such as Nikolai Bukharin who *simultaneously* lived the role of 'policeman' *and* heretic in the years leading to his execution.

The Marxist, Jacques Camatte, like Camus, also abandoned a combative *revolutionary* position several decades ago in favor of indicating a process whereby people might 'simply' abandon, or leave, 'the world.' Unlike Camus, however, Camatte, in his opposition to 'enmity,' abandoned *all* combat and *all* revolt, including the writing of polemics.[1] In 2020, Camatte describes this leaving as a process of 'inversion' but makes it clear that he is not offering a blueprint, or plan of action: "Inversion is not a strategy, it is totally outside of politics, which is the dynamic of organizing people, of controlling them. We must abandon everything that is part of this world."[2] His idea, generally speaking, is that one must first abandon *enmity* in every single area of one's personal life — as he writes on the front page of his website, indicating that he has achieved the first stage: "*I have no enemies: the shutting-in is abolished*"[3] — and then one can join with others of the same mind and begin to lead a different life. However, the goal of a new world will take "a few thousand years" because it will also be dependent on the human population slowly decreasing, thereby allowing all life-forms to flourish.[4]

Rejecting feelings or expressions of *enmity* toward other people or things (such as the social structure, 'injustice,' etc), and accepting the enmity of others towards oneself as their problem, not yours, is also a focus of *Zen Buddhism*. But even if one does feel that one has abandoned enmity on all levels, has one actually escaped it? Simply by continuing to live in the world — paying taxes, educating or bringing up children, living on welfare benefits or a pension, not intervening to resist things getting worse, etc — one's daily decisions help prop up the enmity that the world rests on: the enmity towards the poor which is expressed by fiscal policies; the enmity toward children expressed in the education systems across the world (Ansgar Allen insists that it is a violent act[5]; Camatte himself offers an insightful perspective on, what he terms, 'parental

---

[1] "[E]nmity is linked to competition and the need for recognition. But it also operates in politics and in the field of knowledge with the polemic," *Inimitié et extinction*, Jacques Camatte, 2019, *Revue Invariance* website (R.I.).

[2] '*Inversion is not a strategy*,' interview and translation by Gerardo Muñoz, *Ill Will Editions* website, 2020. Camatte wrote *Ce Monde Qu'il Faut Quitter* in 1974, the English translation, *This World We Must Leave*, is still in publication.

[3] The French original of 'I have no enemies: the shutting-in is abolished' is *Je n'ai pas d'ennemis: l'enfermement s'abolit*. Camatte translates the word *enfermement* as *shutting-in* in English (personal correspondences, 9 July, 23 August 2020). The concept of *enfermement* reflects his conception of a humanity that closes itself up against everything as part of its 'wandering' from its own 'nature' and 'nature' itself.

[4] '*Instauration du risque d'extinction*,' fn. 14, Camatte, R.I., 2020.

[5] See, Allen, A., 2014, *Benign Violence: Education in and Beyond the Age of Reason*, Palgrave Macmillan.

repression')[6]; the enmity toward 'the Other' that is expressed in the persistence of imperialist and colonialist strategies favoring the economies of the West; and so on.

Camatte views himself as faithful to the 'invariance' identified by his mentor, Amadeo Bordiga, in Marxism, as well as faithful to Bordiga himself, and the notions he has developed in the last decades are mirrored by Giorgio Agamben and Franco 'Bifo' Berardi, but before examining these others it is useful to understand just how Camatte sees himself within a larger historical context.

On his website, Camatte includes a short extract from a letter by him from 1978, he writes: "I have included an excerpt from a letter to a comrade because it sets out my position":

> I just want to show that we are in a dynamic of destruction which poses the necessity of another dynamic which must be TOTAL and, therefore, I posit myself directly as a totality, centralized in myself, and thus I am my goal and my movement. If I am right to propose that I cannot merely be 'individuality' but must at the same time be *Gemeinwesen* [community], my position is valid for millions of beings. For it is not I who creates ex-nihilo, rather it is through me that a certain humanity establishes itself. I want to bear witness to this. I am, if you want, like a prophet. In order to bear witness, one must also

---

[6] See, for example, *Inimitié et extinction*, 2019, (R.I.). I would argue that this is the one good idea that Camatte has had. Essentially, he observes that human babies need to be nurtured on the chest of various adults for months after they are born instead of being separated from human contact. Putting them in cots and prams instils in them a sense of insecurity. In other animals it is the young that 'teach' the adults how to raise them, in our civilized society we direct the raising of children instead of following them (Camatte, as far as I know, however, does not explore this comparison). Camatte's argument states that the neglect, distrust, and *enmity* shown to children causes an unarticulated or unconscious resentment to be established which is often expressed in teenage rebellion or an uncaring, or dismissive attitude toward the world of adults. These adolescents are then faced, though they usually do not understand why or how it has come to this, with either becoming 'good citizens' or continuing to express their resentment through a hedonistic, confrontational, or irregular lifestyle. However, Camatte does not follow through with the logic of his narrative and believes that we can abandon this way of bringing up children. To abandon trying to socialize children into the society they are about to enter can only lead to their becoming literally unable to survive. It must also be noted that, since we are created by our society, we cannot help but repeat the parental repression that we ourselves have received, no matter how much we make it kinder. And anyway, children learn from *everything* around them, and so will pick up the dictates and customs of our society through a variety of means.

denounce, bring to light, commend, and sensitize women and men, but I do not proselytize in any way... Our journey must be a call to others...[7]

It would therefore seem that Camatte's Marxism has developed into something comprising distinctly Buddhist[8] and Biblical themes (resisting *enmity* and *bearing witness*). There is also the claim of essentially operating as a prophet. Giorgio Agamben appears to have embarked on a similar journey with his articulation of a — St. Paul inspired — 'messianic destituency' (Aarons: 51: 2020), as a possible means of 'saving' humanity,[9] or escaping the world as it is, though he has not claimed the status of a prophet. Indeed, Agamben has also come to incorporate Buddhist themes. In his book *Karman* (2017), Agamben compares his own conception of *inoperativity*[10] (which is similar to Camatte's *inversion*) with the Buddha's interpretation of *nirvāṇa*, describing the latter as a state "in which imaginations and errors conditioned by ignorance have been suspended and deactivated," and the former as "the space... that is opened when the apparatuses that link human actions in the connection of means and ends, of imputation and fault, of merit and demerit, are rendered inoperative" (Agamben 2017: Ch.4: Sec. 19). *Nirvāṇa*, like inoperativity, is a deactivation of karma, therefore it is a condition that is "no longer the karmic one of merit and demerit, of means and ends" (Agamben 2017: Ch. 4: Sec, 14).

---

[7] 'Extrait de lettre,' 1978, in *Articles d'Invariance serie I* (R.I.).

[8] Though Camatte's perspectives can reasonably be perceived as corresponding to those of Buddhism, he is keen to distance himself from it: "Buddhism for me is unbearable. Buddhism is complete repression," see Interview with Jacques Camatte (2019) on *Libcom*. Buddhism, like all philosophy, is a response to living in a state, or civilization. It is the recognition that life is unsatisfactory and is an effort to make it bearable. As Agamben notes later in this essay, all ethics is a 'doctrine of happiness.' There is no 'philosophy' prior to civilization, by-the-way, or in the non-State societies of the 'uncontacted' tribes.

[9] "Only because I am not alone is there salvation: I can be saved only as one among many, as an other among others" (Agamben: 2020).

[10] Inoperativity is "a form of action that implies neither suffering nor effort" (Agamben, 2007, Ch. 8, sec. 26). In other words, it is activity that is neither *work* nor something designed to accomplish some higher purpose, and it can, Agamben contends, become a 'form-of-life.' It is also a 'pure means.' "The only coherent way to understand inoperativeness is to think of it as a generic mode of potentiality that is not exhausted (like individual action or collective action understood as the sum of individual actions) in a *transitus de*[sic] *potentia da actum*" (Agamben: 40: 1995). Agamben's notion of potentiality is, as is well-known, a consideration of Aristotle's own thinking, but it is also Leibnizean: "[T]here cannot be action without the power of acting [but] potency is worthless which can never be exercised... action and potency are none-the-less different things, the first successive [or momentary], the second lasting" (Leibniz: 125: 1698).

II

It is now time to leave Camatte for a while; indeed, it is Agamben and, even more so, his interpreters who are the principle focus of this essay. Agamben has written extensively on the philosophical background and juridical principles of the phenomenon of the 'state of exception' which "was established by Carl Schmitt in his book *Politische Theologie* (1922)" (Agamben: 2: 2003). Very briefly, Agamben's argument is that in modern times the state of exception (or emergency) has become the norm because of the exponential 'concern' for 'security' (think of the most obvious examples, such as 9/11 and the Covid pandemic). A state of exception arises when a sovereign power suspends the existing rules of law to enforce a situation where the populace must live under degrees of 'emergency' 'legislation.' As Agamben writes: "the entire Third Reich can be considered as a state of exception which lasted twelve years" (Agamben: 2003: 2; repeated in, Agamben: 2013: public lecture in Athens). One can presume that Agamben takes his original inspiration for his investigation into 'the state of exception' from Walter Benjamin,[11] who wrote in the 8th thesis of his *Theses on the Philosophy of History*: "The tradition of the oppressed teaches us that the 'state of emergency' in which we live is not the exception but the rule" (Benjamin: 257: 1940). For Agamben, the phenomenon of the 'security state' or 'state of control,' Benjamin's 'state of emergency,' is one that is increasing in its magnitude and requires, as Benjamin also indicates, new strategies:

> We have to think anew the traditional strategies of political conflicts... The security paradigm implies that each form of dissent, each more or less violent attempt to overthrow the order, becomes an opportunity to govern these actions into a profitable direction. This is evident in the dialectics that tightly bind together terrorism and state in an endless vicious spiral. Starting with the French Revolution, the political tradition of modernity has conceived of radical changes in the form of a revolutionary process that acts as the *pouvoir constituant*, the 'constituent power,' of a new institutional order. I think that we have to abandon this paradigm and try to think something as a *puissance destituante*, a purely 'destituent power' [a deactivating, or dethroning power[12]] that cannot be captured in the spiral of security. (Agamben: 2013)

---

[11] See, Agamben, *State of Exception*, p6-7.

[12] Agamben's notion of 'destituent power' is translated in *The Use of Bodies* as 'destituent potential': "And if to constituent power there correspond revolutions, revolts, and new constitutions, namely, a violence that puts in place and constitutes a new law, for destituent potential it is necessary to think entirely different strategies, whose definition

Part of the strategy Agamben then proposes is to develop a praxis of "exposing clearly the anarchy and anomie [expressed] in the governmental security technologies" which would in itself make possible "a really new political dimension" which could "act as a purely destituent power" (Agamben: 2013). (Perhaps in this Agamben would view the work of radical journalists as a sound beginning step? Of course, his own writings on states of exception would also form part.)

III

Agamben has developed the notion of 'destituent power' through his exploration of the messianism of St. Paul (Cimino: 111: 2016) and his studies of the beginnings of the Franciscan movement: "An example of a destituent strategy that is neither destructive nor constituent is that of Paul in the face of the law [the *Torah*]" (Agamben: 273: 2014). It is about, as Camatte would say, 'leaving this world.' Note, however, that it is important to understand that by this plea Camatte does not only mean 'going to the countryside' as he himself has done, he also means not engaging with the world *as it wants us to engage with it*, for example on the level of enmity. It is the same for Agamben, although he likes the idea of communes the most important thing for him is that we begin to live our lives 'as not': "The 'as not' is a deposition without abdication" (Agamben: 274: 2014)[13]:

> It is not a question of returning to the Franciscan ideal as it once was, but of using it in a new way. My interest in monasticism was aroused by the fact that it was not uncommon for people who belonged to the wealthiest and most educated classes, as was the case with Basil the Great, Benedict of Nursia, the founder of the Benedictine Order, and later with Francis, to decide to leave the society in which they had hitherto lived in order to establish a radically different community of life or, in my view the same

---

is the task of the coming politics" (Agamben: 266: 2014). Agamben may be 'allowing,' as it were, for some kind of straight-forward (albeit destituting) violence, in the formulations of those who will be part of "the coming politics," but it is more likely that he is referencing the "lethal without spilling blood" violence indicated by Benjamin in the *Critique of Violence* (1921), which is explored in detail below.

[13] Agamben continues: "Living in the form of the "as not" means rendering destitute all juridical and social ownership, without this deposition founding a new identity. A form-of-life is, in this sense, that which ceaselessly deposes the social conditions in which it finds itself to live, without negating them, but simply by using them," p 274.

thing, a radically different politics. This began at the same time as the decline and fall of the Roman Empire. What is remarkable about this is that it did not occur to these people to reform or improve the state in which they lived, that is, to seize power to change it. They simply turned their backs on it... already today this model is being practised more or less openly by young people. There are said to be more than three hundred communities of this kind in Italy alone. (Agamben: 2015b)

Once again, it would appear that one of Agamben's core idea is taken straight from Walter Benjamin: "The themes which monastic discipline assigned to friars for meditation were designed to turn them away from the world and its affairs. The thoughts which we are developing here originate from similar considerations" (Benjamin: 258: Thesis X: 1940).[14]

Bifo Berardi also follows the theme of turning the impulse to fight back into an abandoning, and the finding of a path on another level, in a trajectory that would appear to go from Paul to Kafka to Benjamin to Agamben (Camatte remains extramural to these thinkers):

> In order to go beyond resistance, in order to create an autonomous space, we need to create an outside from within. Imagination, poetry: the act of creation of an outside is the poetic act we need now. Call it, if you want, imaginative transcendence. (Bifo: 2012b)

Bifo has decided that, for the purposes of building a new world, economic struggle is a dead end and he suggests a new 'start' can be made in a different field:

> The global collapse of September 2008 marks the impossibility of a new start inside the frame of economic thought. (Bifo: 2010)

---

[14] Benjamin's idea here is not only a 'general' one, it is specifically related to how to deal with fascism, he continues: "At a moment when the politicians in whom the opponents of Fascism had placed their hopes are prostrate and confirm their defeat by betraying their own cause, these [Benjamin's] observations are intended to disentangle the political worldlings from the snares in which traitors have entrapped them." Benjamin is suggesting, in a move that is not altogether dissimilar to Bordiga's, that if one doesn't 'step outside' of 'the world and its affairs' then things like fascism will merely repeat themselves, and the horror will continue to pile up. As I observe elsewhere in this essay, this kind of thinking may lead one to the adoption of Bordiga's *anti*-antifascism, and all of its corollaries.

Nihil Evadere

His disavowal of 'resistance,' has a clear link to the penetrating claim of Jacques Camatte that 'the more we fight against capital, the more we strengthen it,'[15] as well as rephrasing Camatte's urging to 'leave this world.'

Of course, it is also a reflection of Agamben's "movement of messianic destitution" (Aarons: 51: 2020) and Agamben's own formulation:

> I believe that the model of struggle, which has paralyzed the political imagination of modernity, should be replaced by the model of the way out... Of course, this also applies to individual existence. Kafka repeats it constantly: do not seek the struggle, but find a way out. (Agamben: 2015b)

So, it would seem that Camatte's call to leave the world, which he made in the early 1970s, has reappeared in a sector of Italian philosophy close to ultra-leftism, but entirely newly, with no reference to Camatte.

> It is little-known that Franz Kafka entertained neighbors by performing the plié and *arabesque* in the nude at his open bedroom window each morning, often ending on a *turn-out*. He was also an accomplished welterweight boxer, winning three regional trophies.

IV

Returning to Agamben and his study of St. Paul it is possible to discern a vast rhizomic system beneath the topsoil of modern revolutionary and pro-insurrectionist thinking that asserts that *communism* already exists right now. The left-communist and ultra-left claim that there is a 'real movement' actually already in existence that threatens capital — "Communism is not an ideal to be realized: it already exists, not as a society, but as an effort, a task to prepare for" (Dauvé: 7: 1972) — is extended in Agamben's notion of the messianic life, explained here by Kieran Aarons:

> [M]essianic time... *already* has an existence... the Kingdom is already here among us... For Agamben the problem of communism has nothing to do with a future society; it names an ethical process that proceeds from sparks or fragmentary potentials already operative in the present. It is transitional, but not 'toward' anything else — it is *pure transition,* the accomplishing of shared

---

[15] Camatte, 'Mai-Juin 1968: Le dévoilement,' *R.I.*, 1977.

worlds in the process of their own construction, and never a *fait accompli*.[16] (Aarons: 62-63 and 65: 2020: original emphases)

Shailer Mathews, in *The Messianism of Paul*, 1902, draws for us the connections between Agamben's thought and Paul's thought, which Agamben has written on elsewhere. Mathews writes:

> [Paul's] conversion had consisted in the substitution, not of one theology for another, but of one life for another... During the brief period of waiting for [...] deliverance, the Christian was to endeavor to live the sort of live which was to be his in the new kingdom... And perhaps as striking as anything, he repeatedly urges that, as the Christian is a citizen of the new kingdom, he is to live as if he already possessed the privileges of that kingdom... But, however Paul may approach the new life, and however much his expressions may sound contradictory, his ethics is neither archaeological nor heteronomous. On the contrary... he is the very Coryphaeus [chief] of ethical autonomists. How otherwise could one designate the man who declared [that] law had no [...] control over the Christian, and whose letter to the Galatians is a veritable declaration of moral independence? (Mathews: 372-5: 1902)

Paul's ethical system, Mathews insists, is "neither archaeological nor heteronomous," it is not developed through past systems, neither is it contingent on existing moral principles. What this means is that Paul *broke with the Torah*, the Jewish law. In his abandonment of the Torah, Paul therefore sets out a completely separate and new ideological space for Christianity. At the same time as Paul took Christianity in this direction (the first century, CE), Jesus' brother, James, in Jerusalem, was keeping Christianity faithful to the observance of the Torah (this 'Jewish Christianity' effectively disappeared not long after James' death). In traditional Jewish eschatology (declarations and ruminations on the 'end times,' the 'last days,' etc.) there are many messiahs, and the history

---

[16] One might wonder about the semantics of relating the notion of eternal/pure *transition* to the term 'accomplishment,' or how a 'constructing,' can be not *toward* something, though my dialogue is probably more with Agamben here than with Aarons. Perhaps the term "*pure transition*" here means the same as simply living, decaying, or evolving or, in Heraclitian terms, *becoming*. Part of the problem, of course, is that this narrative is also unavoidably set within the 'revolutionary' discussion of whether there needs to be a transition, or not, to communism, despite the communist/messianic claim that "the problem of communism has nothing to do with a future society" because "the Kingdom is already here among us."

of messianism is still not complete, but, in the theology of Paul, Jesus is the culmination of all the past messiahs and the ultimate, or last one. Hence, the fact that Jesus, the direct 'son' of God, was *resurrected* on Earth, is the proof for Paul that one now lives not in the time of *waiting for* the messiah, but in the time *of* the messiah: in 'messianic time.'

Messianic time, and the possibility of the messianic life, is announced by the profound event of the resurrection of Jesus. For Paul, the arrival of Jesus demonstrates that all previous messiahs in the Jewish tradition were simply prophets. To define a prophet Agamben contrasts prophets and apostles (Paul is an apostle, not a prophet). A prophet, he states, is "a man... who receives a word that does not properly belong to him," one who is "an ecstatic spokesperson for God... [unlike] the apostle, who, as an emissary with a determinate purpose, must carry out his assignment with lucidity and search on his own for the words of the message" (Agamben: 60: 2000b). So, Jesus is the messiah, and apostles can only exist after the appearance of the actual messiah, that is, in the time of messiah: in messianic time (Agamben: 1: 2002).

V

But just what is messianic time? Agamben writes: "it is the time we need to make time end: *the time that is left us*" (Agamben: 68: 2000b). In an explanation of what Agamben means, Kieran Aarons writes that it is *a life* in which time can "be seized upon and fulfilled" (Aarons: 76: 2020). This possibility, Aarons indicates, is a 'de-activation' of *law* and sovereignty and corresponds with the suspension of law that exists in what has now become, in our era, a 'permanent state of exception.' It is also, Aarons stresses, not to be confused with time in reference to a coming apocalypse. Messianic time is not a time of *waiting* in a "condition of passivity" (Aarons: 74: 2020) for the apocalyptic, millenarian, solution to the grievances of humanity. Agamben's conception of messianic time is a combining of Paul's conception with the secular messianism of Walter Benjamin ("In any case, I believe that the messianic is always profane, never religious. It is even the ultimate crisis of the religious, the folding of the religious into the profane," Agamben: 2000c). In his notes for the *Theses on the Philosophy of History*, Benjamin writes: "In the idea of classless society, Marx secularized the idea of messianic time,"[17] and in Benjamin's insistence that 'revolution' is a matter of personal

---

[17] Benjamin, W., 'Paralipomena to *On the Concept of History*,' in *Selected Writings, Volume 4, 1938-1940*, H. Eiland and M.W. Jennings (eds.), HUP, 2003.

experience[18] rather than something that humanity has to wait for, he writes in the *Theses* that the astute historian "establishes a conception of the present as the 'time of the now' which is shot through with chips [or splinters] of Messianic time" (Benjamin: 263: 1940).

So, in Agamben's filtering of Benjamin's conception through the writing of Paul, messianic time is neither a time of waiting in hope nor an active attempt to accelerate the arrival of the 'day of judgement,' it is the creation of a kind of life in which one lives in the world as a participant while choosing to present oneself, *to oneself* and to others, as someone who has — in spirit — abandoned one's role. Aarons writes: "Messianic life lives its worldly vocations 'as not'" (Aarons: 79: 2020). This new way of living, as described by Agamben, is taken directly from Paul, who urges his followers to understand that the world they know is disappearing and that they should not feel any sadness, they should live their lives — their vocations, their 'jobs' — as if these are artefacts of a world that has gone... even though in the appearance of reality they do seem to properly exist as a living force (rather than, perhaps, as the zombie carcass they really are?), and, indeed, one has to fulfil certain functions to survive and prosper. (One presumes, then, that Agamben and the followers of his strategy continue their work, and receive their wages, '*as not*'?) The faithful — those who *know*, who accept Jesus as the true messiah, or who agree that we live in messianic time — must, according to Paul initially, participate in these 'appearing-real' residues of *pre-messianic* life as if they no longer exist:

> [So] even those having wives may be as not having, and those weeping as not weeping, and those rejoicing as not rejoicing, and those buying as not possessing, and those using the world as not using it up. For passing away is the figure of this world. But I wish you to be without care. (Aarons: 79: 2020; 1 Cor. 7: 29-32)

Agamben is developing this whole theory within a left-communist, or ultra-leftist, politico-philosophical field, and so his point is to use Paul's vision for secular purposes in order to make a theoretical space for new ideas about what communism is and how it can be accessed.[19] The initial inspiration for his

---

[18] "At its core, Benjamin's idea of revolution is a conception of the fulfilling experience of emphatic meaning." Alison Ross, 2017, 'Walter Benjamin's idea of revolution: The fulfilled wish in historical perspective,' *Cogent Arts & Humanities*, 4:1, p4.

[19] The Agamben-inspired Marcello Tarì, in his recent book, for example, suggests the figure of a revolutionary militant who is a *not-militant*: "[W]e adopt the Pauline strategy of 'as not' so that militants might act *as if they were not* militants," (Tarì: 12: 2017: original

investigations may well be the line from Benjamin: "In the idea of classless society, Marx secularized the idea of messianic time." Remembering Agamben's praise for communes in Italy (above), one would presume that this strategy of living *as not*, or in the "revocation [deactivation or destitution] of every vocation" (Aarons: 66: 2020), is most easily accomplished in communes of like-minded people, although living 'as not' is also, and more importantly, living without abdicating one's current life (Agamben: 274: 2014). And then we can ask whether living this way actually accesses immediately, by way of a 'chip or splinter of messianic time,' the communism that is 'always already' available to us by the eternal presence of messianic time? Such a conception may already have been proposed, in a different form, and involving different strategies, by Amadeo Bordiga (and Jacques Camatte), but without the directly Christian or Jewish inspiration. For Bordiga, in 1960, the true revolutionary was viewed as someone who lived their life *as if the revolution had already arrived*: "A revolutionary — according to us — is someone for whom revolution is as certain as something that has already happened."[20]

> Peter Sellers' most acclaimed role is that of philosopher Giorgio Agamben in the biopic, *Being There*. Sellers boasted, "Once I had got the hair right, the rest was easy." After the movie, the quote "The coming being is whatever being" was seen on tee-shirts across the world.

Agamben is not the only recent thinker to have discovered Paul: "For Giorgio Agamben, Alain Badiou, and Slavoj Žižek the New Testament writings attributed to Paul have much to say on contemporary debates over politics and religious tradition" (Britt: 262), indeed all three have written books on Paul and his relevance to our times. And Agamben and Žižek, at least, have made heavy use

---

emphasis). And this is prefigured by Raoul Vaniegem in 1967: "[A] militant can only be a revolutionary *in spite of* the ideas he has agreed to serve" (Vaneigem: 93: original emphasis).

[20] Camatte, 'Bordiga et la passion du communisme,' *R.I.*, 1972. I have not been able to find this quote from Bordiga in the text that Camatte says it came from. Therefore, I am using it because I feel that it accurately reflects their thinking in the 1950s and 60s anyway, indeed Camatte refers to this idea again in his brief history of Bordiga's thought after WWII, Camatte writes in 'Point de Départ,' *R.I.*, 2003: "The revolution was re-drafted as a *human* revolution and the milieu that would, according to theory, have the task of leading it, was to operate in anticipation of communist society by actualising the social brain. This meant that every member of this milieu in development had to behave as if the revolution were a *fait accompli*."

of the writing of Carl Schmitt and "the omnipresent"[21] Walter Benjamin in the transmission of Pauline interpretations.

In *The Time that Remains*, Agamben sees an actual direct citation from Paul in Benjamin's *Theses on the Philosophy of History* (1940): "You can imagine that I was moved (to quite a degree) when discovering this hidden (although not so hidden) Pauline citation in the text within the *Theses*," (Agamben: 140: 2000b). This citation, by-the-way, is forensically disputed by Brian Britt, in an article in which Britt states that his "primary concern is not Agamben's reading of Paul but his reading of Walter Benjamin as a Pauline thinker through the lens of Carl Schmitt's political theology" (Britt: 263).

VI

There are, for the purposes of this essay, two ways that Agamben's work is interpreted as revolutionary (it is also interpreted in terms of 'pessimism' or 'quietism,' but this judgement does not concern me here), and these are outlined below.

One academic, Antonio Cimino, describes Agamben's "political ambitions" in this way:

> Messianic life is revolutionary precisely because it gives up any attempt to destroy the established order of social and political relationships. It maintains them and at the same time deactivates them by means of the *hōs mē* [as not]. Agamben's basic idea is that Pauline messianism deactivates sovereignty. (Cimino: 112: 2016)

While another, Kieran Aarons, describes Agamben's strategy like this:

---

[21] Carnevali, Barbara, "Contro la Theory. Una provocazione," in *Le parole e le cose*, 19 September 2016: "A simulacrum of philosophy, *Theory*, wanders around [university] departments all over the world... extracted from a canon of disparate authors but which can be combined in a generic radical posture (Marx, Nietzsche, Lacan, Foucault, Deleuze, Bourdieu, Agamben, Said, Spivak, Butler, Žižek, the omnipresent Benjamin, the outgoing Derrida, the new entry Latour...), merged into a single crucible... *Theory* is swift, voracious and cutting-edge... [enabling users to] find a collection of prêt-à-porter ideas with which to fill university papers quickly and superficially." A short version of this article can be found in *The Brooklyn Rail*. It is not clear if this short version is Carnevali's own work/translation, or if it is done by someone else.

What messianism "achieves" is not a magical transfiguration of this world into another one, but a change in our mode of *contact* with this one. Agamben's message is this: stop waiting for another world, learn how to *look* within your situation for the potentialities that allow you to *hold a world in common,* and respond to their call by seizing upon them. In this way, he directs us to where we already are, and tells us something simple: the world is *ours,* but only 'for *use as not-ours'*... [O]nce the violence that deactivates bourgeois society ceases to be conceived as 'maieutic' [rigorously questioning, engaging, and opposing, in order to arrive at 'truth'], i.e. as resulting in a product or 'work', it loses its strictly negative or destructive character and becomes a process that we immediately *inhabit*. (Aarons: 77 and 82: 2020: original emphases)

Aarons' assessment casts Agamben's revolutionary messianism as a violence toward 'bourgeois society,' which is easily identifiable as *insurrectionary*, as opposed to Cimino's conception. Aarons' interpretation is filtered through the work of *Tiqqun* and their own literary exposition of Agamben's concepts which, under their direction, appear[22] relentlessly violent or insurrectionary. But Agamben says:

We are used to understanding radical political change as the result of a more or less violent revolution: a new political subject, which since the French Revolution has been called the constituent or constitutional power, destroys the existing political-legal order and creates a new constituted or constitutional power. I believe the time has come to abandon this outdated model in order to direct our thinking towards what could be called a 'destituent' or 'abolishing power' — that is, a power that absolutely cannot take the form of a constituted power. The constituting force corresponds to revolutions, uprisings and new constitutions; it is a force that enforces new law. For the destituting power, completely different strategies have to be devised, the more detailed determination of which will have to be done by future politics. If power is only overthrown by the constituent power, it inevitably emerges in a different form from the incessant, endless and hopeless dialectic of constituent and constituted, law-making and law-preserving power. (Agamben: 2015b)

Note that Agamben introduces his idea with an observation on violence: "We are used to understanding radical political change as the result of a more or less

---

[22] It will be discussed below as to why *Tiqqun*'s language may not be entirely what it seems to be on the surface.

violent revolution" (my italics). He then makes the point that the 'usual' strategy "corresponds to revolutions [and] uprisings." I am leaving out the part referring to setting up new constitutions and new law because I want to focus on the fact that Agamben is clearly connecting violence to 'revolutions and uprisings' and it is *this* element, *as well as* the constituting one, that he is suggesting is a mistaken strategy for 'a power,' or a movement, that intends to 'deactivate' the state. To understand just where Agamben is coming from one must keep in mind his two, key, historical (as opposed to philosophical) inspirations. Agamben takes his inspiration for "completely different strategies" not only from Paul, but also from the early Franciscans, as mentioned above. At the time of the decline of the Roman Empire they developed what Agamben views as a new approach to power:

> What is remarkable about this is that it did not occur to these people to reform or improve the state in which they lived, that is, to seize power to change it. They simply turned their backs on it. (Agamben: 2015b)

Agamben is not *advocating* violence of any kind (not even the 'violence in reserve' advocated by *Tiqqun*, discussed later):

> The security paradigm [the 'security state,' or 'state of control;' that is, the undeclared 'state of exception' we all now live under] implies that each form of dissent, each more or less violent attempt to overthrow the order, becomes an opportunity to govern these actions in a profitable direction. (Agamben: 2013)

Once again, in a passage that repeats the Camattian observation that 'everything we do to fight capital only strengthens it,' Agamben uses the phrase "more or less violent" to describe actions against the prevailing power. His implication is that violence *and* dissent, in whatever ratio, is counter-productive for those who wish to escape present conditions. This indicates that he views any movement or organization of people for *oppositional dissent* as a form of constituting power (think of 'constituting power' as a kind of mirror of the state, a replacement authority). Agamben does not talk of a 'revolutionary situation' he talks about 'collapse'[23] and the living of a new life. The only way, he argues,

---

[23] See 'Europa muss kollabieren' [Europe must Collapse], interview by Iris Radisch in *Die Zeit* (Zeit Online), 27 August, 2015b; also, *When the House Burns Down*, 2020. It is also interesting, in light of Agamben's use of *Bartleby the Scrivener*, to reflect on the observation of Joyce Carol Oates in her introduction to Melville's short stories: "*Then all collapsed –* this succinct and ominous phrase [from the end of *Moby-Dick*] might be kept in mind as a ground bass to Melville's writing post-*Moby-Dick*" (Oates: viii: 1998). She continues, "As a

that politics can be changed is by walking away from any constituting impulses and abandoning an oppositional 'dialogue' with established power. Agamben does not argue *for* insurrection and revolt, he argues for turning one's back on it all, thereby facilitating "an irrevocable exodus from any sovereignty" (Agamben: 8: 1993 [2000a]).

But this turning one's back does not mean *not carrying on* (it means living 'as not'), Agamben insists that we must 'simply' make use of the world, and its things, without ownership or separation. On top of this, the world as we know it is already falling apart or, in Agamben's metaphor, 'the house is burning'[24] and it has been burning since the two world wars:

> In the coming years there will be only monks and delinquents. And yet it is not possible simply to draw oneself aside, to believe one can pull oneself out from underneath the rubble of the world that has collapsed around us. For the collapse matters to us and calls to us; we, too, are only a piece of that rubble. And we will cautiously have to learn to use it in a more just way, without being noticed. (Agamben: *When the House Burns Down*: 2020)

Agamben's observation that the world is burning, and that dissent does nothing but feed into the protraction of this collapsing phenomena is prefigured by Jean Baudrillard:

> One must not resist this process [of "a dying system"] by trying to confront the system and destroy it, because this system that is dying from being dispossessed of its death expects nothing but that from us: that we give the

---

writer and thinker, Melville was an iconoclast of whom it might have been said, as he'd said so admiringly of Hawthorne: 'There is the grand truth about Nathaniel Hawthorne. He says No! in thunder; but the devil himself cannot make him say *yes*. For all men who say *yes* lie; and all men who say *no*—why they are in the happy condition of judicious, unincumbered travellers in Europe; they cross the frontiers into Eternity with nothing but a carpetbag—that is to say, the Ego." (xi-xii).

[24] This metaphor is a direct reference to the Buddhist *Parable of the Burning House*, a text in which the unaware children of a rich man are 'tricked' by him into leaving their burning home, from which he cannot drag them, by the promise of things outside that they can play with. The notion of *play* is crucial to Agamben's concept of 'use': "The passage from the sacred [or the "serious" p76] to the profane can... come about by means of an entirely inappropriate use (or rather, reuse) of the sacred: namely play... play not only derives from the sphere of the sacred but also in some ways represents its overturning... play frees and distracts humanity from the sphere of the sacred, without simply abolishing it... [Children are particularly good at profanation:] All of a sudden, a car, a firearm, or a legal contract becomes a toy" (Agamben: 75-76: 2005).

system back its death, that we revive it through the negative. End of revolutionary praxis, end of the dialectic. (Baudrillard: 24: 1981)

VII

Agamben's position, as I have described it, makes problematic, or interesting, his well-known relationship with the 'insurrectionist' group, *Tiqqun* (*The Invisible Committee*).[25] *Tiqqun* (a word from Jewish tradition, meaning fix or repair[26]) write:

> We are among those who get organized... We contest nothing, we demand nothing. We constitute ourselves as a *force*, as a *material* force, as an *autonomous* material force within the world civil war... We are not afraid of forming gangs; and can only laugh at those who will decry us as a mafia... we must turn ourselves to the forms of operation peculiar to all guerrillas: anonymous sabotage, unclaimed actions, recourse to easily appropriable techniques, targeted counter-attacks... There are circumstances, like in a riot, in which the ability to heal our comrades considerably increases our ability to wreak havoc. Who can say that arming ourselves would not be part of the material constitution of a collectivity?... This is the way the Party will be built, as a trail of habitable [communized] places left behind by each situation of exception that empire meets. (*Call*: various pages: 2004)

And from *The Coming Insurrection* (a respectful play on Agamben's book title, *The Coming Community*), in which the final slogan is, *All power to the communes*:

> There is no such thing as a peaceful insurrection. Weapons are necessary: it's a question of doing everything possible to make using them unnecessary. An insurrection is more about taking up arms and maintaining an "armed presence" than it is about armed struggle. We need to distinguish clearly between being armed and the use of arms. Weapons are a constant in

---

[25] See: Aarons, 2020, fn 12, p57; Patrick Marcolini, 2009, 'Situationist inheritors: Julien Coupat, Tiqqun and The Coming Insurrection,' NOT BORED! website.
[26] See: 'Who came up with Tikkun Olam?' At *Chabad* dot org. It is highly likely, though, that *Tiqqun* have derived their name from Walter Benjamin who, with his friend Gershom Scholem, studied the notion of *Tikkun Olam*: see Peter Brier, "Walter Benjamin's Sparks of Holiness." *Southwest Review*, vol. 88, no. 1, 2003, p82; Margaret Cohen, in her chapter in the *Cambridge Companion to Walter Benjamin*, 2004, notes the importance of tikkun to the *Theses*, the relevant part of which is quoted on Benjamin's Wikipedia page; in Benjamin's *Task of the Translator* (1921/3), it is claimed that he "evokes the language of Tikkun in Jewish mysticism," by Eiland and Jennings in their biography (*A Critical Life*, HUP, 2014), p160.

revolutionary situations, but their use is infrequent and rarely decisive at key turning points: August 10th 1792, March 18th 1871, October 1917. When power is in the gutter, it's enough to walk over it.

Because of the distance that separates us from them, weapons have taken on a kind of double character of fascination and disgust that can be overcome only by handling them.[27] An authentic pacifism cannot mean refusing weapons, but only refusing to use them. Pacifism without being able to fire a shot is nothing but the theoretical formulation of impotence. Such *a priori* pacifism is a kind of preventive disarmament, a pure police operation. In reality, the question of pacifism is serious only for those who have the ability to open fire. In this case, pacifism becomes a sign of power, since it's only in an extreme position of strength that we are freed from the need to fire. (*The Coming Insurrection*: 56: 2007)

But it appears that one can read these lines, and the works of *Tiqqun* in general, in three ways. Firstly, and perhaps naïvely, at 'face value' as a direct appeal to an extreme militancy of the kind exemplified by Che Guevara. Secondly, and very interestingly, this kind of rhetoric can be viewed as a *literary* work done in the style of the Situationists.[28] Mikkel Bolt Rasmussen, who has written extensively on Debord,[29] gives us a way of approaching *Tiqqun*'s own avant-garde-ism in his assessment of the Situationist project:

Narcissism was never far away in the Situationist's attempt to act critically and to *be* the contemporary avant-garde. The members of the group regarded themselves as a revolutionary elite fighting decadence, but out of fear of recuperation they had to remain invisible and pin their hopes to the proletariat. There was no room for ambivalent utterances… This reduction of society's conflicts to the battle between the working class and capital caused the Situationists to fossilize stylistically… In their writings the denunciation of the spectacle was repeated endlessly, and all non-Situationist activities were redundantly rejected… The monolithic condemnation threatened to pacify the reader who was confronted with the almost impossible

---

[27] Mao wrote: "Every Communist must grasp the truth: *political power grows out of the barrel of a gun.*"

[28] Forgive my attempt at humor, but… it's difficult to resist *simply swooning* when stumbling upon someone who can write: "When power is in the gutter, it's enough to walk over it." For more examples of commandingly sexy *Tiqqunist* language see 'Interview with Julien Coupat,' on the NOT BORED! website.

[29] See, 'The Society of the Accessory,' M.B. Rasmussen, *Parole Compendiums*, 27 April, 2020.

requirement not only to act revolutionary, but also to *feel* revolutionary. (Rasmussen: 14: 2006: original emphases)

Thirdly, one can read the above from *Tiqqun* as a poetical-theological ("Because what critique needs now is poets and theologians, not conscientious functionaries of social intelligence" *Tiqqun 1*, p163),[30] and *philosophical*, foray into *an observation* of the world, the 'global civil war,' as it is. (The 'global/world civil war' concept is briefly explored below.)

The first reading is obvious, of course, and nothing more needs to be said. The second reading is suggested by another scholar of the Situationist International, Patrick Marcolini, who notes the Situationist style of the writing and the repeated references to Debord's formulation of the society of the spectacle.[31] Agamben himself says of *Tiqqun*'s 'Bloom Theory': "Debord is, of course, very present. Sometimes one gets the impression that he has a strong presence, even just on a stylistic level" (Agamben: 2010). This reading is put more explicitly by the French journal, *Le Tigre*:

> [*Tiqqun*'s] style has a lyricism worthy of Cassandra, heralding chaos, and the lyricism is performative: it aims to generate before the eyes of the reader what it designates by its very utterance.[32]

The third reading is Agamben's own, but before I explore that, I think it might be useful to elaborate *Tiqqun*'s notion of "the Party" and the Schmittian/*Tiqqun*ian formulation of the 'partisan.'

> **Pyotr Tkachev, a Russian theorist of revolution and inspiration to Lenin, believed that after the revolution everyone over the age of 25 would have to be eliminated, since they would be unable to assimilate the new ideas. He died aged 41 in a psychiatric hospital in Paris.**

VIII

---

[30] *Theologia Poetica* (poetic theology) is a term associated with Giambattista Vico, and used in his book, *La Scienza Nuova*, 1725-40. For Vico, poets were 'creators.'
[31] Marcolini, Ibid., see fn 25.
[32] 'Du durs Rêveurs,' *Le Tigre*, March/September, 2009.

Traditionally, particularly in non-anglophone European Marxism, there are two types of political party, the actual political party with a membership, and *the historical party* of the working class that will create communism. *Tiqqun* have revealed a new party: *The Imaginary Party*. This conception *reflects* or modifies the idea of the 'historical party of the proletariat' in that the Imaginary Party consists of all the inchoate resentments and hostilities toward modern society that exist within individuals and that are expressed daily. The task *Tiqqun*, or The Invisible Committee, have given themselves is to unite "by any means necessary, all the particular forces currently confronting commodity hegemony — in other words — building the Imaginary Party" (Tiqqun 1: 19). In so doing, "the negative party of negativity [the Imaginary Party] little by little becomes unified and acquires positive content" (*Theses on the Imaginary Party*: Thesis X).

Essential to the notion of the Imaginary Party is the image of the partisan.

The term partisan has entered academic and ultra-left[33] revolutionary circles via the heavy focus on the writings of Carl Schmitt, an unrepentant member of the Nazi Party, by Agamben in his development of a destituent, or *anti-sovereign*, politics. *Tiqqun*'s use of Schmitt's '*The Theory of the Partisan*' (1962) in their core text, '*Theses on the Imaginary Party*' (1999), has, over the years, given the term a new nuance in the academic and anglophone world, and we now see it in much ultra-left or Agamben-inspired literature. *Tiqqun* write:

> It is certainly not a rare thing to see some people take the position of "disappearing into the shadows but transforming the shadows into a strategic space from which emerge attacks that will destroy the place where the imperium has manifested itself up to now, which will dismantle the vast stage of official public life, which technocratic intelligence could not manage to organize" (Carl Schmitt, *Theory of the partisan*). (Thesis XIII)

---

[33] *Tiqqun* portrayed themselves as considering the 'ultra-left' as nothing more than a sad historical artefact: "the ultra-left is a political current that had its moment of glory in the 1920s and [...] subsequently, never produced anything other than inoffensive volumes of Marxology" (Interview with Julien Coupat, 2009, see fn 28). This may, by-the-way, form part of the reason the ultra-left group *Endnotes* never took to them, disliking what they saw as the promotion of a "conceptual miasma" and asking, in 2011, if "these pronouncements amount to anything more than the self-affirmations of a self-identifying radical milieu" (*Endnotes*: 'What are we to do?'). But the term ('ultra-left') persists, and is the easiest way of describing the milieu under discussion.

> The men of the Imaginary Party carry on an irregular warfare. They are engaged in a kind of Spanish War [Schmitt begins his *Theory of the Partisan* with the phenomenon of the Peninsula War in Spain from which the term *guerrilla* entered the English language] where the spectacular occupier bankrupts itself stationing troops and munitions, and a paroxysmal dialectic holds sway within the terms of which "the strength and significance of the irregulars are determined by the strength and significance of the regular organization they attack" (Carl Schmitt) and vice-versa. The Imaginary Party can count on the fact that a handful of partisans is enough to immobilize the whole 'party of order.' [...] These partisans do not oppose the legal order, they depose it. (*Thesis* XXI)

Schmitt's article on partisan or guerrilla phenomena also references a piece written by Lenin. In 1906, Lenin articulated the Party approach to partisan actions in a short article titled 'Partisan War' or 'Partisan Warfare.' This title is usually translated into English as 'Guerrilla War,' but this is a little misleading. The word 'guerrilla' comes from Spanish and is used in western European countries, and anglophone countries, in its original form ('*guerrillito*' means '*little war*'). In Russian, the word 'partisan,' an important word in the 'Soviet' lexicon, is used — *not* the term *guerrilla*. Therefore, I have amended the translation below. Lenin writes:

> The question of partisan actions is of great interest to our Party and the masses of the workers... In the first place, Marxism differs from all primitive forms of socialism by not binding the movement to any one particular form of struggle. It recognizes the most varied forms of struggle; and it does not 'concoct' them, but only generalizes, organizes, gives conscious expression to those forms of struggle of the revolutionary classes which arise of themselves in the course of the movement. Absolutely hostile to all abstract formulas and to all doctrinaire recipes, Marxism demands an attentive attitude to the *mass* struggle in progress, which, as the movement develops, as the class-consciousness of the masses grows, as economic and political crises become acute, continually gives rise to new and more varied methods of defense and attack. Marxism, therefore, positively does not reject any form of struggle. Under no circumstances does Marxism confine itself to the forms of struggle possible and in existence at the given moment only, recognizing as it does that new forms of struggle, unknown to the participants of the given period, *inevitably* arise as the given social situation, changes. In this respect Marxism *learns*, if we may so express it, from mass practice, and makes no claim whatever to *teach* the masses forms of struggle invented by 'systematizers' in the seclusion of their studies. We know — said Kautsky,

for instance, when examining the forms of social revolution — that the coming crisis will introduce new forms of struggle that we are now unable to foresee. (Part I)

We have not the slightest intention of foisting on practical workers any artificial form of struggle, or even of deciding from our armchair what part any particular form of partisan warfare should play in the general course of the civil war in Russia. We are far from the thought of regarding a concrete assessment of particular partisan actions as indicative of a *trend* in Social-Democracy. But we do regard it as our duty to help as far as possible to arrive at a correct *theoretical* assessment of the new forms of struggle engendered by practical life. We do regard it as our duty relentlessly to combat stereotypes and prejudices which hamper the class-conscious workers in correctly presenting a new and difficult problem and in correctly approaching its solution. (Part IV)[34]

If one compares the words of *Tiqqun* and Lenin above one gets the sense that *Tiqqun* give a higher value to 'partisan actions' than Lenin, and, indeed, romanticize 'the partisan' in a way that Lenin does not. *Tiqqun*, of course, define their difference from Lenin in the text above through the word 'depose.' While Lenin aimed to replace 'the legal order' with the 'dictatorship of the proletariat' (however it is defined, and however transitory it was supposed to be), *Tiqqun* do not want to set up a new order, they only want to 'depose.' That is, their strategy is claimed to be *destituent* rather than *constituent* because they do not intend to establish a government (law) that will replace the existing one. So, whereas Lenin's 'partisans' were partisans for the establishment of new law (and effectively they were, even if they didn't intend to be, or didn't like the eventual new law), *Tiqqun*'s 'partisans' are (claimed to be) partisans for the deposition of *all* law. They form, as Aarons writes, channeling his interpretation of Agamben, a "destituent partisanship" (Aarons: 82: 2020).

> *Tiqqun* thinks anyone with a 'disability' or lack of mobility is an enemy of 'the revolution' because they are reliant on the state (eg, for bus passes). In their text, *Theory of The Old Girl*, they claim these social elements are the biggest obstacle to 'the coming insurrection.'

---

[34] As an aside, this text is also interesting because if one replaces the word 'Marxism' with 'communization' this could be an exemplary text of the revolutionary milieu that developed the theory of 'communization' (for example, Gilles Dauvé, *Théorie Communiste*, Evan Calder Williams, Léon de Mattis, *Endnotes*, etc.). One could also, of course, add the word 'destituent' in front of 'partisan' wherever it appears.

IX

It is important to understand that the term just used — *destituent partisanship* — is Aarons' phrase. As far as I know this particular combination of words, which means, of course, 'destituent *guerrilla warfare*,' is not used by Agamben. This extension is typical of a misreading of Agamben that appears to 'want' him to be the philosopher of some kind of violent, and romantic, *insurrection*. For example, using (or misusing) Agambenian categories, Aarons elaborates on insurrection and the tasks of "the revolutionary forces":

> We overcome the *whatness* of our constructed identities, the socio-institutional categories designed to reinforce our separation, by becoming a *how* together in the streets, when our bodies interact by means of a shared gesture[35] of conflictuality (e.g. acting together while rioting, building barricades, looting, fighting the police, defending neighborhoods, etc.).... The legitimacy of 'the people', 'the oppressed', the '99%' is the Trojan horse by which the constituent is smuggled back into insurrectionary destitution. This is the surest method for undoing an insurrection – one that doesn't even require defeating it in the streets. To make the destitution irreversible, therefore, we must begin by abandoning *our own legitimacy*. We have to give up the idea that one makes the revolution in the name of something, that there's a fundamentally just and innocent entity which the revolutionary forces would have the task of representing. (Aarons: 2016: original emphases)

Agamben does use the term "destituent *violence*" (once in *The Use of Bodies*, p269; my emphasis) but this term is directly related to the violence of "a different kind" (Benjamin: 293: 1921) that Benjamin is seeking to reveal in his *Critique of Violence* (1921) through his consideration of Sorel's *proletarian general strike*. This 'divine violence' is an action of pure and immediate *means*, which does not embark on conflict *first* in order to create the space for a new way of life, but *immediately starts living that new way of life*. Agamben writes: "destituent violence, which, insofar as it deposes the juridical order once and for all, immediately inaugurates

---

[35] 'Gesture' is a key Agambenian concept. For Agamben gesture *produces* nothing and, following Aristotle, "good action is itself an end", that is, for Agamben, it is not a means to acquire or achieve some other thing, such as the winning of an argument. Yet gesture is also, for Agamben, *not* an end in itself. Therefore, the gestures in dance, for example, are a "mediality" that expose the *means* (one could also write *ends*) to which 'a dance' is often put, i.e., as an aesthetic (Agamben: 57-8: 2000a/1992).

a new reality," (Agamben: 269: 2014). There is no mention of distributing arms here, or fighting the police, so that a new reality can be established when the forces of authority are defeated, there is only reference to the *immediate* inauguration of "a new reality."

Therefore, the process whereby notion of the 'different kind' of violence that Benjamin is attempting to describe becomes, in Aarons' interpretation (informed by Agamben) 'partisanship' (or guerrilla war) appears shaky, even though that interpretation is essentially supported by other academics (for example, Alison Ross).

There are many claims to the meaning of 'divine violence' in Benjamin's text, from Werner Hamacher's insistence that Benjamin is arguing, following Georges Sorel, that the withdrawal of labor itself is a violence against authority even though it is non-violent (and may attract reprisals, but that is another matter),[36] to Slavoj Žižek's claim that Benjamin's notion of 'pure' or 'divine' violence affirms the revolutionary terrors of the French and Russian revolutions, and can therefore be embodied in the persons of Robespierre, Lenin, and Che Guevara.[37] Agamben writes: "The definition of this third figure, which Benjamin calls 'divine violence,' constitutes the central problem of every interpretation of the essay" (Agamben: 41: 2014).

Benjamin stresses several times in the *Critique* that Sorel's proletarian, or revolutionary, general strike is non-violent, in contradistinction to the repressive force and manipulation organized by political leaders who wish to either preserve the law or enact new law. He notes that "Sorel rejects every kind of program, of utopia — in a word, of lawmaking — for the revolutionary movement" and quotes Sorel directly: "With the general strike all these fine things disappear; the revolution appears as a clear, simple revolt, and no place is reserved either for the sociologists or for the elegant amateurs of social reforms or for the intellectuals who have made it their profession to think for the proletariat." To which Benjamin adds, "Against this deep, moral, and genuinely revolutionary conception, no objection can stand that seeks, on grounds of its possibly catastrophic consequences, to brand such a general strike as violent" (Benjamin: 292: 1921). The blow, the strike, of the unmediated, un-manipulated, withdrawal of labor is the violence of a standstill, and, even though it may lead

---

[36] Hamacher, W., 1994, 'Afformative, Strike: Benjamin's *Critique of violence*,' in *Walter Benjamin's Philosophy: Destruction and Experience*, Andrew Benjamin and Peter Osborne (eds.), Routledge.

[37] Žižek, S. 2008, *Violence: Six Sideways Reflections*, Picador, see the chapter on 'Divine Violence.'

to devastation, for Benjamin and Sorel, this is no reason not to embrace it. Sorel embraces it because it is a pure seizure of life by the proletariat so that daily life can be put to their own use,[38] rather than for the benefit of others. Benjamin embraces it for perhaps slightly more 'mystical' revolutionary reasons, since such an event would be for him an 'opening' to messianic time, or, to stay faithful to his terminology, a massive shard[39] of messianic time slicing into the present.

However, there is a tendency for some to claim that Benjamin is indeed simply advocating revolutionary violence *as combat* rather than as *withdrawal*[40] in his essay, and this view, minus the explicit Leninism of Žižek, perhaps, appears to feed into certain revolutionary or ultra-left discourse.

Alison Ross, for example, decisively dismisses Werner Hamacher's interpretation of Benjamin's divine violence in the *Critique*: "The divine violence that annihilates is replaced, in writers like Werner Hamacher, with a quasi-transcendental operation that is baptized as *nonviolence*" (Ross: 100: 2014). In 2015, Ross writes:

> Such commentary has come at the price of distorting Benjamin's position on divine violence, as if he intended by this term to advocate non-violence. Whatever might be said about the essay's conceptual untidiness, Benjamin nowhere states and defends such a position; it would behove those who advance it on his behalf to explain the omission of any statement to this effect in his essay. (Ross: 40: 2015)

In her book, *Revolution and History in Walter Benjamin* (2019), Ross writes:

---

[38] For Sorel, the revolutionary general strike is something that would operate outside parliamentary process and beyond all political experts and would refuse the reins of the State, it would be *"the passage from capitalism to socialism conceived as a catastrophe whose development defies description."* (Sorel: 140: original emphasis). The true general strike then, for Sorel, consists of a 'collapse,' after which no one can have any idea of what might happen. In a similar, and probably derivative vein (Sorel may have a persistent significance in Agamben's perspectives, curiously finding his way into Marjorana's essay in Agamben's book, *What is Real?*), Agamben views the collapse of Europe, at least, as something imminent.

[39] Agamben, pinning his colors to the Marxian or post-Marxian mast, writes: "In inoperativity, the classless society is already present in capitalist society, just as, according to Benjamin shards of messianic time are present in history" (Agamben: 94: 2014).

[40] Although the kind of withdrawal I mean here is not the same, it is worth keeping in mind how a war can be won by *retreating*, as narrated in the novel *War and Peace*.

Benjamin's remarks on the 'general strike' should [...] be read in the light of the legitimation of revolutionary violence. He classifies the 'proletarian general strike' as a 'nonviolent pure means' as opposed to 'pure immediate violence' (i.e., revolutionary violence) on the one hand, and 'political strikes' that are intended to force concessions from the state, on the other. (Ross: 121: 2019)

Since Benjamin's text is certainly not crystal clear on these matters, as is well-known, it seems risky to demand the text be read as *for* violent acts in the context of a mass stoppage of labor that begins, in Sorelian fashion, the new life *immediately*. Not only should we remember that the 'proletarian general strike' is not a completed fact of history, but only an ideal — though inklings of the *possibility* of it have certainly appeared in history — we should also remember Agamben's observation of its central problem, as well as Ross' advice that the essay is "conceptually untidy."

Ross is, in fact, critical of Agamben's use of the *Critique* to validate his own conceptual elaborations which, she writes, "call on religious faith in order to convey their meaning, and as such [...] demand critical analysis" (Ross: 11: 2008). She is also critical of the possible "quietism" prompted by his "destinal view of politics" (Ross: fn12: 2008). Ross, I presume, regards Agamben as one of those who 'distorts' Benjamin's essay with some kind of "quasi-transcendental operation" (a hippy operation?) that results in it being represented as a piece advocating nonviolence. If this is the case then I am interested in Ross' views on how *Tiqqun*, *Tarì*, and revolutionary academics have used Agamben's concepts to support images of insurrectionary violence.

One of these academics is Thanos Zartaloudis, who effectively demonstrates the connection between this kind of reading of Benjamin's 'revolutionary violence' and Agamben's, even going so far as to claim that Agamben has in mind an image of "the genuine revolutionary":

Revolutionary violence is an extreme act of self-negation: a willing that paradoxically abdicates its own willing. In this manner the genuine revolutionary, for Agamben, casts himself into the absolute which breaks apart the bond between words and deed, will and action, cause and effect, and in this manner violence becomes self-negation in which violence belongs neither to its agent nor its victim. (Zartaloudis: 180)[41]

---

[41] If one is confused as to what exactly Zartaloudis is getting at here, it might be useful to view his 'genuine revolutionary' as some kind of destructive 'Whirling Dervish.'

This intellectual trajectory from a particular reading of Benjamin's *Critique* to an interpretation of Agamben's presumed core theses, results, as noted above in the quote from Aarons, in a validation of violent *insurrection* modified by a *destituent* content (that is, an "insurrectionary destitution"). And this insurrectionary destitution, for Aarons, is "a shared gesture of conflictuality," represented in real terms by, for example, "acting together while rioting, building barricades, looting, fighting the police, defending neighborhoods, etc" (Aarons: 2016).

Firstly, it is important to be clear about what Benjamin means by divine violence, and here it is necessary to use Agamben's interpretation, since it is his those writers such as Zartaloudis and Aarons use: "Benjamin calls this other figure of violence 'pure' (*reine Gewalt*) or 'divine,' and, in the human sphere, 'revolutionary'" (Agamben, 53: 2003).

What is fascinating for me (and should be for Ross) about Benjamin's essay is that it has been filtered through Agamben into radical anglophonic academia to support the idea that the world might be 'saved' through some kind of violent, armed, revolutionary uprising — "a shared gesture of conflictuality" — when neither Benjamin (Ross, of course, disagrees with me here in regard to Benjamin) or Agamben call for an armed uprising.

The important part of Benjamin's consideration on divine violence is that this violence is 'pure means.'

As Valeria Bonacci writes: "It is interesting to note how in his essay Benjamin portrays [the violence of 'pure means'] as essentially non-violent" (Bonacci: 65).[42] Benjamin writes in the *Critique*: "It is true that the omission of an action, or service, where it amounts to a 'severing of relations,' can be an entirely nonviolent, pure means," (Benjamin: 281: 1921). Benjamin writes that whereas partial strikes are a legal right, "a simultaneous use of strike in all industries is illegal, since the specific reasons for strike admitted by legislation cannot be prevalent in every workshop" (283). He argues that such a, general, strike is a

---

Zartaloudis writes: "For Agamben, self-negation becomes genuine when it is elation and dispossession of the self, akin to divine delirium," p180. Agamben explains in more detail this journey to *nirvāṇa* in his book *Karman*, but whether Zartaloudis is being faithful to Agamben, or even making sense, in mixing these categories up in his own mystical way, is another matter.

[42] The original complete sentence is this: "It is interesting to note how in his essay Benjamin portrays such a manifestation of violence as essentially non-violent."

clear 'violence' towards the state that the state may respond to with actual violence, since it is 'illegal.' So, a strike, that exercises 'the right to strike,' "may be called violent if it exercises [that] right in order to overthrow the legal system that has conferred it," and in this case, of a general strike, "the law meets the strikers, as perpetrators of violence, with violence" (283).

Benjamin makes a further distinction between strikes, and in this he follows Sorel. There is the partial strike and the general strike, as noted above. But there is also the "political general strike" and the "proletarian general strike." It is the proletarian general strike that operates as an action of 'pure means.'

Benjamin writes: "We can therefore only point to pure means in politics as analogous to those which govern peaceful intercourse between private persons. As regards class struggles, in them strike must under certain conditions be seen as pure means" (289-291). These 'certain conditions' are that of the *proletarian general strike*, which is "antithetical in [its] relation to violence" in comparison to the *political general strike*.

For Benjamin (still following Sorel) the political general strike aims only at modifying the state, replacing one set of leaders with another, whereas the proletarian general strike (which was expressed in the "abortive German revolution" p291) ignores the state, wants nothing to do with the state, and gets on with living a new life immediately. Benjamin writes:

> While the first form of interruption of work is violent since it causes only an external modification of labor conditions, the second, as pure means, is nonviolent. For it takes place not in readiness to resume work following external concessions and this or that modification to working conditions, but in the determination to resume only a wholly transformed work, no longer enforced by the state, an upheaval that this kind of strike not so much causes as consummates. (291-2)

So, this kind of strike does not *cause* change, or point to a transition to that change, *it consummates the change in one go*, it *is* the revolution completed. If we remember Agamben's note that 'divine violence' in the human sphere is 'revolution,' and if we understand that Benjamin's description of a proletarian general strike is revolution, and then if we remember that the proletarian general strike is pure means, and that pure means is nonviolent... then one has to wonder about Ross' claims and challenge above.[43]

Furthermore, Agamben himself writes:

> Benjamin identifies this violence — or according to the double meaning of the German term *Gewalt*,[44] 'destituent power [It., *potere destituente*]' — in the proletarian general strike, which Sorel opposed to the simply political strike. While the suspension of labor in the political strike is violent, "since it provokes [*veranlasst*, 'occasions,' 'induces'] only an external modification of labor conditions, the second, as a pure means, is nonviolent." (Agamben: 268-9: 2014).

One might also consider how Agamben, in *State of Exception*, uses the term 'human *action*' as a definition of Benjamin's "pure violence." Agamben confirms "in the last analysis, the status of violence as a cipher for human action" (59), and writes, "pure violence [is] the name Benjamin gives to human action that neither makes nor preserves law" (60), and continues:

---

[43] Ross is also concerned to situate Benjamin as 'a revolutionary,' and perhaps even Soviet-*leaning* Marxist. At the beginning of her recent book, Ross writes: "This book does not intend to rehearse a case for Benjamin's revolutionary bona fides. It is not just biographical details such as his friendship with Bertolt Brecht or intimate history with Asja Lacis that can be mentioned in support of his revolutionary sympathies" (Ross: 4: 2019). I agree. However, I think Ross conflates Benjamin's revolutionism with *Jacobinism*. Ross does not properly take into account the object of Georges Sorel's book, *Reflections on Violence*, which was to reveal a different kind of violence, one that, rather than involving a Jacobinist uprising, involved a proletarian seizure of individual and collective daily life — the mass proletarian strike—that *immediately* re-purposes all activity. Sorel is making the point that this act is *a violence* against the established order, but of an entirely different kind to the one advocated by communists who call for the taking up of arms, which is a Jacobinist impulse. The fact that Benjamin, no doubt, considered himself to be a revolutionist or, better, in favor of communism, should not obscure the close relationship of the *Critique* to *Reflections on Violence*. Indeed, as one can see in this essay, through the work of Agamben and Camatte, it is possible to be an advocate for communist life without calling for an insurrection.

[44] There is also a double meaning in Benjamin's use of the word strike: "In the English translation of the "Critique of Violence," it appears as if Benjamin [...] plays with the term strike. Strike means, of course, either a withdrawal of labor (*Streik*) or a blow or hit (*Schlagen*). In comparing state-making, Jacobin, or lawmaking violence with pure immediate violence that is law-destroying and proletarian, Benjamin contends that "if the former threatens, the latter strikes [*schlagend*]; if the former is bloody, the latter is lethal without spilling blood." (Harrison: 197; Benjamin: 297: 1921)

Pure violence exposes and severs the nexus between law and violence and can thus appear in the end not as violence that governs or executes (*die schaltende*) but as violence that purely acts and manifests (*die waltende*). (Agamben: 62: 2003)[45]

X

It is now time to return to Agamben's own assessment of the work of *Tiqqun*. From a 2010 interview:

> I think that the Bloom theory [Agamben and *Tiqqun* worked on this together; Aarons: 57: 2020] is the assessment of a situation, like in the other texts, it's not that we want to push something so far as to provoke a dialectical reversal, because it's true that it is being done a lot and that one can always resort to it. But still I feel that the tone defining those texts is one of 'assessment of a situation.' What is going to happen next is not clear. It's not implicit whether or not, beginning with what Tiqqun calls the Bloom, this 'non-subject' referred to as the Bloom, there will be a revolution. That's always what makes the texts a little difficult, because on the one hand they could be read as a merciless, completely negative analysis and on the other, since it's the assessment of a political situation, one could discover a new set of potentialities. Any situation has its set of potentialities. (Agamben: 2010)

If we read this and take into account that Agamben never calls for violence, and 'only' calls for the turning of our backs on things (this being the revolution required), plus we remind ourselves of *Le Tigre*'s view of *Tiqqun*'s literary style, we can assume that either *Tiqqun* has completely misunderstood Agamben, or they were indeed merely making a Situationist-style avant-garde intervention (Rasmussen: 2006) and a poetical and theological *assessment* of the situation they perceived happening around them, that is, the 'global/world civil war' that was identified by Agamben in 1995:

> The face, truth, and exposition are today the objects of a global civil war, whose battlefield is social life in its entirety, whose storm troopers are the media, whose victims are all the peoples of the Earth. (Agamben: 95: 2000a)[46]

---

[45] "Nothing so aggravates an earnest person as a passive resistance," Herman Melville, *Bartleby the Scrivener*.

[46] In the book *Stasis*, 2015, Agamben reflects on Ancient Greek notions of 'civil war' and the tensions between household and polis, suggesting that current global phenomena exist

But this civil war, as Agamben makes clear here, is a relentlessly one-sided affair, where — if one factors in his notions of the effects of "the security paradigm" (see above) — oppositional dissent, or push-back, only fuels further repression, and Agamben's advice to its victims is drawn from Kafka's, which is to 'find a way out.' Agamben is not advocating an armed insurrection, riots, looting, or the building of the ubiquitous barricade against this machine-like assault from authority, he is advocating a spiritual and physical slipping away from it.

However, there is a good reason for readers of Agamben to misunderstand his own take on the 'global civil war.' In his book, *State of Exception*, Agamben writes, "The expression 'global civil war' appears in the same year (1963) in both Hannah Arendt's *On Revolution* and Carl Schmitt's *Theory of the Partisan*" (Agamben: 3: 2003), but he makes no qualification of this observation. For both these writers this conception of civil war was formulated through a consideration of the cycle of war-and-revolution/revolution-and-war that was witnessed in the 20th century (Arendt: 17-19; Schmitt: 67-8). And Schmitt extended the notion to the proliferation of 20th century colonial wars of liberation, describing Lenin as "the professional revolutionary[47] of the world-wide civil war" (Schmitt: 66). Thus, *Tiqqun* are able to claim, "We constitute ourselves as a *force*, as a *material* force, as an *autonomous* material force within the world civil war" (*Call*: 13: Proposition 11). This could be read as *Tiqqun* stating that there is an actual civil war going on, in which 'troops' on either side are already mobilized or, perhaps more correctly, as *Tiqqun* claiming ("We are among those who get organized," *Call*: 3: Proposition

---

outside of both, at "a threshold of politicization/depoliticization," in which the private and the political are both "exceeded" or negated; this territory is described as a "a zone of indifference" (p12), and he claims that the 'global civil war' of the present is represented, or actualized, by terrorism (p18). Compare with Jean Baudrillard: "as everywhere else...the media...precede...terrorist acts" (Baudrillard: 91: 1995); and, *yet*, "Against the hegemony of [the] system, one can exalt the ruses of desire, practise revolutionary micrology of the quotidian, exalt the molecular drift or even defend cooking. This does not resolve the imperious necessity of checking the system in broad daylight. This, only terrorism can do" (Baudrillard: 163: 1981).

[47] Readers today may view the term 'professional revolutionary' as a derisory one, and, indeed, Schmitt may also be using it pejoratively, but it was used by Lenin in 1902, at the beginning of Part IV of *What Is To Be Done?* to encourage the eradication of 'amateurishness' amongst revolutionaries. As Albert Camus informs us in *The Rebel*, the originator of the term 'professional revolutionary,' as used by Lenin, was probably Pyotr Tkachev (1844-86), who, until Stalin implemented the 'Lenin Cult,' was often considered to be the first Bolshevik.

I) that they are *endeavoring* to mobilize, at least, themselves and, perhaps even, 'the masses.'

Though, again, perhaps one should not read *Tiqqun* literally. *Tiqqun* introduce their *Theses on the Imaginary Party* with a quote from Hannah Arendt on thinking as "a kind of action," which, once again serves to help situate their work and purpose within a literary/philosophical, or as they put it, "poets and theologians" field, rather than one of actual revolt in the here and now, even though by the term 'poet' they may mean 'creator.' In *The Coming Community*, Agamben writes: "At the point you *perceive* the irreparability of the world, at that point it is transcendent" (Agamben: Appendix, Sec. 3: 1990; my emphasis).

The revolutionary 'task,' we have before us, then, if we insist on being revolutionaries, is to *think* our way out. This, Agamben suggests, can be done by starting with Benjamin:

> The aim of my essay [*Walter Benjamin and the Demonic: Happiness and Historical Redemption*] [is] to trace the fundamental [lines] of Benjamin's ethics. Here the word 'ethics' is intended in the sense it had when it made its appearance in the Greek philosophical schools as a 'doctrine of happiness.' For the Greeks, the link between the demonic (*daimonion*) and happiness was evident in the very term with which they designated happiness, *eudaimonia*. (Agamben: 138: 1982)

Agamben is still thinking through this relationship of the demon, or *daemon*, to happiness in 2015:

> Remaining faithful to one's own demon does not in fact mean blindly abandoning oneself to him and being confident that he will in any case lead us to success — that he will make us write the most beautiful poems, if we are poets; that he will grant us happiness and pleasure, if we are sensual beings. Poetry and happiness are not his gifts; rather, the demon himself is the ultimate gift that happiness and poetry award us at the point where they regenerate us and give us new birth... It is said that the demon is not a god but a demi-god. Yet 'demigod' can only mean the potency and possibility, not the actuality of the divine. Insofar as maintaining a relation with potency is the most arduous undertaking, the demon is something we incessantly lose and to which we must try to remain faithful at all costs. A poetic life is the one that, in every adventure, obstinately maintains itself in relation not with an act but with a potency, not with a god but with a demigod. (Agamben: 86-88: 2015a)

> Mallarmé once wrote a poem with a comma after every word to emphasize the elusive nature of truth, or the problem of 'certainty.' He also invented an early version of hypertext using a fountain pen, three chopsticks, and a balloon, but failed to sell the idea to publishers.

It is also useful to note that Agamben indicates several times that what he is suggesting has not yet fully 'emerged,' or, rather, that its emergence is the task of a future generation, despite our apparently living in messianic time, and Aarons' claim that, "For Agamben the problem of communism has nothing to do with a future society" (Aarons: 65: 2020). For example, Agamben writes: "for destituent potential it is necessary to think entirely different strategies, whose definition is the task of the coming politics" (Agamben: 266: 2014), *and*, "The profanation of the unprofanable is the political task of the coming generation" (Agamben: 92: 2005). Ross, for example, therefore, regards Agamben's work as comprising of a "destinal view of politics" (Ross: fn12: 2008). The notion of things being 'coming' but 'already here' is part of the philosophical field of the 'always already,' developed from Martin Heidegger's (another unrepentant Nazi, and to whose memory Agamben dedicated his book, *Stanzas*, 1977/93) use of the concept in *Being and Time*. But to return to Agamben:

> [N]ot work but inoperativity or decreation is the paradigm of the coming politics (*the coming* does not mean *the future*). Redemption, the *tiqqun* that is at stake in the book [*The Coming Community*], is not an operation or work, but a particular kind of sabbatical vacation. It is the insalvable that renders the salvation possible, the irreparable that allows the coming of the redemption. (Agamben: Postface to 2001 edition of *The Coming Community*: original emphases)

This, I think, indicates the 'collapse' that makes possible the letting go of all purpose, and the making use of the things of the world for no other purpose than the using of them, which may happen in moments in the present, for individuals, but is, for Agamben, more likely to happen when Western civilization, or at least Europe, actually collapses. Once again following Benjamin (*Theses*: 11), Agamben is concerned with happiness and redemption. Agamben sets "Benjamin's warning — who recommends we not confuse life with work" (Agamben: 58: 2015a) in opposition to Kant's "determination of the human being as moral [and which] thus coincides with the definitive triumph of purposiveness [operativity] in the sphere of action" (Agamben: Ch. 4: Sec. 11: 2017). Only through a letting go can the kind of *nirvāṇa* Agamben envisions be achieved.

XI

So why is it that Agamben's concepts and terminology are used so much by those who advocate the idea of violent insurrection?[48] In the case of *Tiqqun* it is not only that they have utilized Agamben's ideas, they have, with *Bloom theory*, formulated them together. This has perhaps given a credibility to Agamben within the ultra-left, as well as amongst anarchists, that ignores key elements in his writings. Maybe Agamben is happy to be associated with left-communists, insurrectionist partisans, and others, because, although they don't quite 'get him' they are, perhaps, *on the way*, or close. As Agamben says of *Tiqqun*, indicating that, while their journal is "very political," it has "taken on a messianic tone" and has asked *the right question*:

> In this regard, I am thinking of a review which has just been published in France, by young people I know, which is called *Tiqqun*. [It] interests me because it's an extremely critical, very political journal, which takes on a very messianic tone, but always in a completely secular manner. Thus, they call Bloom the new anonymous subjects, the unspecified singularities, hollowed out, ready for anything, which can be diffused everywhere, but remaining elusive, without identity but re-identifiable at every moment. The problem they ask themselves is: "How to transform this Bloom, how will this Bloom operate the leap beyond itself?" (Agamben: 2000c)

One should also consider that his own political and philosophical trajectory perhaps began from a similar place. His 1970 essay, *On the Limits of Violence*, an engagement with Benjamin's *Critique* that treats the notion of 'revolutionary violence' with less of his later nuance, is quite separate to the perspectives of his more recent oeuvre, but some of his later ideas are embryonic in the piece.

It may well be that Agamben himself has political views or sympathies that don't entirely 'fit' with his writing as such, but without knowing him we can't know what these are or might be (as an analogy: an anarchist might produce texts urging people not to vote in elections, but then might privately hope that a particular candidate or party is elected), and anyway they would be irrelevant for the purposes of this essay. Yes, he might talk to students contemplating a sit-in, or give talks to anarchists in Athens, and others, but this does not necessarily mean he is demonstrating unqualified support for their actions and

---

[48] See, for example, the site *Ill Will Editions*.

perspectives, he may be trying to get them to think beyond their current ideas. In the same way, he might speak at Roman Catholic events (Notre Dame Cathedral, for example, where he presented at a Lenten conference, in 2009), and engage in dialogue with the Church, over for example, its 'mysteries' and the recent Pope who resigned (Benedict XVI). But this does not necessarily mean that he supports the Catholic Church in all its activities and all its perspectives, it may be, once again, that he is trying to get them all to go beyond their current thinking.

Indeed, this possible strategy of 'forging alliances with anyone who might listen,' if I may put it like this, was promoted by the famous theoretician of Italian *operaismo*, Mario Tronti, in a joint manifesto in 2011:

> The manipulation of life, brought about by technical developments and the violence inherent in the processes of globalisation, in the absence of a new international order, confronts us with an unprecedented anthropological emergency. It appears to be the most serious manifestation, and at the same time the deepest root, of the crisis of democracy. It poses challenges that call for a new alliance between men and women, believers and non-believers, religions and politics. (Tronti, *et al*: 12-13: 2012; first published in the Italian Catholic daily newspaper, *Avvenire*, 2011)

There is one further thing of interest in the Camattian/Agambenian turn toward a philosophy of leaving, or turning one's back on, the world. This is the connection it has to the Bordigan position on anti-fascism.

The left-communist Otto Rühle was entirely correct when he asserted that fascism stole its ideas from Bolshevism, in 1939 he wrote:

> Nationalism, authoritarianism, centralism, leader dictatorship, power policies, terror-rule, mechanistic dynamics, inability to socialize — all these essential characteristics of fascism were and are existing in bolshevism. Fascism is merely a copy of bolshevism. For this reason, the struggle against the one must begin with the struggle against the other. (Rühle: _The Struggle Against Fascism Begins with the Struggle Against Bolshevism_)

Amadeo Bordiga, who persisted in his fondness for Lenin and Bolshevism and so did not equate these dictatorial forms as Rühle did, campaigned from the 1920s for a position that viewed anti-fascism as a pro-capitalist strategy:

> We steadfastly maintained that the real enemy and foremost danger was not Fascism, much less Mussolini the man, but rather the anti-fascism that

Fascism – with all of its crimes and infamies – would have created. This antifascism would breathe life into that great poisonous monster, a great bloc comprising every form of capitalist exploitation, along with all of its beneficiaries: from the great plutocrats down to the laughable ranks of the half-bourgeois, intellectuals and the laity. (Bordiga: *Against anti-fascism: Amadeo Bordiga's last interview (1970)*, at *Overland*, 24 November, 2017)

He is also right, and history has proven him right. But he is only *practically* right if one thinks one can escape or abolish capitalism within a time frame in which fascism doesn't kill us all. In the meantime, the only *humane*, and practical, response to fascism is to join with others to resist or defeat it, even if it means the return or strengthening of social democracy.

It is this position of Bordiga's that underpins the whole of Camatte's approach to the way capital has come to dominate our lives. Camatte developed Bordiga's *anti-antifascist* position so that it became 'the more we fight capital the stronger it gets.' He is right of course. But what can we do? Wait? Tend our gardens, as Voltaire suggested? His argument is that instead of fighting capital, instead of opposing fascism, instead of opposing Bolshevism, instead of opposing *anything*, we slip away from it, or, as Agamben concurs, spiritually turn our backs on it all and live *as not*.

Nowhere in their writing do either Camatte or Agamben call for an uprising, the taking up of arms, the throwing of rocks, looting, or any kind of oppositional dissent.[49] They call first and foremost for an inner change within each individual, a change in perception that enables a transcendence (specifically for Agamben: "a deposition without abdication"), and secondarily for a 'reconnection' with 'nature,' or, effectively, the setting up of communes. They urge us to 'leave this world' or to find a way out. Echoing *Bartleby the Scrivener*'s desire to 'not to',

---

[49] The closest Agamben gets to speak of what might be interpreted as some kind of violent resistance to authority is in a brief reference: "The subject... is what results from the hand-to-hand confrontation with the apparatuses in which it has been put—and has put itself—into play," in *Profanations* (Agamben: 72: 2005), and he repeats it in *What is an Apparatus?* where he writes: "the strategy that we must adopt in our hand-to-hand combat with apparatuses cannot be a simple one" (Agamben: 17: 2006). But he is talking about the constant battle one has with 'technology' and the devices of government (that is, the network of actual practises, and actual things, that govern us) and how we are transformed by the 'technology,' the devices of governmentality, and our resistance to them. ('Apparatus' is the English translation of Foucault's *dispositif*.) For most readers, apart from *the partisans*, of course, his image of 'hand-to-hand combat' would not make them think that Agamben is saying: "praise the lord and *pass the ammunition*."

Agamben writes that in the future we must recover ourselves and the things of the world "without being noticed."[50] In possibly Agamben's most lucid book (*What is Real?*) there is even the faint, though highly alluring, if equally impossible, implication that perhaps we should 'just' disappear.

Yet several interpreters of Agamben's work use his writing to validate their energetic literary fascination for revolt, insurrection, the arming of the partisans, looting and destruction; and this "monolithic" (Rasmussen: 14) rhetoric ultimately serves only to maintain a readership, and academic niche, that increasingly becomes the passive object, or target, of 'revolutionary discourse.'

The consequences of the *Tiqqun* avenue are that those who *might* engage in a proper ongoing and active critique of the world either end up on the trajectory of "police rule or insanity," as Camus insists, or, and this is the most likely outcome, they will simply become enervated by the performative oratory, thereby becoming inactive and silent. The consequence of following Camatte or Agamben is that one might be transported away toward a *nirvāṇic* cloud of philosophical and revolutionary purity thereby, again, becoming inactive and silent. Both consequences are therefore an effective, if not actual, sanctioning and facilitation of reactionary politics.

Postscript, September 2021:

As I indicate above, it *is* possible that Agamben, since he has a 'voracious curiosity' for political struggles, as Negri posits below, has — in conversation that has so far been unrecorded or transcribed — offered some kind of verbal support for the notion of violent insurrection. But this is unknown to us, is not anywhere within his texts or interviews, and is not given in evidence, for example, by Kieran Aarons.

This commentary below was published by Antonio Negri in 2004, after the writing of 'Bloom Theory,' 2000, which *Tiqqun* and Agamben are understood to have worked on together.

> "Agamben is one [of] my best friends, one of my most intimate friends. I have known him for roughly two decades. We often spend summer vacations together; we get together for Christmas every year; we are basically family. In short, we love each other very much. I am older than he is. And unlike

---

[50] The story of *Bartleby*, by Melville, is central to Agamben's thesis, see the chapter in *Potentialities*. The quote from Agamben is from *When the House Burns Down*, 2020.

myself, he was never involved in political struggles, for which he has an incredibly voracious curiosity, as they constitute a great lack in his life — and he very much regrets not having had such experiences. He is quite limited when it comes to understanding politics — and in his work this limitation takes the form of a radical Heideggerism." (Casarino, C., and Negri, A., *In Praise of the Common: A Conversation on Philosophy and Politics*, University of Minnesota Press, 2008, p152)

Certainly, it is true that since 2004 Agamben has spoken in the Notre Dame to Catholics, and to anarchists in Athens and student demonstrators in the Sorbonne, been interviewed occasionally in leftist circles, but nowhere has he advocated violence or any kind of active insurrection. Instead, as he explains in an interview from February 2021, published on his blog at *Quodlibet*, his advice is to give testimony of the truth:

"[Jesus said:] 'for this I have come into the world: to testify of the truth.' In fact, there is no experience of truth without testimony: true is that word for which we cannot but commit ourselves to bear personal witness. Here, the difference between a scientific and a philosophical truth emerges. In fact, while a scientific truth is (or at least should be) independent from the subject who enunciates it, the truth we are talking about is such only if the subject who pronounces it is wholly at stake in it. Indeed, it is a veridiction and not a theorem. Faced with a non-truth imposed by law, we can and must testify of the truth." (Agamben, G., *Where is Science Going?*, 17 February 2021)

The word 'veridiction,' here, references Foucault's use of the word in *The Birth of Biopolitics*. Veridiction is a kind of 'truth' dependent upon the worldview of the individual or subject that states it, or the social system that observes and 'uses' it for their own purposes. It is not an objective truth. Foucault uses the example of the 'truth' of 'the market' as the grounds upon which modern government is founded, rather than on notions of justice or being 'just.' 'Truth,' therefore, for government, becomes more overtly and explicitly related to the motions of the economy than to the (usually deceitful) ideal of social justice. Agamben uses this conceptualization to affirm that truth is one's own individual 'truth,' and that it is only verifiably 'true' when one 'testifies' it.

This mix of 'fact' and 'truth' — or 'knowledge' and 'truth' — that affirms that one's own version of the truth is as valid as anyone else's is the basis of Donald Trump's belief that 'truth' can be generated with a 'positive' attitude (see *The Power of Positive Thinking*, by Norman Vincent Peale), and led to Rudy Giuliani arguing on television in 2018 that it was pointless for Trump to attend the

Mueller inquiry because it would just be a competition between different viewpoints. When the interviewer wondered what the problem with attending the inquiry could be and stated that, after all, "Truth is truth," Giuliani famously replied: "No, it isn't truth. Truth isn't truth."

Giorgio Agamben, in similar vein, ends his February interview with: "We can only, in an unjust and false society, attest to the presence of the right and the true. We can only, in the middle of hell, testify of heaven."

Despite the association with *Tiqqun* and other occasional public appearances, by far his most decisive political intervention to date has coincided with the Covid-19 pandemic, during which he has contributed numerous texts and been the lead signatory of at least one petition to the Italian government. Throughout his pandemic interventions he has demonstrated a close spiritual alignment with the forces of the reactionary right, in Italy and beyond, who are against lockdowns, masks, and vaccines, who are 'covid-skeptic,' and proponents of various 'conspiracy theories.' Much of the 'anti-political' 'left' — who have been reading Agamben for two decades now, and of whom many appear to share a Christian outlook — are therefore seeing in the pandemic a 'state of exception' forming as a conspiratorial highpoint in their narrow perception of modern 'statecraft,' and this aligns them, too, with the reactionary right, and 'Trumpists' in general, who speak of the same conspiracy.

But maybe this political intervention is finally revealing some sort of support for violence, insurrection, and 'underground resistance'? In a text published at *Quodlibet* on the 17th September 2021, he writes that "the dissidents [must] think of creating something like a society within a society, a community of friends and neighbors [which will form a] new clandestinity."

This feels very much like a reference to the Italian resistance movement to Mussolini's fascism, a phenomenon that has been widely referred to as an exemplar for action by the reactionary right in Italy, as explained in an article by Donatella Di Cesari published in the same month: '*Denialists, conspiracy-theorists, and the hyper-credulous: The reactionary battle for 'No Pass.' This is not a liberation struggle: it prioritizes the individual over the many*' (*Negazionisti, complottisti e ipercreduli*, La Stampa, September 8, 2021).

Three towering philosophers: Heidegger admired the quality of Hitler's hands; Wittgenstein worked as a hospital porter delivering prescriptions but advised patients against taking them; when Jean-Luc

Nihil Evadere

Nancy was told he needed heart surgery, Agamben recommended he refuse it.

References:

Aarons, K., 2016, 'No Selves to Abolish: Afropessimism, Anti-Politics and the End of the World,' Mute magazine, 26 February 2016.

Aarons, K., 2020, 'Destitution and Creation: Agamben's Messianic Gesture,' in *Journal of Italian Philosophy, Vol. 3*, 2020, UK. Can be found online.

Agamben, G., 1970 (2009), On the Limits of Violence, in *Diacritics*, Vol. 4, Winter 2009, pp.103-111, Lorenzo Fabbri (ed.), Elisabeth Fay (trans.), John Hopkins University.

Agamben, G., 1982 (1999), 'Walter Benjamin and the Demonic: Happiness and Historical Redemption,' in *Potentialities: Collected Essays in Philosophy*, Daniel Heller-Roazen (trans. and ed.), SUP, 1999.

Agamben, G., 1990 (1993), *The Coming Community*, Michael Hardt (trans.), University of Minnesota Press. The *Postface* of 2001 can be found online at The Anarchist Library.

Agamben, G., 1995 (1998), *Homo Sacer*, Daniel Heller-Roazen (trans.), SUP, 1998.

Agamben, G., 2000a (1992-6), *Means Without End: Notes on Politics*, V. Binetti and C. Casarino (trans.), Uni of Minnesota Press. *Note on Gesture*, 1992; *Form-of-Life*, 1993.

Agamben, G., 2000b (2005), *The Time That Remains: A Commentary on the Letter to the Romans*, Patricia Dailey (trans.), SUP. One can find an early draft translation of part of this book online: Agamben, G., 2002, 'The Time That Is Left,' *Epoché*, Volume 7, Issue 1 (Fall 2002).

Agamben, G., 2000c, A Minor Biopolitics: Interview with Giorgio Agamben, *Vacarme*, 2 January, 2000.

Agamben, G., 2003 (2005), *State of Exception*, Kevin Attell (trans.), Chicago University Press.

Agamben, G., 2005 (2007), 'In Praise of Profanation,' Kevin Attell (trans.), in *Profanations*, Jeff Fort (trans.), Zone Books.

Agamben, G., 2006 (2009), *What is an Apparatus?* David Kishik and Stefan Pedatella (trans.), SUP.

Agamben, G., 2007 (2011), *The Kingdom and the Glory: For a Theological Genealogy of Economy and Government*, 2011, SUP.

Agamben, G., 2010, interview transcript at: https://anarchistwithoutcontent.wordpress.com/2010/04/18/tiqqun-apocrypha-repost/. Also referenced in Aarons, 2020.

Agamben, G., 2013, 'For a Theory of Destituent Power,' public lecture in Athens, 16th November, 2013, published by Chronos (ΧΡΟΝΟΣ) 2014, also at Roar Magazine. Can also be found at the The Anarchist Library in PDF form with the title: *From the State of Control to a Praxis of Destituent Power*.

Agamben, G., 2014 (2016), *The Use of Bodies*, Adam Kotsko (trans.), SUP, 2016.

Agamben, G., 2015a (2018), *The Adventure*, Lorenzo Chiesa (trans.), MIT Press, 2018.

Agamben, G., 2015b, 'Europa muss kollabieren' [Europe must Collapse], interview by Iris Radisch in *Die Zeit* (Zeit Online), 27 August, 2015.

Agamben, G., 2015c (2015), *Stasis: Civil War as a Political Paradigm*, Nicholas Heron (trans.), Edinburgh University Press, 2015.

Agamben, G., 2016 (2018), What is Real? Lorenzo Chiesa (trans.), SUP.

Agamben, G., 2017 (2018), *Karman: A Brief Treatise on Action, Guilt, and Gesture*, Adam Kotsko (trans.), 2018, SUP.

Agamben, G., 2020 (2021), *When the House Burns Down*, Kevin Attell (trans.), *Diacritics*, 6 January 2021.

Arendt, H., 1963/65, *On Revolution*, Penguin, 1990.

Badiou, A., 1997, 'Politics and Philosophy: An Interview with Alain Badiou,' Peter Hallward, *Angelaki: Journal of the Theoretical Humanities*, 3:3, 1998, can be found online.

Baudrillard, J., 1981 (1994), *Simulacra and Simulation*, Sheila Faria Glaser (trans.), University of Michigan Press, 1994.

Baudrillard, J., 1995 (2002), *Screened Out*, Chris Turner (trans.), Verso, 2002.

Benjamin, W., 1921 (1986), 'Critique of Violence,' in *Reflections: Essays, Aphorisms, Autobiographical Writings*, Peter Demetz (ed.), Edmund Jephcott (trans.), Schocken Books.

Benjamin, W., 1940, 'Theses on the Philosophy of History,' in *Illuminations*, Hannah Arendt (ed.), Harry Zohn (trans.), Schocken Books, 2007.

Berardi, Franco 'Bifo,' 2010, "Precariousness, Catastrophe and Challenging the Blackmail of the Imagination," *Affinities: A Journal of Radical Theory, Culture, and Action*, Volume 4, Number 2, Fall 2010, pp. 1-4.

Berardi, Franco 'Bifo,' 2012b, *Transverse*, short piece, available on the Internet.

Bonacci, V., '*State of Exception* or *Threshold of Indiscernibilty*? A study on the Beginnings of Giorgio Agamben's *Homo Sacer* Project,' in *Ethics and Politics XXII*, 2020, 3, University of Trieste. Can be found online.

Britt, Brian, 2010, 'The Schmittian Messiah in Agamben's The Time That Remains,' *Critical Inquiry*, 36(2), 262-287, University of Chicago Press.

Camus, Albert, *The Rebel*, Anthony Bower (trans.), Penguin, 1982.

Cimino, A., 2016, '[Agamben's political messianism in The Time That Remains](),' *International Journal of Philosophy and Theology*, 77:3, 102-118.

Dauvé, Gilles, and François Martin, 1972, *Eclipse and Re-emergence of the Communist Movement*, PM Press, Oakland, CA, 2015.

Endnotes, 2011, 'What are we to do?' in *Communization and its Discontents: Contestation, Critique, and Contemporary Struggles*, Benjamin Noys (ed), Minor Compositions, New York, 2011. Pages 29-30. Can be found online.

Harrison, P., 2017, *The Freedom of Things: An Ethnology of Control. How the Structure of Dependence in Modern Society has Misinformed the Western Mind*, TSI Press.

Leibniz, G.W., 1698 (1908), 'On Nature in Itself,' in *The Philosophical Works of Liebnitz*, Second Edition, George Martin Duncan (trans.), Tuttle, Morehouse and Taylor, New Haven, 1908.

Mathews, Shailer, 1902, The Social Teaching of Paul. IV. The Messianism of Paul, in *The Biblical World*, May, 1902, Vol. 19, No. 5, pp. 370-377. University of Chicago Press. Available online.

Oates, J.C., 1998, 'Introduction,' to *Herman Melville: Billy Budd and Other Tales*, Signet, 1998.

Rasmussen, Mikkel Bolt, 2006, 'Counterrevolution, the Spectacle, and the Situationist Avant-Garde,' *Social Justice* 33, no. 2 (104) (2006): 5-15.

Ross, A., 2008, 'The Agamben Effect,' *South Atlantic Quarterly* 107:1, Winter 2008, Duke University Press.

Ross, A., 2014, 'The Distinction between Mythic and Divine Violence: Walter Benjamin's *Critique of Violence* from the Perspective of *Goethe's Elective Affinities*,' in *New German Critique* 121, Vol. 41, No. 1, Winter 2014. Available online.

Ross, A., 2015, 'The Ambiguity of Ambiguity in Benjamin's *Critique of Violence*,' in *Towards the Critique of Violence: Walter Benjamin and Giorgio Agamben*, Brendan Moran and Carlo Salzani (eds.), Bloomsbury, 2015.

Ross, A., 2019, *Revolution and History in Walter Benjamin: A Conceptual Analysis*, Routledge.

Schmitt, C., 1963, *The Theory of the Partisan*, A.C. Goodson (trans.), Michigan State University, 2004. Can be found online.

Sorel, G., 1908 (2004), *Reflections on Violence*, Jeremy Jennings (ed. and revised trans.), Cambridge University Press.

Tarì, Marcello, 2017 (2021), *There is No Unhappy Revolution: The Communism of Destitution*, Richard Braude (trans.), Common Notions.

Tiqqun 1, 1999, *Tiqqun: Conscious Organ of the Imaginary Party*. This can be found online; the *Theses* are also here.
The other texts by *Tiqqun* can be found online.

Tronti, M., *et al*, 2012, *Emergenza antropologica: Per una nuova alleanza tra credenti e non credenti* [*Anthropological Emergency: For a new Alliance Between Believers and Non-Believers*], P. Barcellona, P. Sorbi, M. Tronti, and G. Vacca (eds.), their 2011 manifesto introduces the collection, Guerini e Associati, 2012.

Vaneigem, Raoul, 1967 (2012), *The Revolution of Everyday Life*, Donald Nicholson-Smith (trans. 1994/2012), PM Press.

Zartaloudis, Thanos, 2015, 'Violence Without Law? On Pure Violence as a Destituent Power,' in *Towards the Critique of Violence: Walter Benjamin and Giorgio Agamben*, Moran, B. and Salzani, C. (eds.), 2015, Bloomsbury.

Žižek, S. 2008, *Violence: Six Sideways Reflections*, Picador.

Translations, unless otherwise stated, are by the author.

3 Wandering: Camatte, Millenarian Confusion, and the Humans who Escaped his Notice

[This article was originally written in 2020 with the title: "The *Gemeinwesen* Has Always Been Here: *An Engagement with the ideas of Jacques Camatte*." I have since developed my knowledge and thinking on Camatte's 'politics' and have now re-written the piece somewhat. This may make the article feel a little disjointed, but if one reads the rest of this book, then my arguments should demonstrate a sufficient coherence.]

> The less you *are*, the less you express your own life, the more you *have*, the more pronounced is your alienated life, the greater is the aggregate of your alienated being.
> Karl Marx, *Economic-Philosophical Manuscripts, 1844*[1]

Jacques Camatte's writings, which are regularly added to, can be found on the website *Revue Invariance*. Born in 1935, he was a radical Marxist theoretician in European left-communist circles during the fifties and sixties, mentored by Amadeo Bordiga. However, the events around 1968, particularly in France, caused him to shed his left-communist affiliations. So much so, in fact, that he collaborated with *Jaca Books* (a right-wing, traditionalist, Catholic publishing house in Italy) in the 1970s to have his pieces published, and currently he is working with *Il Covile* (another traditionalist Italian grouping on the far-right) to have his writings translated and archived. In 2019 he conducted a friendly interview with the French group *Cercle Marx*, who have, at least, far-right connections.[2]

---

[1] Economic-Philosophical Manuscripts, 1844. All translations by author, unless indicated by a footnote reference.

[2] Until the 1980s *Jaca Book* was the publishing house for the reactionary 'Communion and Liberation' movement — *Comunione e Liberazione* (CL). In 1975 the *Red Brigades*

The recent emergence of a 'traditionalist' worldview is filtered through an 'anti-left Marxism' and expressed, for example, by *Jaca Books* and *Il Covile*, and people like Diego Fusaro and Elena Louisa Lange. Camatte's involvement with publishers of the "extreme Catholic right" and the "reactionary far-right" (as he, himself, describes them) should not, however, be regarded as inconsistent or dubious on his part. Indeed, Camatte is quite open about his associations. Camatte is not demonstrating any kind of 'betrayal' in working with these groups since his project is to go beyond the left, and beyond all *enmity*. He is following the logic of Bordiga's 'anti-anti-fascism,' which extends out, in Camatte's perspective, to become a project for the complete salvation of 'humanity.'

So, a first point of interest is just why the extreme right is fascinated with Camatte. Perhaps this has much to do with his problematic positions on 'woman' (derived from Jacob Bachofen),[3] 'artificiality,' and 'homosexuality,' which are all touched upon in his article *Amour ou combinatoire sexuelle*, 1978. My contention, in this piece, and other texts I have written on the politics of Camatte, is that the original positions, which he has inherited from Bordiga, and which also find expression in much of the ultra-left, and in the development of the ultra-left into an 'anti-political,' or 'anti-left Marxist,' milieu have borne a misunderstanding of social relations in capitalist society that have led to key and significant elements of the ultra-left slipping into the arms of not only the reactionary far-right, but also conservative Christianity. Furthermore, this kernel of 'traditionalism,' or 'reaction,' begins in our modern era with the work of Karl Marx himself. I do not really discuss this here, but an indication of how 'resistance' to the modern world has formed itself, and how it has led to the reactions of Nazism, the Taliban, and even covidskepticism, can be sensed if one wonders just how close

---

described CL as "a clerical-fascist campaign unleashed by the Vatican against the danger of communism." Camatte had *Capitalism and Communism in Russia* published by *Jaca Book* in 1974, and *Towards the Human Community* in 1978. I must point out again that Camatte is quite open about this, like his current work with *Il Covile*, it is by no means a secret (http://www.jacabook.it/ricerca/main-aut.htm). The interview with *Cercle Marx* is here https://www.youtube.com/watch?v=EKC007KoIew (transcription: https://libcom.org/library/interview-jacques-camatte-2019). *Cercle Marx* appear to be 'red-brown confusionists' and are linked with the far-right figure, Francis Cousin, who refers to himself as such (for a little history: https://www.liberation.fr/debats/2019/01/16/le-confusionnisme-est-il-le-nouveau-rouge-brun_1703403/; and here: https://paris-luttes.info/une-analyse-critique-des-theories-14329?lang=fr). The *Libcom* site describes *Cercle Marx* as "a racist pseudo-Debordist/Bordigist group."

[3] See Cynthia Eller, *Gentlemen and Amazons: The Myth of Matriarchal Prehistory, 1861-1900*, 2011, UCP.

Marx's conception of 'species-being' is to Martin Heidegger's concept of 'being-with.'

The second point of interest is just how Camatte's logic finds itself aligning, or at least 'falling-in-with,' with the traditionalism of the extreme right. If this is the case, and it is, then has Camatte made a deep theoretical mistake? If he has, then so too have also the entire 'ultra-left' and the whole school of Continental Philosophy (*SouB* to *Endnotes*, and Deleuze to Agamben). Indeed, the 'mistake' begins with Marx himself, and specifically the failure of Marx to understand his own position within the millenarian tradition that repeatedly, inevitably, sets itself *against* the State and *for* the (re)creation of a 'garden of Eden.'

But to properly understand what I am claiming here (one does not have to agree with it, of course) one will need to have read much else in this book. Anyway, I have now made this essay something of a mess, but never mind, let's continue...

Like much of the left after 1968, Camatte decided that humanity was now caught in an impasse. There could no longer be any overthrowing of the bourgeoisie by the proletariat because all of humanity had now become 'domesticated' by capital. Therefore, any organized revolt *against* capital now only helped it develop. His proposal is that instead of fighting capital — a strategy that, if 'successful,' only returns capital to us in a stronger form — we must, somehow, *abandon* it. The taking leave of this capitalist world entails recreating connections with the natural world... it does not mean going to war against capital in order to topple it.[4]

The abandonment of '*this world*'[5] and all it stands for, including the human *enmity*[6] for all things (other animals, other things, other humans) — something that has become embedded in the modern human psyche and which causes us to repeatedly create situations of 'battle' or *discontinuity* — will, he argues, begin a process that leads to the formation of a genuinely human community, one that is *continuous* with nature and itself. It will transform *Homo sapiens* (literal meaning: 'wise man') into a new species: *Homo Gemeinwesen*. This process, Camatte insists, is immanent to our current condition and is perpetually re-

---

[4] Camatte's notion of 'domestication' under capital has been a popular trope of 'anti-capitalists' for nearly fifty years, but it isn't really any more interesting or informative than this from Nietzsche: "The meaning of all culture is simply to breed a tame and civilized animal, a *domestic animal*..." (*The Genealogy of Morality*)

[5] See: *This World We Must Leave*, 1974.

[6] See *Inimitié et extinction*, 2019.

emerging. Indeed, Camatte views himself as a kind of vessel for the emergence of the new human: "it is not I who creates ex-nihilo, rather it is through me that a certain humanity establishes itself. I want to bear witness to this. I am, if you want, like a prophet."[7]

Camatte takes the term *Gemeinwesen* from Marx. *Gemeinwesen* translates as 'community' but Marx insists that the true essence of *individual humans* is their immutable existence as *social beings*, and this confers another significance to the word. As he wrote, following Feuerbach[8]: "The individual *is* the *social being*."[9] *Gemein* translates as 'common,' and *wesen* as 'being,' or 'essence'. So, it can also be read as 'common essence,' or 'common being' and it is via these avenues that Camatte uses the term Gemeinwesen to mean the true human community, or the immediate, or *unmediated* community... in other words, the true goal of communism as envisaged by Marx.

Marx writes:

> "This communism is humanism as a perfect naturalism and naturalism as a perfect humanism [it is important to recognize that Marx understands that this can only be achieved through empiricism, or 'the scientific method'[10]]. It is the genuine dissolution of the conflict between man [sic] and nature, and between man and man, the true resolution of the conflict between existence and being, between reification and identity, between freedom and necessity, between individual and species. Communism is the riddle of history solved, and it knows itself to be this solution."[11]

---

[7] 'Extrait de lettre,' 1978, in *Articles d'Invariance serie I, Revue Invariance* (R.I.)

[8] Feuerbach, L. 2012, *The Fiery Brook: Selected Writings*, Zawar Hanfi (ed. and trans.), Verso, London, P98.

[9] *Economic and Philosophical Manuscripts 1844*.

[10] See The German Ideology, Part 1, A, and Engels on Ludwig Feuerbach, Part 4. Both on *Marxists Internet Archive*.

[11] "Dieser Kommunismus ist als vollendeter Naturalismus = Humanismus, als vollendeter Humanismus = Naturalismus, er ist die *Wahrhafte* Auflösung des Widerstreites zwischen dem Menschen mit der Natur und mit dem Menschen, die wahre Auflösung des Streits zwischen Existenz und Wesen, zwischen Vergegenständlichung und Selbstbestätigung, zwischen Freiheit und Notwendigkeit, zwischen Individuum und Gattung. Er ist das aufgelöste Rätsel der Geschichte und weiß sich als diese Lösung." From: *Ökonomisch-philosophische Manuskripte aus dem Jahre 1844*.

Marx asserts that, "The _human being is the true community_ of humankind."[12] Camatte has utilized this particular phrase throughout his work as a touchstone for his ideas (although, as he wrote in 2010,[13] he has tried to mitigate the anthropocentric and humanist connotations associated with the term 'human being' by stressing that it is the particular species' 'life form,' or the individual itself, that is, at one and the same time, the true community of humankind).

To better understand this phrase – which is another version of 'the individual is the _social being_' — it is useful to know that Marx is here using it in the context of revolts against "dehumanized life"[14] – whether they be in France in 1789, or across the USA in 2020. He is arguing that such revolts against _things as they are_, constitute a deep psychological attempt by people to reconnect to the original human community that most of us lost long generations ago. They are attempting to reverse the conditions of their lives, which are marked by an ever-increasing separation from _a human life_, from human nature, _from themselves_, in fact. These regular expressions of discontent and revolt occur because _humans are separated from the community that enables them to be fully, or properly human_. The discontent of even one small district — "because it starts from the standpoint of the _single, real individual_" — is enough, he asserts, to expose the tragedy of our separation from the communal essence of human nature. Camatte clarifies the nature of these kinds of revolts by stating that such "rebellion is largely a rebellion of bodies;" they are, "an act of understanding that takes place not only on an intellectual level, but also sensorially."[15]

Indeed, Camatte used the original longer quote containing these ideas (from _The Economic and Philosophical Manuscripts of 1844_, and which is interpreted in the above paragraph) in a leaflet distributed during the French strikes in May 1968.[16]

What Marx is arguing, and what Camatte pursues in his own theory, is that humanity has lost its own community. The community of humans has been replaced, for example, with the community of money, or the community of capital and, because of this, humans have become wretched and lost, and not even properly human... and they sense this loss. Camatte argues that the loss was initiated when humans first began to separate themselves from nature, millennia ago. From that time, they have become increasingly detached from the

---

[12] 'Critical marginal notes to the article: The King of Prussia and Social Reform. From a Prussian,' _Vorwärts!_ 60, 1844.
[13] https://revueinvariance.pagesperso-orange.fr/glosesprussien.html
[14] See fn10 above.
[15] Camatte, _Errance de l'humanité_ (The Wandering of Humanity), RI, 1973.
[16] Camatte, _À propos de la Semaine rouge_ (About the Red Week), 23 May 1968, RI.

world and from themselves — since their own nature is as a social being — and this has led to an incessant *wandering*.

The concept of a 'wandering' humanity was explored by Emil Cioran in 1949, in *Précis de Décomposition*[17] (*A Short History of Decay*). What Marx refers to as a sense within the species of *the loss of community*, Cioran refers to as *nostalgia*, by which he means a yearning for a *place* and a home, a 'homesickness.' Cioran writes:

> "Since Adam all the endeavor of mankind [sic, et al] has been to modify *the man*. [...] While all beings have their *place* in nature, man remains a metaphysically wandering[18] creature, lost in Life, peculiar in Creation. No one has found a valid goal for history, but everyone has proposed one, and in the abundance of such a plethora of disparate and fanciful goals the idea of purpose is cancelled out and vanishes like a ridiculous product of the mind."

Cioran asks how humanity can find a compromise between the unremitting, *interior* longing, or nostalgia — he uses the words, "*Sehnsucht, yearning, saudade*" — for a home, or a *place*, and the rootless, peripatetic condition of our existence. His answer is that there is no compromise: there is no remedy for the affliction:

> "On the one hand we have the yearning to be immersed in the indivisibility of the heart and hearth, while on the other we absorb space in a never-satiated hunger. And the space we consume offers no limits since it only generates new wanderings, though the goal recedes ever further as we move forward. [...] There is no solution to the tension between the Heimat

---

[17] Emil Cioran, 1949, *Précis de Décomposition*, Éditions Gallimard (1978), Paris. Translations by Moosenhauer. All quotes used are easily locatable in the book, in French or English, so I have refrained from adding even more footnotes.

[18] Cioran uses the word 'divagante' here, which is best translated as wandering, or straying. Elsewhere he uses the term *divagation* in a variety of contexts, all of which also translate as wandering, straying, rambling, etc. Divagation is also a word used in English, meaning digression, detour, tangent, etc. Camatte prefers the word, *errance*, which means wandering also, but can also mean vagrancy. Camatte does use the word *divagation* as the title for one text, ([Divagation](), 2010) in which he states that he is using it because of its old meaning: *errer çà et là*, 'to wander here and there.' [Later note: I have since discovered that the concept of wandering was used by many in the early 20th century to describe 'the predicament of humanity,' including Martin Heidegger, who wrote of 'not being at home in the world.' Camatte has also read Heidegger, of whom he says: "To see what there is of interest, of importance in Heidegger, you have to really mine his thought to the end, it's complicated," see [Interview with J. Camatte](), by *Cercle Marx*, on *Libcom*]

[home/homeland] and the Infinite: it is to be rooted and uprooted at one and the same time."

While, probably unknowingly, echoing Marx, Cioran also prefigures Camatte's depiction of the trauma — "the founding *trauma* of discontinuity"[19] — embedded in the human psyche when they separated from, or became discontinuous with, nature, when he writes:

> "To be torn from the earth, enduring in exile, cut off from one's immediate roots... is to yearn for a rehabilitation with the originary source, to yearn for a return to the time before the rupture of separation."

Camatte has expanded and re-articulated this notion of separation and wandering. By 'wandering' Camatte insists that, since their separation from nature, humans have felt the need to *justify their existence*: they are constantly searching for a meaning to their lives and a purpose for their existence. For Camatte, the dilemma revolves around the centuries-old question of whether humans are part of nature or outside of it. The 'wandering,' as both Cioran and Camatte affirm, is an expression of the profound identity crisis that afflicts the species: if humans are part of nature then *how* are they part of it, and if they are above or beyond nature then *where exactly* is humanity located? (The *content* of wandering, by-the-way, can be understood effectively and usefully, as *history*.)

Whereas Cioran sees no hope of an escape from the current human condition, Camatte, now having abandoned his Marxist and 'revolutionary' credentials, sees the possibility of the emergence of a new type of human being. Camatte envisages that *Homo Gemeinwesen* will be "the successor species to Homo sapiens. It will be in continuity with nature and the cosmos. Its processual knowledge [its *becoming* or, perhaps crudely, its *consciousness*], will not have a justificatory function, as it will operate solely within the dynamics of enjoyment."[20]

In 'The Wandering of Humanity' (1973), Camatte goes into a little more detail as to what the new society of the Homo Gemeinwesen will look like, although, since he hadn't properly formulated the concept of the Homo Gemeinwesen at that time, he simply refers to the new society as 'communism':

> "Communism puts an end to castes, classes, and the division of labor (onto which was grafted the movement of value, which in turn animates and exalts

---

[19] Camatte, *Surgissement de l'ontose*, 2001, RI.
[20] Camatte, *Point de Départ*, 2003.

this division). Communism is, first of all, union. It is not domination of nature but reconciliation, and thus regeneration of nature: human beings no longer treat nature simply as an object for their development, as a useful thing, but as a subject (not in the philosophic sense) not separate from them, if only because nature is in them. The naturalization of man [sic] and the humanization of nature (Marx) are realized; the dialectic of subject and object ends. What follows is the destruction of urbanization and the formation of a multitude of communities distributed over the earth. [...] Only a communal (communitarian) mode of life can allow the human being to rule his reproduction, to limit the (at present mad) growth of population without resorting to despicable practices (such as destroying men and women)."

He continues...

"It is obvious that this cannot be a return to the type of nomadism practised by our distant ancestors who were gatherers. Men and women will acquire a new mode of being beyond nomadism and sedentarism. Sedentary lives compounded by corporeal inactivity are the root cause of almost all the somatic and psychological illnesses of present-day human beings. An active and unfixed life will cure all these problems without medicine or psychiatry."[21]

Writing on the pandemic in 2020 it is clear that Camatte sees this process of leaving the world of capital and arriving at the destination of a new species — the Homo Gemeinwesen, or the true human community, as involving a reduction in population, but over thousands of years. He writes: "From the moment we start the inversion, it will take us a few thousand years for the number of human beings to begin to fluctuate between 250 and 500 million."[22] So, one should not make the mistake of thinking that Camatte is proposing any kind of 'forced' population reduction.

It is also useful to be reminded that he is not proposing any kind of confrontation with the world as it is. He explicitly states that constructing an 'enmity' to capital in order to topple it will merely make it stronger. This was

---

[21] The Wandering of Humanity, in *This World We Must Leave and Other Essays* (1995), Alex Trotter (ed.), Fredy Perlman and Friends (trans.), Autonomedia, New York. Quotes are from P66 and 67 respectively. The ignorance regarding 'our distant ancestors' in this last insight should not obscure the profound implications of the rest of the thesis.

[22] Camatte, footnote 14, in <u>Instauration du risque d'extinction</u>, 2020, RI.

the conception he formed on reflection of the events around 1968: "The more we fight against capital, the more we strengthen it."[23]

So, the key is to begin, somehow, to create new ways of living: "The problem is to create other lives."[24] Indeed, Camatte appears to find interesting any new social experiments that indicate a different way to live, or which contain a refusal of aspects of this society, such as the hippie movement,[25] or alternative agricultural methods,[26] although he is, of course, aware how these movements can become re-incorporated into capital. But there is also an urgency attached to this abandonment of things as they are, since the choice is now hurtling toward that between "communism or the destruction of the human species."[27] And these refusals or revolts are always susceptible to *recuperation* by capital: "Capital can still profit from the creativity of human beings, regenerating and resubstantializing itself by plundering their imaginations."[28]

The impulse to begin a regeneration of community and nature is not a simple or straightforward one for Camatte though. As it is not a 'political' alternative, it is not a toppling of the old regime and a replacement with a new one, it is not a revolution as commonly understood. More recently, Camatte uses the term 'inversion'[29] to describe the leaving of this world. This concept is not meant to imply a *simple* reversal of things as they are, nor does it mean a return to a time prior to our dehumanization. It is the accessing of the seed of naturalness inside us, which has long been repressed and concealed, and helping it to germinate. In this way, the new species of Homo Gemeinwesen will begin to emerge. One can see how this idea is closely linked to the way Marx described the essence of revolt above, but in Camatte's conception all 'politics' is removed. As Camatte insists: "Inversion is not a strategy, it is totally outside of politics, which is the dynamic of organizing people, of controlling them. We must abandon everything that is part of its world."[30]

---

[23] Camatte, <u>Mai-Juin 1968: Le dévoilement</u>, 1977, RI.
[24] Wandering of Humanity, 56.
[25] Ibid., 168.
[26] Camatte: "The disappearance of agriculture will probably take centuries," <u>Inversion et Dévoilement</u>, 2012, RI.
[27] Ibid., 34.
[28] Ibid., 63.
[29] <u>Inversion et Dévoilement</u>, 2012, RI.
[30] Interview with Camatte, '<u>Inversion is not a strategy</u>,' May, 2020.

A Millenarian Residue?

Jacques Camatte has come from the modern revolutionary tradition encompassed by Marxism that Yuri Slezkine describes, in his monumental work, *The House of Government*,[31] as *millenarian*. Millenarianism, which can be religious or secular, is the belief that human society is in need of a great transformation and that after this transformation people will live in peace and harmony. It is the eternal recurring impulse of those who live within exploitative and hierarchical societies, by which is meant, of course, *a State*.

The conditions of life within a State – work, exploitation, hierarchy, ennui, poverty, wealth, despair — are the causes of millenarianism and, as the anthropologist Pierre Clastres has suggested with the social movement of the *karai* prophets in the Amazon, even *the threat* of a burgeoning State can produce millenarianism.[32]

Very significantly, Clastres further suggests that the *karai* millenarians — who "mobilized" more than 10,000 people to migrate toward the Land Without Evil, in the direction of the setting sun — accomplished "that impossible thing in primitive society: to unify, in the religious migration, the multifarious variety of the tribes. They managed to carry out the whole [unifying] program of the chiefs with a single stroke."[33] Clastres' startling and profound observation is that millenarianism — the revolutionary overthrow, or escaping, of existing conditions — contrary to what it pretends to be, is actually the most efficient way to homogenize people, to unify them for a cause external to themselves. Revolutionaries then, and one can glean it from history if one looks properly, are the State-builders *par excellence*.

Millenarianism, therefore, is a recurring response, in various forms, to the State, which is a society that is deeply unsatisfactory. When historian Christopher Hill assessed contemporary historical analysis in 1972, in *The World Turned Upside Down: Radical Ideas During the English Revolution*, he wrote that: "we now see millenarianism as a natural and rational product of the assumptions of this society." Millenarianism — another term for 'revolutionism' — is then, objectively, *a function of the State*. Millenarianism also, invariably, has some kind

---

[31] Yuri Slezkine, 2017, *The House of Government*, Princeton University Press.
[32] Pierre Clastres, 1981, *Archeology of Violence*, Jeanine Herman (trans.), Semiotext (2010), P160-162.
[33] Pierre Clastres, 1974, Society Against the State, Robert Hurley and Abe Stein (trans.), Zone Books (2013), Brooklyn, P217-8.

of relationship to the idea of a 'fall from grace,' or a loss of naturalness and community... and so one can see that the millenarian impulse comes from the same standpoint as that of those whom Marx describes above as *rebelling* — because they sense that they are *dehumanized* or, at least, bereft of the community that makes them human. We all contain the germ of millenarianism inside us, it is a facet of our response to an unsatisfactory life... Albert Camus, in *The Rebel*, advises us not to "unleash" it.[34]

Perhaps the first evidence of millenarianism we have in history is from Iran with the arrival of Zoroaster, some three thousand years ago. As Karl Jaspers argued, this era in the development of civilization – which he termed 'the axial age' – was one of flux and uncertainty, in which there was a proliferation of radical thinking and the expression of discontent. Slezkine writes:

> "Zoroaster made history — literally as well as figuratively — by prophesying the absolute end of the world. There was going to be one final battle between the forces of light and darkness and one last judgement of all human beings who had ever lived — and there would be nothing but an all-encompassing, everlasting perfection: no hunger. No thirst, no disagreement, no childbirth, and no death. The hero would defeat the serpent one last time; chaos would be vanquished for good; only the good would remain — forever" (Slezkine: 76-77).

"Millenarianism," Slezkine affirms, "is the vengeful fantasy of the disposed, the hope for a great awakening" (Slezkine: 99). This vengeful fantasy, of course, is entirely understandable, and probably inevitable, and therefore impossible to prevent from returning in new forms... but the problem with it is that it never leads to peace on earth, and usually makes things far worse. Slezkine continues the history:

> "Most millenarian sects died as sects. Some survived as sects, but stopped being millenarian. Some remained millenarian until the end because the end came before they had a chance to create stable states. Christianity survived as a sect, stopped being millenarian, and was adopted by Babylon as an official creed. The Hebrews and Mormons survived their trek through the desert and traded milk and honey for stable states before being absorbed into larger empires. The Muslims created their own large empires bound by routinized millenarianism and threatened by repeated 'fundamentalist' reformations. The Münster Anabaptists and the Jacobins took over existing

---

[34] Albert Camus, *The Rebel*, (1951), Anthony Bower (trans.), Penguin, 1982, P265.

polities and reformed them in the image of future perfection before losing out to more moderate reformers. Only the Bolsheviks destroyed 'the prison of the peoples,' vanquished the 'appeasers,' outlawed traditional marriage, banned private property, and found themselves firmly in charge of Babylon while still expecting the millennium in their lifetimes. Never before had an apocalyptic sect succeeded in taking control of an existing heathen empire (unless one counts the Safavids, whose millennial agenda seems to have been much less radical). It was as if the Fifth Monarchists had won the English Civil War, 'reformed all places and all callings,' contemplated an island overgrown with plants that the heavenly father had not planted, and stood poised to pull up every one of them, *'root and branch, every plant, and every whit of every plant.'*[35] The fact that Russia was not an island made the challenge all the more formidable" (Slezkine: 180).

All serious *movements* that seek to radically alter, abolish, or escape State societies are millenarian movements. Millenarianism is a product of the critique of the State in which the masses are perceived to be the dupes of evil. The remedy necessitates the sweeping away of all the mechanisms of evil – the laws, the norms, the traditions – along with all those who, through pure malice, weakness, or sloth, facilitate or maintain the evil. Only the good in heart – that is, the most loyal to the cause — will arrive safely at the other side of the revolution.

But less dramatic versions of millenarianism also exist: some religious sects insist on simply waiting — and being ready — for the apocalypse, which will be delivered when God decides. This strategy mirrors the belief of far-left, or ultra-left revolutionaries, or anarchists who wait in readiness — remaining close to 'the cause' and engaging others, perhaps to convince them — for the confluence of events that will give them the opportunity to become the midwives of communism.

This strategy of far-left communist groups is (equivocally) endorsed by, for example, the group *Endnotes*,[36] in 2019, who describe the apparent, but *false* — as

---

[35] Slezkine, Ibid., P180. Quotes are from Thomas Case, in addresses to the House of Commons, 1641. See also House of Government, p122. See also Bernard Capp, *The Fifth Monarchy Men: A Study in Seventeenth-Century English Millenarianism*, Faber and Faber, 1972/2011.

[36] *Endnotes* is a group that has existed since 2005, with a prehistory (to 1992, in a UK group called *Aufheben*), which has become, as they write in their 'about themselves', "increasingly international." In their agonising over who they are and how they relate to "the class struggle" in the article We Unhappy Few, they have decided that they are

they regard it — choice for contemporary ultra-left, far-left communist, or left-communists, etc.,[37] as being between "'revolutionary intervention' or *attentism* (wait-and-see-ism)." That is, "there is either a revolutionary communist way of relating to struggles or one should not be involved at all." They solve the false choice by referring back to Marx and Engels' notion of communism as 'the *real movement*'[38] and stating that, "it is not *we* but class struggle that produces theory [understanding]." But *Endnotes* do not seem to recognize that there is *no such thing* as being able to 'not be involved at all.' Even the dead are involved in our present life, as Marx noted: "*Le mort saisit le vif!*" (The dead seize the living!)[39]

In practice, of course, both quietist millenarians and non-party, anti-'political,' or anti-vanguard revolutionaries (like *Endnotes*) are always involved *in events* whether it be in *preparing themselves* by learning how to be closer to God, or by

---

theoreticians of current conditions and their abolition (not recruiters to a cause), and that the group should last "only so long as they feel they are contributing something useful" (P53). But how are they to know if they are contributing something 'useful,' even if it is just 'a feeling,' and useful to whom? What do they mean by 'useful'? Are things only 'important' if they have 'a use'? Their quietist millenarianism, though they insist they have never been a sect "in the normal sense," (P21) is explained in this sentence: "A purpose that we have found that takes our interest[,] indeed to which we have found ourselves driven[,] is communist theory, the thinking about capitalism and its overcoming" (P53). This is the waiting, in studious and steadfast readiness, for the arrival of 'God.'
Non-hyperlinked quotes from 'We Unhappy Few,' the first (unsigned — perhaps 'group editorial'?) article, in *Endnotes #5: 'The Passions and the Interests,'* 2019, UK/USA.

[37] It is always difficult to make this kind of list for readers who may not already be 'in the know' as to the milieu I am referring to, which includes anarchists, councilists, left-councilists, situationists, Bordigists, and the libertarian left as well. The easiest way to imagine this milieu is to think of everyone that Lenin was attacking in his work of 1920, *'Left Wing' Communism: An Infantile Disorder.*

[38] One must understand the notion of 'the real movement' in the context of Marx and Engels' whole-hearted support for 'the scientific method,' which is how they developed their notion of *the dialectic* as the driving force in 'history.' A famous line from Marx is rarely understood: "Philosophers have hitherto only *interpreted* the world in various ways; the point is to *change* it." This line was never a simple urging of philosophers to 'get active' for the good of things, it meant that philosophers had to abandon the world of 'universal absolutes' (think Plato's 'theory of Forms') and work within the social and environmental processes that were *actually in existence*. If they did this, Marx believed, they would no longer be 'idle philosophers,' they would be *scientists* – in Marx's era it was the scientists who were seen to be changing the world, and proletarians and philosophers would be able to do likewise if they became 'scientists' too or, more precisely, dialecticians of the materialist conception of history (historical materialism). See, for example, Engels' *Ludwig Feuerbach and the End of Classical German Philosophy, Part 4: Marx*, from the paragraph beginning: "But what is true of nature..."

[39] Marx, K. 1867, *Capital Volume 1*, Penguin Books, 1976, P91.

getting closer in understanding to, as Marx put it, 'the *real* [concrete] movement [*becoming*] that abolishes the current conditions'[40] — or in simply attempting to attract others to one's point of view in order to increase the number of the blessed... so that at the appointed hour — when either God appears in His fury, or the Proletariat rise in Theirs — there will be enough believers to get those who are worthy to the other side.

I should note that, as one half of the producers of the book — or "archaeological artefact,"[41] — *Nihilist Communism*, I too have been millenarian. Our advice to those who, like us (we called ourselves *Monsieur Dupont*), wanted *the great transformation that will bring peace and harmony* but saw its arrival as coming from the class struggle and the intervention of 'revolutionaries,' rather than God, was to: "be ready for a long wait, to have no great expectations, to be ready for failure, and to keep going for decades."[42]

Compare this last instruction, or appeal, with the *Parable of the Sower*, from *The King James Bible*: "Now the parable is this: The seed is the word of God... [and it is deemed to have fallen on good ground when those that hear the word] keep

---

[40] There are several references to 'the *real* movement' in *We Unhappy Few*. The quote from Marx is usually translated as something like: "the real movement which will abolish the present state of things,' and is used frequently in the literature of 'communization' theory. The whole sentence from Marx is "Communism is for us the *real* movement which will abolish the present conditions." Since the early 1970s the line, starting at 'the real movement...,' has become something of a magical incantation for left communists. The notion of 'the real movement' was referred to, but not referenced, in *Eclipse and Re-Emergence of the Communist Movement*, by the ultra-leftists, Gilles Dauvé (Jean Barrot) and François Martin, and it was here that the notion of *communization* first appeared. In 2000, Dauvé indicated that communization theory emerged from the Situationist International's 'critique of separation' (see 'Back to the SI' on *Troploin*). Amusingly, in 1983, Camatte described 'Dauvé and his companions' as "the living dead" (see *La Mort Potentielle du Capital*, RI) in response to their criticism of Camatte's 'optimism' (see *La Banquise* #1, available at archivesautonomies.org).

[41] Preface to second edition of *Nihilist Communism: A Critique of Optimism – the religious dogma that states there will be an ultimate triumph of good over evil – In the Far Left*, Ardent Press, 2009, p ix.

[42] Ibid., 101. It should also be noted that *M. Dupont*, the collective name for the two people who produced NC, was never 'a group.' The book was assembled from correspondence between us (and with others who were generally hostile to us), it was an expression of a friendship, a kind of romance, now lost in time, especially so since the other Dupont has since had a 'theological turn' and become a peddler of far-right propaganda in a possibly confused, but certainly very odd, attempt to use the tools of 'neo-reaction' for the sake of 'communism' (see the self-reverential and Agamben-inspired text, *I am not Chuang*, by Frère Dupont.)

it, and bring forth fruit with patience." Or this from the *Book of Revelation* (*Apokálypsi*), in which God writes letters to 'seven churches' through visions given to a prophet, probably in 95CE: "I know thy works, and thy labor, and thy patience... And [how thou] hast borne, and hast patience, and for my name's sake hast labored, and hast not fainted." Perhaps the unconscious repeating of such a directive, almost 2000 years later, is an example of *eternal recurrence*...

The State — or that which oppresses us, whatever it is — will always be *critiqued*. The State necessarily, or naturally, creates the conditions for this critique, and, therefore, millenarians — that is, *revolutionaries* — are *functions* of the State. They do not appear where there is no State. They do not appear in non-State societies. But, counter-intuitively, the critique of the State or 'present conditions' is not harmful to the State (though it may prove so for particular elements in the State hierarchy). In fact, it is necessary to its objective development, as recorded examples beginning with the English Civil War at least, attest.

Wherever there has been a revolution the State has become stronger, and the exploitation of the working classes has been escalated, become more brutal, and made more efficient, for a short time at least. The English and French Revolutions enabled the institutional ascendency of the bourgeoisie: the new ruling class, as well as the new middle class, the bureaucrats. Both revolutions enabled both countries to maintain and expand their position as a world power. The Russian Revolution is easily recognizable, ultimately, as the revolution of the children of the emergent middle-classes — the bureaucrats — and they introduced industrialization at an unprecedented speed and on an unprecedented scale.[43] The Chinese Communists also introduced industrial capitalism at breakneck speed — don't be deceived by the fact that they called themselves 'communist.' The same can be said for those 'developing' countries, such as Cuba, where industrialism was introduced to a rural region under the banner of communism or socialism. Revolutionaries then, in the grander scheme, are not *counter-functions* of the State and capital, they are just functions — they *aid* the development of the economy and the control of the laboring classes.

Camatte, observing the history of the twentieth century, discovered that in this period the nature of capitalism changed so that, as noted above, 'the more we fight against capital, the more we strengthen it,' but one could also have made that observation from all the revolutions in the capitalist era, beginning with the

---

[43] See, *Fascism is not a Pathology*, in this volume.

English one. So perhaps it is more correct, or at least universal, to say: the more we fight against *the State*, the more we strengthen it. Of course, in our era there is no clear dividing line between State and economy — or State and capital, indeed, in capitalism the State found its perfect marriage — and the all-consuming, global, and ubiquitous nature of our economic system means that the imagining of a State existing in the world that is *not capitalist* constitutes a laughable and ridiculous whimsy.

Camatte has certainly tried, consciously or otherwise, to shy away from the millenarian bases of his original political adherences. This is demonstrated by his absolute refusal to be part of any 'organization,' and his insistence that what he is now arguing for is not a politics of any kind. Yet still, in his vision of the arrival of a new human species he fulfils the millenarian criterion: millenarianism, which can be religious or secular, is the belief that human society is in need of a great transformation and that after this transformation people will live in peace and harmony. And he still engages his vision with people, he still produces texts, and informs others of a better way to think.[44] His millenarianism though, like that of *Endnotes*, as well as *Monsieur Dupont*, is effectively a quietist one.[45]

A Contradiction?

Camatte argues that the class struggle is long finished because, as those involved in the 'revolutionary' events around WW1 demonstrated, the only thing

---

[44] It would seem that many of us, I include myself here, have an inbuilt urge to endlessly *proselytise*. Emil Cioran writes, in *A Short History of Decay*, that people "are the chatterboxes of the universe" and that many insist on speaking for others... they use the word 'we, for example,' to describe what *they themselves* think. Anyone, he continues, "who speaks in the name of others is an imposter." But we can temper our proselytism by refusing the diktats of serious, political, or academic prose by writing *I* instead of *we*, and never starting sentences with phrases such as: "Our task is to..." or "We need to..."

[45] Although those around *Endnotes*, from behind their academic parapets, do also seem keen on *a degree* of *boy's own* activity. *Monsieur Dupont/Frère Dupont*, Agamben, Camatte, *Endnotes*, etc, are poles of attraction, or *rivals*, in the tent of millenarian communism. The *Endnotes* pole is the boys dream of "hijacking trucks" (see J. Bernes, Endnotes 5), the MD/FD pole is the narcissistic lament of 'failure.' Meanwhile, Agamben flirts with Diego Fusaro, and Camatte flirts with *Cercle Marx*.

the working class is now able to achieve is not communism but *self-managed capitalism*, since its aims are 'full employment and self-management.'[46] Therefore, he is claiming that any revolutionary struggle against capital that is based on the (now-defunct-as-a-potential-creator-of-communism) *working class* will only return capital to us, after the glorious deception of the revolutionary moment, in a stronger and more vicious form.

But it is worse than this. Just as there is no genuine working class anymore – it has been absorbed into capital – there are no classes at all, society is no longer organized on the basis of a living social relationship (bad though it was)... capital has 'run away' from the control of the bourgeoisie and is now operating as an autonomous system. All humans, are now capitalized, that is, they are all hanging desperately off the coat-tails of the "automated monster"[47] of capital that proceeds — robot-like, or zombie-like (because it is a dead thing, it is no longer a social relation) — on its own course.

How to stop the monster? Camatte has already discounted opposing it, since that will just strengthen it – because in our opposition we are acting within its terrain, that is, on its own terms. Camatte therefore argues that to stop the monster we have to abandon it, and not in an organized political way – because that would be an immediate creation of an opposition: an enmity. We all have to begin abandoning 'this world as it is,' somehow organically, by choosing to live different lives. If we do this then not only will zombie-capital die of starvation, but after a few thousand years the new species will have fully emerged, and humans will live in community with nature and themselves.

But if people are already capitalized (Camatte describes it as *their madness*), meaning that if they fight the system they only bring it back stronger, then would not that also imply that if they left the system they would just take their capitalist brains with them, even though, like the oppositionists, they do not intend to?

Is it not the case that every escape from capital or the State, or *things as they are*, every sect, or movement — from the Vikings who escaped the burgeoning power of Harald Finehair's expanding kingdom by settling in Iceland, to the tragedy of Jonestown — that has gone somewhere else to found a new world has just brought the sickness with them?

---

[46] Camatte, *Contre la domestication*, 1973, RI.
[47] Camatte, *La Mort Potentielle du Capital*, RI.

Nihil Evadere

The problem is centered on whether one can will a genuine *change* in one's life, as an individual or as a group. If one is *willing* the change then it is logical to assume that the imagining of the change emerges from the very circumstances of the thing one is opposing – the desired change is bound by the parameters of the original thing one is trying to escape. We are social beings, we are socially constructed, we can only see the world through our own perspective, though we can recognize that there may be other perspectives.

It is useful here, in order to explain what I mean, to think about how the concept of *time* is perceived in two different eras: the modern era (capitalism), and the European Middle Ages (feudalism).

We can, for example, *understand* when someone tells us that medieval peasants lived by a cyclical calendar derived from agrarian existence but, despite this, we are unable to view time as *a rotation* because we cannot look up from this page and comfortably accept, or throw out the notion, that time is not *linear*. As historian A. J. Gurevich writes of the transition from feudal to urban capitalist conceptions of time: "The alienation of time from its concrete content raised the possibility of viewing it as a pure categorical form, as duration unburdened by matter."[48] It was the success of the modern economy, which needed coordination to operate efficiently, that changed our conception of time. It was the introduction of supply chains, distribution, and factory work, culminating in railway timetables, that led to the abandonment of any sense that time was 'cyclical,' 'seasonal,' or connected to the earth. This linear expression of time is now hard-wired into our brains because it reflects our everyday existence, therefore this interpretation of time also affects how we act in the world. How we are created is how we create.

We cannot see through the eyes of a person inhabiting a different mode of living. Our consciousness is determined by the daily life we live, and the principles and values generated by and acting upon this actual daily existence. Once a society is established, then that society becomes an organic whole, a *mode of living* (not necessarily an 'economy'). A twenty-first century Parisian can as little *decide* to understand time as cyclical as a medieval European peasant could decide to understand time as a separate linear category of the universe.

One can also see how change in oneself is often impossible through simple *willing*. Genuine, grief, over the death of a loved one, for example, cannot just be wished away, it slowly lessens over time, or is forgotten in other pursuits (as

---

[48] A.J. Gurevich, *Categories of Medieval Culture*, G.L. Campbell (trans), Routledge, 1985, p150.

long as those pursuits are not taken up specifically to forget about one's grief, in which case the pursuit itself is a constant reminder). Therefore, it would be true to say that the solution to disabling grief does not come from our thinking about it and putting it into perspective, but from *time*. Genuine changes — or *solutions* — are always delivered to us on levels other than our conscious willing.

In an articulation, or extension, of Marx's historical materialist proposition — "People make their own history, but they do not make it freely, and not in circumstances of their choosing, but under circumstances that are proximate, pre-existing, and handed-down"[49] — the Marxist scholar Ernest Mandel formulated the term *parametric determinism*. This is a useful concept to utilize when thinking about the limits of our possible understandings of other eras, or other cultures... or other animals. He argues:

> "Most, if not all, historical crises have *several possible outcomes*, not innumerable fortuitous or arbitrary ones; that is why we use the expression 'parametric *determinism*' indicating several possibilities within a given set of parameters."[50]

We could substitute the words 'historical crises' with 'situations,' or even 'imaginings.' The point being that we are products of the society we are born into. We cannot simply *will ourselves* to be the products or functions (or reproducers) of another society (for example, 'a truly communist' society), no matter how close we feel to understanding the particular social organization we are observing or considering. Radical changes in society – such as the transition from feudalism to capitalism — do not happen via human will, they happen on other levels. The revolutions that made capitalism official – such as the English, French, and Russian – were the institutionalizing, or ratifying, of an economic force that had *already* achieved actual predominance. Of course, Camatte does stipulate that the emergence of the new human being will take thousands of years and perhaps, therefore, he is recognizing the problem involved in changing one's perspective or changing one's entire way of living. And perhaps he is arguing that if we just make certain changes now — changes that are connected to the 'naturalness' that still lingers inside us — then we will set ourselves on the way to becoming the new species... I am not so certain in my 'resistance' to Camatte's particular ideas here, and am reminded of Voltaire's solution in *Candide*, which I will come to below.

---

[49] Marx, *The 18th Brumaire of Louis Bonaparte*, 1852.
[50] Ernest Mandel, *How To Make No Sense of Marx*, 1989, at *Marxists' Internet Archive*.

In the end, there is still a 'problem' in Camatte's urging of us to *leave this world*... the logic of his writings compel us to wonder how, in 'leaving the world', we will not just take the world with us. If we can't fight it without making it stronger, then maybe we can't leave it without making it stronger either. Capital is, after all, the recuperator *par excellence*. Even *détournement* became a means for making money.

The Already Existing Human Community

Camatte proposes that all rebellion that is linked to a yearning for human community, that is, those rebellions, or movements, that called for 'universal brotherhood [sic]' or mutual aid in the past, for example — since these calls are a connection to the lost Gemeinwesen — are beginnings of the *inversion*: the process of regaining a true human community. The problem, for Camatte, is that capital has developed so much that most of these beginnings are now completely useless if they exist as organized political projects. For such *beginnings* — as we have seen with the mutual aid and solidarity in the recent events around covid-19 and the Black Lives Matter movement — to be effective and unrecuperable they must, according to Camatte, develop into situations where ordinary people no longer appeal to or confront the system in order to change it. For Camatte, people must instead start living different lives, lives that embrace these human values. Inversion can only be begun[51] when there is no feeling of *enmity*, and when there is no feeling that some ideological prop, such as 'the working class,' or 'justice,' is needed to justify one's actions. If we dispense with the damaging notions and images of *enemy* and *friend* — for example, *the bosses* and *the working class* — we can get on with trying to live. Camatte's hope is that there will be a mass abandonment of our current way of living when people realize the madness they have had to endure.

As already noted, Camatte predicts that the new human species will take thousands of years to come fully into being. To assist with the emergence of the new being Camatte suggests a number of practical measures that need to be somehow implemented as soon as possible. In *Emergence and Dissolution*, Camatte lists some of these changes, which include: "The immediate cessation of the construction of roads, highways, airfields, ports, and cities;" the abolition of tourism, "the most elaborate form of the destruction of men, women and

---

[51] Camatte, *Il divenire all'inversione*, 2017, RI.

nature;" and the abolition of sport, "an absurd activity, a theatrical form of capitalist competition, and a fundamental support for advertising."[52]

When one reads Camatte's 'list of demands' from this 1989 article it is difficult not perceive them as potentially authoritarian measures to be put in place for the good of the planet, and in a footnote added in 2008 Camatte notes this: "It would have been better to have [only] written 'cessation,' because 'prohibition' inevitably evokes and calls for repression." Still, one has to wonder how we can stop things like construction projects, tourism, and sport without either becoming part of a government, or without fighting against these phenomena. Unless all the construction workers, tourists and sports fans stay at home to tend their vegetable gardens and allotments, and don't turn on their televisions... causing those industries to collapse.

There is a strangely powerful allure in this vision of a mass of humanity just 'leaving the world' to tend their own gardens, a phenomenon that would, of course, require a collective effort, or communal cooperation. Maybe the essence of the beginning of Camatte's 'inversion' — as a 'leaving of this world' — can be understood in practical terms by reference to Candide's advice at the end of Voltaire's novel of the same name — which is that while we can wonder about the world all we like, the most useful thing is to 'cultivate one's own garden.' Candide says this after he and his *'petite société'* have withdrawn from worldly pursuits and are concentrating on sustaining themselves by their own means, learning all sorts of skills, and being useful to one another. As one of them remarks: "Let us work without calculation (*travaillons sans raisonner*), for that is the only way to make life bearable." If one decides to follow Camatte, is one also following *Candide*? With the difference that Candide did not profess to be "like a prophet," or engage with the far-right to put forward his views.

Returning to the notion that it will take thousands of years for this new communal species of human being to grow to maturity, one must perhaps — despite Camatte's indicating that the species will form a true human community — sense that we cannot really know what this new community will truly be like. I think Camatte would agree with this. The new community — the new species — he predicts is something impossible to describe beyond partial indications, and this has profound implications once one remembers the societies of 'tribes' around the world who have little or no contact with the global economy: it is

---

[52] Camatte, *Émergence et Dissolution*, 1989, RI.

impossible for us to fully understand these peoples either. These are the societies that, as Pierre Clastres has shown, are 'against the State.'[53]

Camatte does refer to the work of Pierre Clastres a couple of times, but only briefly. In *The Integrated Revolution* (1978),[54] Camatte appears to recognize the centrifugal social organization of 'primitive' (non-State) societies, described by Clastres, as valuable in resisting the threat of homogeneity and the loss of diversity between communities — which is carried out through 'violence,' or 'war' — but he does not think that this is an appropriate strategy 'for us' since society has already been homogenized and any recourse to a diversity-amplifying violence would simply be a "blind" violence without any proper context. It is unfortunate that Camatte only considers Clastres' observations and theories as a tool for rectifying the ills of civilized society, therefore rejecting them quickly, rather than exploring them further. Clastres himself never suggested that the social organization of the non-State societies he encountered in the Amazon should be taken up by radicals in civilization. He merely noted that 'the savages' had resisted the State — somehow — for *a long time*, and that they effectively represented the last real humans.

What might one learn — using a Camattian lens — from the ethnography of those peoples who live beyond the State?

Clastres suggests that the goal of these societies is not 'peace and harmony,' it is not unification. The 'community' that exists within groups and between groups is operational on different levels to the ones we might understand. Their 'enemies' are closer to them than our 'friends' ever will be, enmity is bound up in their conception of the relations with themselves, and others, even the dead.[55] This is one indication of the problem in Camatte's defining of what a true human community will look like... he cannot know. The foundation of his notions of true human community come from the Enlightenment and the ideas of democracy. He is the inheritor of the ideas of Spinoza and Marx, who reflected the radical implications of the Enlightenment, a phenomenon that itself reflected the growth of capitalism as a form of society. 'The savages,' as Clastres has observed, do not want peace. Peace, since the establishment of the first State, has always been the prize of slaves. As subjects of a State this is, naturally, what both Camatte and I want too. But one should keep this aim for oneself, and not bring it to non-State peoples.

---

[53] For a detailed exploration of Clastres' thought see *The Freedom of Things*.
[54] Camatte, La révolution intègre, 1978, RI.
[55] For a detailed review of the anthropological literature, see the section, "*Enemy Relations,*" in *The Freedom of Things*.

The other thing one might discover, if we extend Camatte's, or Cioran's, analysis — which concludes that humans are discontinuous with nature and therefore psychologically traumatized, and now even *obsolete* — to the 'uncontacted tribes,' is that there are two types of 'human being' on the planet... but only one type can truly call itself 'human.'

The Second Type

The 'human beings' who *cannot* truly call themselves human, according to Camatte, include myself and all the others who are products and functions — not of the earth from which we originate — but of the economy we know as capitalism... whether they reap the benefits of the demented 'wealth' that capitalism generates, or whether they struggle to survive in the depths of the madness that is the flipside of the madness of progress and technological advance. I agree whole-heartedly with Camatte here, these so-called humans (you and I) are fictions, or creations — or the hollowed-out drones — of an uncontrollable and autonomous economy that has severed all their links — beyond romantic fancies and false claims — to other animals and the earth itself.[56]

How did this human come into existence? Since I am talking about the kind of human who lives in a State I must then ask why and how the State emerged. There is a lot of mystification from all sectors of the political and academic spectrum on this but, as I have attempted to demonstrate elsewhere, while we cannot know the specific circumstances by which original — 'pristine,' they are called — States came about, we can understand why: the State is a managerial solution for the problem of a population that has become too large for the maintenance of traditional ways of living.

Most narratives of the emergence of the State begin with the rise of a chief who bullies people, which leads to a Royal Family, which leads to a retinue that eventually forms a bureaucracy. It is this bureaucracy that then wields the real power. The bureaucracy spreads out over the land and becomes a kind of closed proto-democracy. Eventually there are so many people helping to run the State directly through supervisory – the nascent 'middle class' — and entrepreneurial means that it becomes clear to them that the real power is in their hands and that they should have that power recognized. They begin a movement based on

---

[56] Much of this and the next section is taken from the article, *The Last Humans*.

the new circumstances. Oliver Cromwell was landed gentry. Gerrard Winstanley — the leader of the Diggers, the far left of the revolutionists of the 'English Civil War' — was a middle-class businessman. Robespierre was a lawyer. Lenin was famously middle-class. Castro was born into a prosperous farming family and studied law at university. Guevara was a doctor. The workers and peasants get behind them because they also like this new 'democratic' idea and because they need some improvement in their lives – in fact, of course, the vocational revolutionaries can only *appear*, and fulfil their function, if the workers and peasants are already at some level of revolt. Then there is a revolution (we are not talking about 'revolts' here), sometimes it is bloody. The new leaders realize that the workers and peasants had a slightly different idea about how things should proceed and begin a clampdown. Often the first leaders of the revolution are kicked out, and new people, with a more reasonable agenda step in.

I agree with the whole of this narrative except for the very first part. My research into how peoples prior to the rise of a State (including present-day 'uncontacted tribes') organized themselves socially shows how one of the priorities was to keep group numbers small, and if numbers did start to escalate these groups would 'fission' — they split. Robin Dunbar has famously done work on optimal group sizes and he argues that for humans to operate successfully without coercion they must be able to have regular face-to-face interactions — everyone must know everyone else. Once the group becomes too numerous for everyone to know each other it becomes necessary for laws to be laid down.

My research[57] suggests that the key element in the emergence of a new State — Mesopotamia, the Indus, Mesoamerica, etc — was not agriculture or alluvial valleys but the fact there was a rise in the population and for some unknowable reason the group was unable to split.

The classic narrative for the rise of a chiefdom/State is that a rapacious thug organizes a group and takes over the tribe. But the anthropological record suggests that humans were able to resist vainglorious thugs for thousands of years. And how come there are 'egalitarian' tribes outside of States right now? There must be something else. Many anthropologists and historians suggest that advances in technology — for example, irrigation — led the way for numbers to rise and for people to become enslaved. But how come modern 'uncontacted tribes' haven't invented modern farming techniques, increased their numbers and set up a ruthless dictatorship to serve under? Are they just *stupid*?

---

[57] See *The Freedom of Things*.

The reason powerful Chiefs emerged was because the populace reluctantly agreed that the new circumstances demanded a new way of organizing things. Everyone did not know everyone else anymore and so people could get away with things, cliques could form, 'crimes' could be committed. Laws had to be made and people had to follow them – but the people who didn't like the laws just ignored them. Finally, and this probably happened very quickly, a charismatic person seized the chance for self-aggrandizement... and in the end the populace agreed. A strong leader backed up by thugs would at least keep some peace.

Of course, the power would usually go to the Chief's head and atrocities would be normalized, and if the people weren't totally downtrodden they might support a rival Chief's bid to topple the present one... and so history was written... right up to Representative Democracy.

The State itself is neither evil nor good, it is a managerial solution to the problem of a large population. Imagine the scene, two people sitting under a rockface discussing the future: "Yeah, Enki and his gang reckon they can sort out all the problems as long as everyone does what he says and gives him a tribute by sending daughters and sons to work for him, and building him a really good place to sleep in. The whole place will be a lot easier to live in, less chaos, but we'll have to stay where we are and work harder to make sure he gets enough recompense for his trouble. We don't want him to put his thugs on us, but it will be good if he sorts out those lazy thieving bastards who live up by the chickpea bushes..."

The State is often viewed as an obstacle to the ideals of peace and love — and communism — but maybe there is no escaping an authoritarian State when there are so many people jammed together? Perhaps this is one of the many lessons of the Russian Revolution? (Anyone who suggests here that perhaps the way to peace, love, and communism is therefore to reduce the human population is — apart from articulating real evil — missing the point that as functions of capitalism they would merely be recreating capitalism in a new situation, just as the Bolsheviks did in 1918.)

Jean-Jacques Rousseau opined for the freedom had before the advent of the State and civilization, but he recognized that living in a society where everyone

Nihil Evadere

— no matter their place in the hierarchy — was dependent upon everyone else meant that humans could not go back.[58]

He decided that we had to make the best of a bad job,[59] and this was the message in his book *'Of the Social Contract.'* Rousseau's book, of course, was used by the Jacobins to justify their Parisian dictatorship in 1793-4, but as David Wootton writes in his introduction to Rousseau's *Basic Political Writings*: "Robespierre and the Jacobins admired him greatly, but they misunderstood him profoundly (their Rousseau was invented to serve their own purposes)."[60] Rousseau's practical and humane — and anti-millenarian — approach to being trapped, in what might be ironically termed, *a less-than-satisfactory society* has been echoed much later by writers who have witnessed or considered the millenarian outcomes of the Russian Revolution, such as Albert Camus.

In 1951, arguing in favour of *rebellion* – that is, an opposition to all forms of dictatorship — as opposed to *revolution*, he writes, "Instead of killing and dying in order to produce the being that we are not, we have to live and let live in order to create what we are." He continues:

"The revolutionary is simultaneously a rebel or he [sic] is not a revolutionary, but a policeman, or a bureaucrat, who turns against rebellion. But if he is a rebel he ends by taking sides against the revolution. So much so that there is absolutely no progress from one attitude to the other, but co-existence and endlessly increasing contradiction. Every revolutionary ends by becoming either an oppressor or a heretic. In the purely historical universe that they have chosen, rebellion and revolution end in the same dilemma: either police rule or insanity."[61]

Vasily Grossman, writing about Soviet Collectivization and the Terror Famine in the Ukraine in 1932-3 through the character Anna Sergeyevna, in *Everything Flows*:

---

[58] For a detailed discussion see *The Freedom of Things*.
[59] See Rousseau's *Discourse on Inequality*, for his analysis of civilization as a society of centripetal *dependence*, from which we cannot escape. Discussed in *The Freedom of Things*.
[60] D. Wootton, Introduction, *Basic Political Writings*, J-J Rousseau, 2011, Hackett, p ix.
[61] Quotes are from pages 215 and 218 respectively, from *The Rebel* by Albert Camus, Anthony Bower (trans.), Penguin, 1982.

"When I look back now, I see the liquidation of the kulaks[62] very differently. I'm no longer under a spell... 'They're not human beings, they're kulak trash!' – that's what I heard again and again, that's what everyone kept repeating. And when I think about it all now, I wonder who first talked about kulak trash. Lenin? Was it really Lenin? How the kulaks suffered. In order to kill them, it was necessary to declare that kulaks are not human beings. Just as the Germans said that Yids [sic] are not human beings. That's what Lenin and Stalin said too: The kulaks are not human beings. I can see now that we are all human beings."[63]

The First Type

The other type of human is the one that still lives in the forests, in the hills, or on the plains, avoiding the advances of civilization. But their existence is precarious and is becoming more fragile with each passing day. These peoples are the last humans.

---

[62] The kulaks were portrayed by the Bolsheviks as 'rich' peasants who were in the way of the socialisation of the land but, in reality, they were simply *all* peasants. The peasantry – and the relationship between the land and the city – has been a perennial problem for revolutionaries, as Marx wrote in 1875: "The peasant exists on a mass scale as a private land proprietor, where he even forms a more-or-less considerable majority as in all the countries of the West European continent, where he has not disappeared and been replaced by agricultural laborers, as in England – the following will take place: either the peasants will start to create obstacles and bring about the fall of any worker revolution, as he has done before in France, or else the proletariat (for the peasant proprietor does not belong to the proletariat; even when his situation places him in it, he thinks that he doesn't belong to it) must, as the government, take steps as a result of which the situation of the peasant will directly improve and which will therefore bring him over to the side of the revolution." (quote is from *The Marx and Engels Reader*, 1978, Robert Tucker, but can also be found at marxists.org.)

The group, *Théorie Communiste* (Roland Simon) who are close to the group *Endnotes*, wrote in 2011: "The essential question which we will have to solve is to understand how we extend communism... how we integrate agriculture so as not to have to exchange with farmers" *Communization and its Discontents*, B. Noys, p58.

Maxim Gorky is reported as having once said: "You'll pardon my saying so, but the peasant is not yet human... He's our enemy, our enemy" (Lynne Viola, *The Unknown Gulag*, 2009, OUP).

[63] Vasily Grossman, *Everything Flows*, Robert and Elizabeth Chandler with Anna Aslanyan (trans.), Vintage, 2011, P128-9.

We cannot know who these peoples really are because to go to them is to bring all our psychological and biological sicknesses to them. But what we can know, from the literature of anthropologists (and we have enough of that – there is no need for any other budding student of anthropology or professor of 'the exotic' to invade the space of these peoples), is that these peoples do not work; they do not have an economy; they do not have hierarchies; they do not have social control as we know it;[64] they do not have money; they do not have history, but they do have collective memory; they do not seek to conquer the world; they do not have books; they do not destroy nature; they do not treat each other with disrespect; they do not treat other animals with disrespect; they live for enjoyment...

On the Homo Gemeinwesen, the 'successor species to Homo sapiens,' Camatte writes, as noted above:

> "It will be in continuity with nature and the cosmos. Its processual knowledge [its *becoming* or, crudely, its consciousness], will not have a justificatory function, as it will operate solely within the dynamics of enjoyment. [...] It is obvious that this cannot be a return to the type of nomadism[65] practised by our distant ancestors who were gatherers. Men and women will acquire a new mode of being beyond nomadism and sedentarism. Sedentary lives compounded by corporeal inactivity are the root cause of almost all the somatic and psychological illnesses of present-day human beings. An active and unfixed life will cure all these problems without medicine or psychiatry."

Camatte's description is remarkable because it describes communities that already exist, present-day uncontacted tribes – *these peoples are already here.* They live alongside us.

The quote from Marx used at the beginning of this text is also usefully repeated here — "The less you *are*, the less you express your own life, the more you *have*, the more pronounced is your alienated life, the greater is the aggregate of your alienated being" — because the list above of what non-State peoples *have* can

---

[64] The notion of 'reverse-dominance hierarchy,' for example, as expounded by Christopher Boehm, is contested in *The Freedom of Things*. There is also an in-depth examination of 'the feud' in non-State societies that shows why this phenomenon is/was also not an exercise in 'social control.'

[65] While 'hunter-gatherers (my, less pejorative term, is *wild-fooders* – see *The Freedom of Things*) were certainly not sedentary by our standards they also were not nomadic in the way this term is generally understood.

only be written by civilized people like ourselves as what they, in the main, *do not* have. This is an indication of how separate we are from them in all respects.

The uncontacted and Indigenous peoples (who are defended by the organization Survival International) are the last humans. They are the revolution that has always been here. They have had no 'fall from grace' in the way we have. They have not embarked on a relentless *wandering* — or *history* — that has brought the world to the point of complete ecological collapse. They do not live in drudgery and empty despair; they have not had their spirit and humanity hollowed out of them.

As for us, we are trapped in a world that can never be made perfect because it will always need to be *managed*. And maybe we don't really have much control over what we do, over the choices we can make... since we have no control over *who we are*. Perhaps the best one can do 'politically' is to keep trying to oppose injustice, and oppression, to keep resisting dictatorship, even though it will inevitably keep returning. One could also try to help non-State peoples remain in their lands, separate from our world. As Camus advises... keep on pushing that rock back up the hill, no matter what.

> Eleanor Rigby, having the same name as the unfortunate character in the *Beatles* song, successfully sued the group for defamation in 1969. Tragically, in 1983, she was run over by a car at a bus stop. She was buried alone at her church with her name; nobody came.

4 Translating and understanding "die *wirkliche* Bewegung"

In the original German, the sentence, written by Marx: "We call communism the real movement which abolishes the present state of things," is "Wir nennen Kommunismus die *wirkliche* Bewegung, welche den jetzigen Zustand aufhebt."

This line is from the first part of *The German Ideology*, 'The Contrast of Materialist and Idealist Perspectives' (1846) and can be found online, in German, at *MLwerke*. Note that the word *wirkliche*, which is usually translated as 'real,' is emphasized in Marx's original.

Marx was a philosopher and a (social) scientist, and he wrote very carefully. The term 'real movement' here does not imply a 'true' or 'genuine' social movement of the peoples. The term is related explicitly to his notions of 'species being,' *Gemeinwesen*, and a development in history that has ignited a '*real* movement' within humans, as the social beings that they are, against their conditions.

The English translation — real movement — is comprised of two words that, in the present era at least, do not help us to understand Marx's meaning. We need to understand the word 'real' here as actual, or concrete, *not* as genuine, or true. And we need to understand the word 'movement' in relation to dialectical materialism. Therefore, we should understand the word 'movement' here as *becoming* (a 'moving toward' in the dialectical process), *not* as a socio-political phenomenon.

Therefore, it makes much more sense to dispense with the term '*real* movement' and replace it with '*concrete* becoming.' If we translate Marx's phrase this way then it not only fits perfectly within his dialectical method; it is also instantly comprehensible to anyone who has some knowledge of the conceptual work done around the terms *becoming* and *immanence*, within what is known as 'continental philosophy.'

The immanence of communism, for Marx, is not an evolution of the species, and it has not been immanent since the dawn of time, it is a *becoming* that was initiated at the time capitalism emerged as the dominant social system. This is because, in Marx's view, capitalism created the very contradictions that would lead both to its destruction and its replacement by communism (capitalism, for Marx, simultaneously exacerbates the alienation of human beings while materially returning them to their social essence). And to emphasize that this becoming is related to the material world and not to the world of ideas, that is, to *reality*, Marx stresses — italicizes — the word *wirkliche*.

The sentence, "We call communism the real movement that abolishes the present state of things," therefore, is better understood conceptually by translating the original of it into English as:

"We call communism the *concrete* becoming that abolishes the current conditions."

5 What is so Special about Relative Surplus Value?

I

In 'Capital,' Marx defined two ways of creating a surplus from exploiting the labor of others. The first is the extraction of *'absolute surplus value.'* Extracting absolute surplus value means profiting from the labor of others by making them work longer or harder or getting more of them to work. This economic model comes up against predictable limits: people die from overwork; you can't get enough of them; they cost too much to keep healthy; and so on. The second way of creating a profit is to make improvements in the organization of their tasks, and to introduce machinery to enable labor time to be more productive. This second way is called the extraction of *'relative surplus value'* — and it is the prime motor of capital-ism. The profits available from this second way of doing things are dependent not upon absolutes like the number of workers, or the availability of a resource, but upon the entrepreneurs' ability to innovate production, supply, and distribution methods so that profits increase *relative* to other factors that remain constant or that might even be reduced. New methods or machinery, for example, and as we all know, may mean less workers are needed.

The word capitalism is hyphenated throughout this piece in order to stress the fact that 'having capital' means one intentionally builds funds for making future investments in industry. Capital is not just money under the bed, it is profit that is specifically to be used to go back into the further production of wealth. The term 'capitalism,' therefore, is better thought of as a verb — capitalism does not exist without the relentless circulation of money — rather than a noun.

II

I remember once seeing a single-frame cartoon which depicts a middle-aged couple in a bedroom in a medieval setting. One of them is looking out at the glorious sun rising over the hills and exclaims something like: "Thank goodness! Look dear! At last, the Reformation has arrived!"

This cartoon says everything I have ever wanted to say about the tendency we have to view 'the past' as if it is always waiting for 'the future.' This is a narrative of history that academics call 'teleological' — meaning that 'the present' is the 'purpose' of the history leading to it. But even though they have a term for it many academics lazily go along with the idea that history is something like a conscious spirit in society struggling for a higher good. It is no coincidence that this idea was expressed — in the midst of Europe's technological irruption — by the philosopher Hegel, who argued that "the absolute rational final goal of the world" is the transcendent synthesis of "the plan of divine Providence" with *reason*.

We are, it seems, locked into the progressivist notion that history, despite being a bumpy ride (Hegel suggested that it could be even regarded as a "slaughtering block" of sacrifices for the future), is a narrative that ultimately shows how humans are becoming more intelligent. True there are the old folk who pine on myopically about the past of their youth being better than now, unaware that their parents also complained, and their parents before them... but generally most of us would still agree that today's society is the peak of progress so far, only to be eclipsed by the next big technological shift. (Well, a lot of us now suspect that instead of a future of flying cars we are now fast-tracked to ecological Armageddon, but that is another matter.)

The Reformation cartoon is premised on the fact that we tend to think of people in the past as just waiting for things to get better. In the same vein, we have the common idea that 'people who lived in caves' must have been simply desperate for improvements to their lives between being chased by saber-toothed tigers. Something key to these interpretations of the past is that humans then are thought of as just like us now, as if *we* were suddenly transported back 100,000 years.

There are four problems with this view. The first is that if we think that 'uncivilized' humans struggled to survive, then how come they did so for at least 200,000 years before the rise of the first States and early civilization?

The second problem is that if it was so hard for humans to survive without civilization then how do other animals survive now? Is life for them really a daily unrelenting struggle? Maybe we might argue that they do not have the consciousness that would tell them that their lives are brutish and short... but then how did conscious humans cope with 200,000 years of the knowledge that their lives were terrible, and how do present-day uncivilized tribes cope? These people must have been constantly beset by depression and suicide, and therefore the tribes that live outside of States on the planet now must also suffer this malaise. Of course, they weren't, and they don't. And the only reason tribespeoples and Indigenous peoples of today suffer from depression and suicide is because they have been dragged into civilization and have had everything they once had taken away. As Émile Durkheim noted in 1893, one of the gifts of modern civilization is "the suicide of sadness."

The third problem with this notion is that it mixes in unsavory depictions of the past — such as in the 'Middle Ages' in Europe, and the beginnings of Industrialization — as if it was *always* like this. In his book, *Better Angels*, eminent philosopher Steven Pinker, for example, snobbishly objects to the Middle Ages in Europe on the grounds that "habits of refinement, self-control, and consideration that are second nature to us had to be acquired", and that people then, "were, in a word, gross." Although we can look back on aspects of the hardships of *civilizations* and be thankful that we don't have to endure *particular* rigors now, should we paint *the whole* of the past in that way?

The fourth problem is that by looking at the past like this we are forced to logically conclude that all previous societies were a little misguided about things or, simply, a bit *stupid*. The flip side of such a self-congratulatory view of our towering present-day 'wisdom' is a dangerously pejorative judgement of those 'uncontacted tribes' who live without civilization. Think Bolsonaro and Modi.

III

Instead of viewing the story of humanity as a continuous narrative with progress as the underlying motor I would argue that there are two world-significant physical events that happened in the past that are crucial to understanding present-day human society. These events were both 'misfortunes,' as Étienne de La Boétie wrote in 1553 of the first one. The first was the emergence of hierarchy and exploitation that is expressed in the formation of a State or civilization — an environment where people submit to 'voluntary servitude,' as La Boétie observed. The second was the emergence of capital-ism as the globally dominant economic form. It is this second one that I want to elaborate on.

We all probably have a vague idea of what capital-ism is: private — or State — ownership of the means of production, wage labor, a money-economy, alienation, 'consumer society,' supply and demand, and so on. But capital-ism did not always exist, something specific brought it into existence, and we can sense that capital-ism is different to all previous economic forms because of the remarkable phenomenon of the Industrial Revolution. Suddenly three hundred years ago the scene was set for going from handloom to power-loom weaving... then to trains, cars, to splitting atoms, to computers, smart phones, etc.

But the Industrial Revolution was not the natural culmination of five thousand years of the rise and fall of civilizations since Mesopotamia, it was not the result of a growing intelligence in humanity that enabled individuals to master what we call science and technology: it was the coming together of the weaving industry, dominated by work-ethic oriented Protestants; gold from the Americas; and the Atlantic Slave Trade.

The key factor in this revolution of human and planetary existence was the profit-making strategy developed by the weaving entrepreneurs of Northern and Western Europe. These merchants set up efficient supply and distribution networks around the core productive unit of the woollen weaver who worked at home, and crucially they ensured their weavers had efficient handlooms to enable higher productivity. The gold and the slavery, and the Protestantism, only helped support the new economic method and ensure that it had the space and time to spread to other ventures and become universally successful. The new economic method was the extraction of *'relative surplus value,'* as Marx termed it. The method fitted in perfectly with the emergent work ethic of the Protestant movement in Europe — and the gold and the slavery buoyed up the new environment until it was fully established. But it was the extraction of 'relative surplus value' — in a word, *capital*-ism — that ultimately and essentially triggered the Industrial Revolution.

Jairus Banaji in his book, *Theory as History*, which examines agrarian societies prior to their being fully capital-ist, particularly in 19th century India, argues, as does Marx, that whether workers are slaves or peasants or hired labor is not the issue for defining a capital-ist enterprise — it is the fact that profits are used to generate even greater profits by investing in improved production methods, *and that money is not left idle.*

IV

In capital-ism people became a special type of resource in an enterprise — one that can be eternally adapted to work at different rhythms, in new situations, with new machinery and processes — this happened because entrepreneurs realized that humans were adaptable and could learn new skills. The historian E.P. Thompson has written extensively, by the way, on worker resistance to the new forms of labor, and how these resistances were broken down by factory discipline. By the time the European working class emerged from the 19th century, even though many dreamed of a better world, they had all absorbed the work ethic promoted by the ruling classes. Slaves and newly colonized peoples — who had perhaps been warriors and suchlike in their previous lives — often simply died from the incessant work they were forced to do.

The Industrial Revolution was the culmination of various chance forces combining, rather than the expression of a triumph of concerted human will. The social organization and astonishing technology we see in the world around us is less the invention of bright people who have been well-educated and more the product of the imperative to increase relative surplus value, the particularly capital-ist way of increasing profits. The appearance of the steam engine owes more to the strategy of acquiring relative surplus value than it does to the acclaimed genius of James Watt.

And the consequences of the emergence of the systematic acquisition of relative surplus value were increased monetary wealth for *a whole class* — who, crucially, now knew that to stay rich they had to keep innovating and investing. The emergence of the 'science' we have today was, also, not the culmination of eons of human ingenuity — it was the result of this same particular method of pursuing wealth, as it still is.

It was only during "the great watershed of the sixteenth century," as Banaji writes, that it became apparent that capital-ist production had become the dominant economic mode in western Europe. It is only in a fully capital-ist mode of production that the whole of society is geared towards, as well as determined by, the raising of the relative productivity of each worker. This is the motive for technological innovation. It is why today, when capital-ism has become part of our very DNA, we witness a proliferation of James Watts'.

So, the enormous technological 'achievements' during and after the Industrial Revolution are not some magical culmination of human history — they are the specific result of a society that emerged by organizing itself on the principle of being able to extract an infinite sum of profit from the ever-adaptable resource of the human being.

References:

Anderson, S. 2009, The Two Lives of Narcisse Pelletier, in *Pelletier: The Forgotten Castaway of Cape York*, Stephanie Anderson (ed. and trans.), Melbourne Books, Australia.

Banaji, J., 2011, *Theory as History: Essays on Modes of Production and Exploitation*, Haymarket Books, Chicago.

Boétie, É. de La, 1553 (2008), *The Politics of Obedience: The Discourse of Voluntary Servitude*, Harry Kurz (trans.), Ludwig von Mises Institute, Auburn.

Durkheim, E., 1893 (1997), *The Division of Labour in Society*, W. D. Halls (trans.), The Free Press, New York.

Hegel, G. W. F., 1822-30 (2011), *Lectures on the Philosophy of History*, Ruben Alvaredo (trans.), Wordbridge Publishing, Aalten. (Quotes are from, pp 12, 13, and 20.)

Mandel, E. 1976, Introduction, in *Capital, A Critique of Political Economy, Volume I*, Ben Fowkes (trans.), Penguin Books.

Marx, K. 1867 (1976), *Capital, A Critique of Political Economy, Volume I*, Ben Fowkes (trans.), Penguin Books.

Pinker, S., 2012, *The Better Angels of Our Nature: The Decline of Violence in History and its Causes*, Penguin Books.

Survival International, survivalinternational.org

Thompson, E. P., 1967, Time, Work-Discipline, and Industrial Capitalism, in *Past and Present*, No. 38. (Dec., 1967), pp. 56-97.

Weber, M., 1904-5/1920 (2003), *The Protestant Ethic and the Spirit of Capitalism*, Talcot Parsons (trans.), Dover Publications, New York.

6 The Society of Self-Realization

Marx wrote, "The individual *is* the social being" (1844). He viewed the distant past of humanity as a condition in which community was pre-eminent and insisted that the organization of life through community aligned to the essence of what it is to be human. His perspective defined the emergence of class societies (i.e., civilization, beginning with a chiefdom) as operating against this deep need within human beings, and instances of revolt against hierarchical and exploitative societies throughout history repeatedly demonstrated the desire to be truly human.

With the arrival of capitalism great numbers of people were alienated from their daily existence even more, indeed to an astonishing extent. No longer were the lowest classes of people able to use the land they lived on to feed and clothe themselves. The common lands were enclosed, and the humans were driven off, initially replaced by sheep. Their lives became even more precarious, and then became the resource for industrialization. They were given freedom from the bondage of serfdom and from ties to the land; they were now free to sell themselves in a market as labor, competing against each other even more directly than previously. Another group of people, of course, were, later, brutally ripped from their homelands and enslaved for as long as the slave owners could get away with it; they were eventually granted the freedom of wage slavery too, though they have, in the West, generally, due to the embeddedness of racism in modern society, remained third class wage slaves. Thus, Marx argued, by the mid-19th century human separation from each other, and from nature itself, was almost complete. No longer were humans dependent upon one another, now they were free-floating slaves to money, or wages (their freedom was an illusion, or rather, the freedom of a commodity), and they had become pure atoms in the process of creating wealth.[1]

---

[1] But industrialization, according to Marx, had ushered in a threat to capital and the persistence of class society. By concentrating workers in such large numbers in factories, where they were bound to feel dissatisfied, humans were able to rediscover their social essence and the strength they had if they organized themselves communally against the dictates of an oppressive system. At the same time, the wealth that capital was able to produce made it possible, with a different organization of work, for a revolutionary class to sustain a new world society based on equality and freedom. So, for Marx, capitalism

Jean-Jacques Rousseau, before, and contrary to Marx, regarded the emergence of civilization as a transformation of human conditions from one of 'freedom' as *self-sufficiency* to one of *dependence*. He regarded civilization as an inescapable social construct because every member of a civilization becomes wholly dependent on the activities of a mass of unknown, or faceless, others for their survival, from the most impoverished to the most powerful. Modern society, for Rousseau, was a complex web of dependence. Pre-empting the Hegelian 'master-slave' construct, but in a more straight-forward form, he described the social relations of those within civilization as *dependent* on others in every direction: "He who believes himself the master of others does not escape being more of a slave than they" (Rousseau: 156: 1762).

Rousseau viewed civilization as the separation from 'nature' and the expression of human submission to dependence, a social form in which we are all bound together in our lack of self-sufficiency. Marx, on the other hand, considered humans to be separated from nature from their beginnings (through the activity of 'labor' and their 'consciousness') and therefore — in a dissemination of the trope of the 'helpless' 'cave-man' — dependent upon one another for their survival, but, more importantly for the discussion here, he viewed civilization as the *separation* of people, a social form that increasingly, as it develops, sets people apart (alienates them), first from the ownership of their own activity, then from each other. Under capitalism, according to Marx, this process is ratcheted up a great number of notches and is endowed with the 'progressive' ideological mantle of *Bourgeois Individualism*.

Lawrence Krader, in his *Introduction* to Marx's *Ethnological Notebooks*, writes:

> Rousseau's notion of the chains of civilization as opposed to the primitive state of freedom was reconceived by Marx as the chains of primitive bondage which were, rather, satisfying and comforting. Despotic, dissatisfying, discomforting are the bonds of civilization. (Krader: 60: 1974)

The ideology of individualism emerged in the Enlightenment in opposition to 'tradition.' (We should always remember, by-the-way, that the period of *the Enlightenment* falls within the period of the *Atlantic Slave Trade*, and is, no doubt,

---

was the means, horrendous as it was, and is, by which they could abolish their atomized existence. No longer would they be at the service of money, bosses, and machines, they could create an egalitarian and communal society, a true human community, that ensured all the means required for a happy existence were available for all.

as linked to that phenomenon as it is to the rise of capitalism itself, of which, of course, slavery played such a monumental part.) Individualism soon became a 'right': "the right of the individual to freedom and self-realization" (Meiksins Wood: 6: 1972). But there were two notions of this 'right' for the individual. The first was the bourgeois one which defined the right as emanating from a free market and the ownership of property. The second was a social ideal that claimed that a reorganization of society — the redistribution of property — would give everyone freedom, and from there self-realization would follow. The second conception was taken up by everyone — from Max Stirner, to Marx, to Oscar Wilde — who wished to see an end to the ignorance and bondage characterized by *traditional*, as well as *bourgeois*, society. The anarchist Peter Kropotkin wrote in 1884, "No society is free so long as the individual is not so."

Both these conceptions, the economic and the social, come straight out of the Enlightenment battle against 'traditional' society, which was also, of course, the *process* of the economic institutionalization of capitalism. But both conceptions of individualism ultimately only serve the concept of the market, if not the market itself.

The anarchist, Emma Goldman, in 1910, demonstrated how the project of the Enlightenment had been channeled into radical politics — and how it repeats and supports the trope of people prior to the modern day being intellectually inadequate — but also how it indicates the birth of the notion of the possibility of a personal identity:

> The primitive man, unable to understand his being, much less the unity of all life, felt himself absolutely dependent on blind, hidden forces ever ready to mock and taunt him. Out of that attitude grew the religious concepts of man as a mere speck of dust dependent on superior powers on high, who can only be appeased by complete surrender. All the early sagas rest on that idea, which continues to be the *Leitmotiv* of the biblical tales dealing with the relation of man to God, to the State, to society. Again and again the same motif, man is nothing, the powers are everything. Thus Jehovah would only endure man on condition of complete surrender. Man can have all the glories of the earth, but he must not become conscious of himself. The State, society, and moral laws all sing the same refrain: Man can have all the glories of the earth, but he must not become conscious of himself... [Anarchism's] goal is the freest possible expression of all the latent powers of the individual. (Goldman: *Anarchism: What It Really Stands For*)

But, as decolonizing academic, Linda Tuhiwai Smith writes:

The individual, as the basic social unit from which other social organizations and social relations form, is another system of ideas which needs to be understood as part of the West's cultural archive. Western philosophies and religions place the individual as the basic building block of society. (Tuhiwai Smith: 49: 1999)

Philosopher Alasdair MacIntyre elaborates this theme:

In much of the ancient and medieval worlds, as in many other premodern societies, the individual is identified and constituted in and through certain of his or her roles, those roles which bind the individual to the communities in and through which alone specifically human goods [benefits] are to be attained; I confront the world as a member of this family, this household, this clan, this tribe, this city, this nation, this kingdom. There is no 'I' apart from these. (MacIntyre: 201: 1981: see *References* for more on this)

The French group *Tiqqun* write:

Thus, in the bourgeois republic, where man is a true, recognized subject, he is cut off from any quality of his own, he is a figure without reality, a 'citizen', and there, where, in his own eyes and in those of others, he passes for a real subject in his everyday existence, he is a figure without truth, an 'individual.' (*Tiqqun*: 34: 2000)

The difference between the society of capital and all other societies that we know of is that every single facet of it is facilitated by money and the market, and this includes all its cultural forms. The culture, or ideology, of *the Individual* is an aspect of the universal market inside of which we are trapped. It has been helped in its development, or growth, by all those, from whatever part of the political/philosophical spectrum, who have championed the righteousness of individualism, or the goal of the *free individual*.

Though Marx, following the ideals of the Enlightenment, also put the notion of self-realization, or individualism, on a pedestal, and he asserts that it is *only* possible in the developments following a communist revolution, he also presciently observed the fact that *everything* human was now, under capitalism, being mediated through a market:

Finally, [in 'the history of exchange'] there came a time when everything that men had considered as inalienable became an object of exchange, of traffic and could be alienated. This is the time when the very things which till then had been communicated, but never exchanged; given, but never sold; acquired, but never bought — virtue, love, conviction, knowledge, conscience, etc. — when everything, in short, passed into commerce. It is the time of general corruption, of universal venality, or, to speak in terms of political economy, the time when everything, moral or physical, having become a marketable value, is brought to the market to be assessed at its truest value. (Marx: 1847)

In this quote Marx is indicating the chronology, which he described in more depth elsewhere, from the 'formal' to 'real' domination of capital, or the formal to *"real subsumption of labor under capital"* (Marx: 1035: 1867). In the *formal* phase, existing labor processes are directly subordinated to capital, in the *real* phase, they are transformed into specifically capitalist production. But this higher stage of capitalism has certain fundamental implications for production, and therefore society, as a whole: "Capital must increase the value of its operations to the point where it assumes social dimensions, and so sheds its *individual* character entirely" (Marx: 1035: 1867). Capitalist production, therefore, in the *real* phase becomes *the character of society itself.*

Jacques Camatte, who has explored in great depth the notion of the real domination of capital, notes, in *Forme-Realité-Effectivité-Virtualité*, 1997, that the terminology can be confusing and it would have been better to have used the terms 'superficial' in place of 'formal,' and 'substantive' in place of 'real.' Even more simply, one can reasonably frame Marx's periodization of capital's expansion under the terms 'emergent' and 'comprehensive,' or perhaps 'complete.' For a way to visualize this two-stage development of capital — from first taking control of existing mercantilist and labor practices, to then reshaping them, as well as *all other aspects* of social and intellectual life, both collective and individual, to its requirements — use the analogy of the [zombie ant fungus](#).

Guy Debord elaborated on the theme of the total domination of capital — of capitalist production becoming the society itself — in the *Society of the Spectacle*, 1967. He writes:

In societies where modern conditions of production prevail, all of life has become an immense accumulation of *spectacle*. All that was once lived directly has passed into a representation (Thesis 1). The spectacle subdues living human beings to the extent that the economy has totally subjugated them. There is now nothing but the economy developing for itself (Thesis 16).

So, for Debord and Camatte, capitalism is a totalizing social form... but as indicated above, and as Foucault asserts, *all* societies are, by definition, totalizing. It is therefore no surprise that capital, having become the society itself, compels society to continue to reproduce itself *as capital*.

Jacques Camatte and Gianni Collu make this clear:

> Capital, as a social mode of production, accomplishes its real domination when it succeeds in replacing all the pre-existing social and natural presuppositions with its own particular *forms of organization* which mediate the submission of the whole of physical and social life to its own needs of valorization. The essence of the *Gemeinschaft* [community] of capital is organization. (Camatte and Collu: 1969-73; original emphasis: also see *References*)

So, if all societies are totalizing, if all societies own their subjects in such a way that they can only say what they can say and only see what they can see... what is it that differentiates our modern society from all previous ones?

> In the 60s Guy Debord wrote, "all of [modern] life presents itself as an immense accumulation of spectacles." Fortunately, spectacles can nowadays be donated for recycling, and the discarded eyewear Debord complained of littering the streets of Paris is a thing of the past.

First of all, it is the generation of 'relative surplus value.' This is the key, mostly neglected or misunderstood, economic mechanism of capitalism and that which makes it different from all other economic forms (which means all other *State* forms). Once the process of acquiring relative surplus value becomes the reproductive mechanism of society then the society is definitively *capitalist* — capital has achieved real domination (Camatte and others are mistaken in their timelines because they do not have a sufficient grasp of the significance of relative surplus value), the Industrial Revolution is possible. (For the supreme importance for capitalism of the acquisition of what Marx terms 'relative surplus value,' which would take up too much space here, see *Capital Vol 1*, and *What is so Special about Relative Surplus Value?*)

Second, it is the totalization of the market, the totalization of competing interests. The special core value of our society is not the obedience to a higher authority, or the knowing of one's place, or the identification with specific ancestral connections, or one's place in and on the land (as Aboriginal people in Australia say, 'we don't own the land, the land owns us') — it is that every aspect of our lives is mediated through money and a market. It is through this market that we acquire our *individualism*.

We are now encouraged to pick our own identity, our own individuality, from the market of identities on offer to us. How did we acquire such an untethered freedom? (To be lost in space, affirming one's existence to the void, must then be the apotheosis of this kind of freedom.)

Ironically, we acquired this immense and useless freedom through a 'shrinking' of the world into something that can only be viewed through a European lens. As Achille Mbembe writes:

> Over the course of the Atlantic [Slave Trade] period... the small province of the planet that is Europe gradually gained control over the rest of the world. In parallel, particularly during the eighteenth century [the Enlightenment], there emerged discourses of truth relating to nature, the specificity and forms of the living, and the qualities, traits, and characteristics of human beings. Entire populations were categorized as species, kinds, or races, classified along vertical lines.
>
> Paradoxically, it was also during this period that people and cultures were increasingly conceptualized as individualities closed in upon themselves. Each community — and even each people — was considered a unique collective body endowed with its own power... The expansion of the European spatial horizon, then, went hand in hand with a division and shrinking of the historical and cultural imagination and, in certain cases, a relative closing of the mind. In sum, once genders, species, and races were identified and classified, nothing remained but to enumerate the differences between them. (Mbembe: 16-17: 2013)

We acquired this freedom following the demand of capital that *everything* be placed for sale in the market as a commodity — we acquired the insensible and lifeless freedom of *a thing*, a dead thing, a commodity. Thus, all the varying, elusive, and contradictory modes of what it is to be human were at first repressed by capital because such fluidity was perceived as interfering with the work ethic, and then, after the First World War, they began to find a commodity status and became part of marketing campaigns. After struggles for recognition and equality, coinciding with developments in capital that turned more and more toward the mining of the human being itself, these fluid 'divergences' were encouraged to return, but only on the condition that they constituted *identities* that could be commodified and put to work in the circulation of money. After the establishment of the principle of identity, given to us by the Enlightenment and bourgeois ethics, as described by Mbembe above, the first identity to construct itself *from within itself* — and then to operate, naturally, in the service of capital and society — was the identity of 'the working class' (although, part of its self-formation was helped, for example, by the fact that 'the working class' was viewed as the vessel for the salvation of humanity by Marx). From there all other identities could establish themselves and function usefully for society, and, in this, the cultural work of capital — its colonization and re-directing of our very desires — became complete.

Jean Baudrillard recognized how deep this process had become entrenched in modern thought when he objected to the concepts of 'desire' and 'difference' as formulated by Gilles Deleuze.

In his work with Guattari, Deleuze develops a definition of desire as positive and productive that supports the conception of life as material flows. (Ross: 66: 2010)

In diametric opposition, as Franco 'Bifo' Berardi (2007) notes, "Baudrillard... argued that desire is the driving force of the development of capital."

Baudrillard had already criticized the notion of 'desire' in *Symbolic Exchange and Death*, 1976, but in *Forget Foucault* he makes his critique more explicit:

> This is the nature of desire and the unconscious: the trash heap of political economy and the psychic metaphor of capital. And sexual jurisdiction is the ideal means, in a fantastic extension of the jurisdiction governing private property, for assigning to each individual the management of a certain capital: psychic capital, libidinal capital, sexual capital, unconscious capital. And each individual will be accountable to himself for his capital, under the sign of his own liberation. (Baudrillard: 40: 1977)

As for the notion of 'difference,' this too is an accelerator for the culture of capital in our society, as Baudrillard observes (2002), the proliferation of *difference* is the sign of our modern *undifferentiation* (not to be confused with *indifferentiation*). Deleuze and Guattari's categories of 'difference' and 'desire' are the most recent and most powerful endorsements of the individualism capital provides for us, and part of the reason for this is that these categories were intended to indicate some kind of way out of capital. The problem is, if one tries to indicate a way out of capital one only gives capital and money new avenues to explore.

Nihil Evadere

But there is something very important here to note. Baudrillard may be right that Deleuze and Guattari's formulations — against their intentions — give a philosophical and political impetus to the undifferentiation that capital appears to 'desire,' but, if so, they are only going along with the development of capital (the development of our society) that is already in process, while Baudrillard, in contrast, is offering a critique and resistance to this development that, ultimately, coincides with the *traditionalist* critique of 'modernity' offered by reactionary thinkers (and Heideggerian communists/leftists) — because his critique is against the equality that capital offers us all through the very process of undifferentiation. Therefore, his thinking on 'sexuality' is approved of by the far-right.

In 1924, Otto Rühle, a left-communist Marxist, wrote against the notion that 'the working class' was a social category:

> Only in the factory is the worker of today a real proletarian, and as such a revolutionary within the meaning of the proletarian-socialist revolution. Outside the factory he is a petty-bourgeois, involved in a petty-bourgeois milieu and middle-class habits of life, dominated by petty-bourgeois ideology... In the factory the worker is another person. There he confronts the capitalist face to face, feels the fist on his neck, is irritated, embittered, hostile. (Rühle: 1924)

By the end of the 1950s, certainly in the UK, a great many individuals from working class backgrounds were becoming academics, acclaimed writers, and pop stars. Many of those within this new social phenomenon found themselves in a confusing position. They had 'escaped' from what was regarded as a 'working-class environment' (in fact, they had often escaped from a 'lower middle-class environment'). They now had more money, more recognition from society, and they mixed in different social circles to their parents. They had to contend with the condescension of many in their new social circle. This caused some to nurture a resentment. This resentment, along with new sources of artistic creativity derived from a 'working-class' upbringing, enabled them to make a profound impact on the culture. In the UK this was exemplified by playwrights of the 'kitchen sink' drama — a phenomenon parodied by *Monty Python* in 1969 in their television sketch, [Working Class Playwright](). But it was probably in academia, and other traditionally middle-class professions, that the parvenu middle-class had the greatest impact. In general, any pop star, or professor at a university, or politician, who claims to be working-class, or to be able to speak for the working class, will be looked at askance by anyone occupying a low-paid, non-managerial job. In their claiming to have retained their status as working-class — and many academics and other professionals still make this claim — they helped build the idea that one could create one's *identity*... or pick one from the equivalent of a supermarket shelf.

Many years later, Rühle's notion was consciously reformulated in the book *Nihilist Communism*:

> We do not know what anyone means when they describe the proletariat as a social category. If they are implying that members of the working class as a social body have something between themselves other than their experience of work, then we utterly reject this. We have a penchant for champagne and Tarkovsky movies whereas our neighbors prefer White Lightning and WWF wrestling, our economic position, however, is identical. We refute all identity politics as ideology and we absolutely refuse to view the proletariat as a political/sociological constituency equivalent to ethnicity, gender, or sexual preference. The proletariat has no existence independent of capitalism. (Monsieur Dupont: 50: 2003)

In 1999, Jean Baudrillard wrote:

> Identity is a dream that is pathetically absurd. You dream of being yourself when you have nothing better to do. You dream of yourself and gaining recognition when you have lost all singularity... Identity is this obsession with appropriation of the liberated being, but a being liberated in sterile conditions, no longer knowing what he is. It is a label of existence without qualities. Now all energies — the energies of minorities and entire peoples, the energies of individuals — are concentrated today on that derisory affirmation, that pride-less assertion: I am! I exist! I'm alive, I'm called so-and-so, I'm European! A hopeless affirmation, in fact, since when you need to prove the obvious, it is by no means obvious. (Baudrillard: 70-1: 1999)

Giorgio Agamben and *Tiqqun* have also tried to critique and demolish the concepts of individualism and identity. In 1990, Agamben wrote:

> A being radically devoid of any representable identity would be absolutely irrelevant to the State. This is what, in our culture, the hypocritical dogma of the sacredness of human life and the vacuous declarations of human rights are meant to hide... [Whatever, in this time,] rejects all identity and every condition of belonging, is the principal enemy of the State. (Agamben: 86-7: 1990)

Indeed, to claim that one belongs to 'the working class' or to any other such fictional category — to self-identify as anything — is to, of course, do the State's work for it.

The last part of this quote is used by *Tiqqun* in their first journal issue, and it forms a basis for the theory of *Bloom* (see note in *References*), on which *Tiqqun* and Agamben collaborated (Agamben: 2010). And *Tiqqun* extend the theme, though they have perhaps jumped the gun with their declaration that 'the individual' has already disappeared — "The fiction of the individual has decomposed at the same speed that it was becoming real" (*Tiqqun*: 7: 2007) — but their critique of individualism and identity aligns with others here. They write:

> The more I express myself, the more I am drained... The injunction, everywhere, to 'be someone' maintains the pathological state that makes this society necessary. The injunction to be strong produces the very weakness by which it maintains itself, so that *everything seems to take on a therapeutic character*, even working, even love... Our feeling of inconsistency [our failing at living our identity] is simply the consequence of this foolish belief in the permanence of the self and of the little care we give to what makes us what we are... [T]he connection of cybernetic solitudes... sometimes condense into a *milieu*, where nothing is shared but codes, and where nothing is played out except the incessant recomposition of identity. (*Tiqqun*: 13,14 and 17: 2007; original emphases)

Tiqqun and Agamben are right in their critique of individualism, but their cure for it relies on the millenarian success of a genuine world revolution that instaurates 'communism,' which could be achieved, as *Tiqqun appear* to suggest, by an armed globalizing insurrection (*Tiqqun*: 56: 2007) or, as Agamben insists, by a 'turning of one's back on the world,' in the manner of the early Franciscan monks, which he supports by quoting Franz Kafka: "Kafka repeats it constantly: do not seek the struggle, but find a way out" (Agamben: 2015). If the cure is so fantastically remote — the majority of us forming self-sustaining communes in the countryside, or a global armed revolution — then it is likely that, for all our critiques of individualism, the pathology of individualism is likely to continue... Of course, what they also do, again by indicating *an escape*, is to provide new avenues for capital to explore, certainly the fascination for Giorgio Agamben has, until recently, sustained many salaries in academia. Both the emergence of 'individualism' (for example, in the work of Emma Goldman) and the opposition to it are factors in the renewal of our social forces.

The opposition to individualism was formed by Western thinkers, such as the ones above, long after individualism had already become the ethos and *doxa* of capitalist society, and so, such critiques are as ineffectual as the critique of, for example, advertising, which will always be one step ahead of its detractors (the SI and Marshal McLuhan, for example), and will even 'recuperate,' almost immediately, their critiques to develop new strategies. This happens not because capital is some kind of relentless sandstorm that we cannot halt or escape, it happens because our society is — organically — capitalist, and *we* are the very motors of its reproduction, in the same way that *any* member of *any* society cannot fail to reproduce *their* society.

Ironically, perhaps, but really *of course*, 'capital' beat Karl Marx and Emma Goldman to the goal of 'free individuality' by a country mile and didn't even need a revolution to do it, but it could be argued that without the help of Marx, Goldman, and others, the victory may not have been so swift. Today, each of us is 'free' to choose an identity from the cultural marketplace, this being the ultimate bourgeois liberation from *tradition*. And we are applauded, though the applause is unavoidably hollow, deceptive — and *bored* — for 'speaking' what we are encouraged to believe is 'our truth.'

As the academic, Ansgar Allen, observes, such encouragements, such demands for self-realization, echoing *Tiqqun*'s description of the 'citizen in the bourgeois republic,' belie an insidious coercion:

> The popular phrase, *be true to yourself*, serves as a violent constraint. Those who attempt to obey this command search in vain for their inner self (which must, of course, remain elusive). They satisfy themselves with imported ideas that provide a sense of depth. Their inner self arrives as a constructed and constraining illusion. (Allen: 20: 2014)

The quest for our *individuality*, our *desire*, our *difference*, our *truth*, is exactly what capital 'wants' in order to maintain the continued expansion of the market, which now focusses so clearly on the human commodity and the creation of "social persons" (Cesarano and Collu: *Thesis 66*), the growth of all kinds of human factories — from schools, to universities, to child-care, to aged-care, to entertainment, to social media — being an example. This manufacturing of *apparent* individuality and *apparent* difference is, of course, as Baudrillard observes, the acceleration of the 'goal' of capital, which is humanity's complete homogenization or *undifferentiation*. It is something, moreover, that we cannot resist, except through the bloodshed of a *talibanistic* seizure of power. It is true that once one's identity is set one becomes a fossil, and a liar. But lying is a fundamental requisite for survival in our society; we are all liars; we are raised to be liars by the adults around us; by the society we cannot help but reproduce. Our journey of lies begins with our earliest observations of adults and the lessons they provide regarding how it is that we must live. After this we daily recreate this society by everything we do, and if we tried to create a new society, either in a small cult form, or a religious, fascist, or 'proletarian' dictatorship, it would be a worse terror, so the question is: how do we use this knowledge to guide our actions?

> As the planet heads toward ecological Armageddon two questions remain unresolved: do trees have free will and whose fault is it?

References:

Agamben, G., 1990 (1993/2003), *The Coming Community*, Michael Hardt (trans.), University of Minnesota Press; in the chapter, *Tiananmen*, which can be found online here.

Agamben, G., 2010, interview transcript at: https://anarchistwithoutcontent.wordpress.com/2010/04/18/tiqqun-apocrypha-repost/

Agamben, Giorgio, 2015, 'Europa muss kollabieren' [Europe must Collapse], interview by Iris Radisch in *Die Zeit* (Zeit Online), 27 August, 2015.

Allen, Ansgar, 2014, *Benign Violence: Education in and Beyond the Ae of Reason*, Palgrave Macmillan.

Baudrillard, Jean, 1977 (2007), *Forget Foucault*, Nicole Dufresne (trans.), Semiotexte.

Baudrillard, J., 1999 (2001, 2011), *Impossible Exchange*, Chris Turner (trans.), Verso.

Baudrillard, J., 2002, YouTube video, check between 1min 58 secs and 3 mins.

Berardi, F. 'Bifo,' 2007, 'In Memory of Jean Baudrillard,' *Rebelión* website.

Camatte and Collu: 1969-73.

This quote originally appeared in *Transition*, in the journal *Invariance* #8, 1969, in French, and is signed on Camatte's Internet site (*Revue Invariance*) by 'Jacques Camatte and Gianni Collu.' Originally articles in *Invariance* were unsigned. The quote was later used in the Italian book *Apocalisse e rivoluzione* (1973) by Giorgio Cesarano and Gianni Collu (see below), where the quote is attributed to Collu and, as Camatte confirms on his website, the beginning was written by Collu and the rest by Camatte. My translation.

Cesarano, G., and Collu, G., *Apocalisse e rivoluzione*, Dedalo, 1973. Can be found online. My translation.

Camatte, J., 1997, 'Forme-Realité-Effectivité-Virtualité,' *Revue Invariance*.

Debord, Guy, *La société du spectacle*, 1967. My translation.

Dupont, Monsieur 2003 (2009), *Nihilist Communism: a critique of optimism — the religious dogma that states there will be an ultimate triumph of good over evil — in the far left*, Ardent Press, San Francisco.

Goldman, Emma, 1910, 'Anarchism: What It Really Stands For,' in *Anarchism and Other Essays*, 1910, available on the Internet.

Krader, Lawrence, *The Ethnological Notebooks of Karl Marx*, (transcribed, edited and introduced by Krader), 2nd Edition, 1974, Assen, NL.

Kropotkin,P., 1884, *The Place of Anarchism in Socialistic Evolution*, Part One, available on the Internet.

MacIntyre, A., 1981/2014, *After Virtue: A Study in Moral Theory*, Bloomsbury.
The quote above from MacIntyre continues:
"To this it may be replied: what about my immortal soul? Surely in the eyes of God I am an individual, prior to and apart from my roles. This rejoinder embodies a misconception which in part arises from a confusion between the Platonic notion of the soul and that of Catholic Christianity. For the Platonist, as later for the Cartesian, the soul, preceding all bodily and social existence, must indeed possess an identity prior to all social roles; but for the Catholic Christian, as earlier for the Aristotelian, the body and the soul are not two linked substances. I am my body and my body is social, born to those parents in this community with a specific identity. What does make a difference for the Catholic Christian is that I, whatever earthly community I may belong to, am *also* held to be a member of a heavenly, eternal community

in which I also have a role, a community represented on earth by the church. Of course, I can be expelled from, defect from or otherwise lose my place in any of these forms of community. I can become an exile, a stranger, a wanderer. These too are assigned social roles, recognized within ancient and medieval communities. But it is always as part of an ordered community that I have to seek the human good [individual and collective benefit], and in this sense of community the solitary anchorite or shepherd on the remote mountainside is as much a member of a community as is a dweller in cities... The Individual carries his communal roles with him as part of the definition of his self, even into isolation" p201-2.

Marx, K., 1844, *Economic Manuscripts*, Private Property and Communism, Sec 3.

Marx, K., 1847, *The Poverty of Philosophy*, Chapter 1, Part 1.

Marx, K., 1867 (1976), *Capital, A Critique of Political Economy, Volume I*, Ben Fowkes (trans.), Penguin Books

Mbembe, Achille, 2013 (2017), *Critique of Black Reason*, Laurent Dubois (trans.), Duke University Press.

Rousseau, J.-J., 1762 (2011), 'On the Social Contract,' in *Jean-Jacques Rousseau: Basic Political Writings, Second Edition*, Donald A. Cress (ed. and trans.), Hackett.

Ross, Alison, 2010, 'Desire,' in *The Deleuze Dictionary, Revised Edition*, Adrian Parr (ed.), Edinburgh University Press.

Rühle, O., 1924, [From the Bourgeois to the Proletarian Revolution](), Marxists' Internet Archive.

Smith, Linda Tuhiwai, 1999, *Decolonizing Methodologies*, Zed Books.

Tiqqun, 2000 (2012), *Theory of Bloom*, Michael Hurley (trans.), can be found online.

Tiqqun, 2007, *The Coming Insurrection*, can be found online.

Wood, Ellen Meiksins, 1972, *Mind and Politics*, UCP.

7 The Language and Discourse Trap

Discourse: communication in speech or writing; a speech or piece of writing about a particular, usually serious, subject; spoken or written discussion – from the Cambridge Dictionary, online.

Sermon: a part of a Christian church ceremony in which a priest gives a talk on a religious or moral subject, often based on something written in the Bible; a long talk in which someone advises other people how they should behave in order to be better people; a lecture — from the Cambridge Dictionary, online.

Doxa: a Greek word meaning common belief or popular opinion or, as Allan Bloom explains in his notes to Plato's Republic: "what is popularly held and is based upon the appearance or seeming of things, as opposed to their reality."

The civilizing discourse which, like all discourse, expresses itself almost exclusively as a sermon, urges us relentlessly and in every sphere to believe that humans have developed — *rather than lost* — skills for social organization. In our very language 'primitive' means backward; 'savage' means brutal; 'uncivilized' means barbaric; 'simple' means less intelligent; and 'non-literate' means 'uneducated.' There is no word or phrase for a society that is not a State that doesn't define that society in terms of its existing at 'a lower stage of development,' whether it be the whole of humanity prior to five thousand years ago or those peoples outside States now. There is also no word for the time before written history that doesn't define that period by its incompleteness. We are trapped by the discourses that generate our language.

The term 'discourse' was embedded in academic jargon — *understood* is another matter — after Michel Foucault ruminated on the limits and possibilities of thought in the late 1960s. Foucault argued that a 'discourse' consisted of a series of "statements" that provided a broad rationale within various intellectual, academic, or scientific fields. But he also warned that these discourses are — following Nietzsche's work on the genealogy of morality — "from beginning to end, historical" and that we who participate in them are "governed by rules which are not all given to [our] consciousness." Foucault was arguing that we are functions of our time and environment, and he suspected that although many scholars and activists formally went along with this materialism they didn't actually understand its proper implications. So, there are a multitude of discourses that reflect and shape our views of the world, one of which is the civilizing discourse. Marx had already written — somewhat obliquely, it turns out — "Men make their own history, but they do not make it as they please." Foucault, channeling Nietzsche, took it to another level: we are functions of the society we are born into and any notion that one can, as an individual, alter the discourse with "a fresh word" that only *we* are able to impart... is a fanciful dream.

More than this, Foucault insists that it is our *body* — above, beyond, and deeper than our 'intellect' — that is formed by the epoch and environment we live in. Our very bodies constitute the discourses of our particular history: "We believe that the body obeys the exclusive laws of physiology and that it escapes the influence of history, but this too is false. The body is molded by a great many distinct regimes; it is broken down by the rhythms of work, rest, and holidays; it is poisoned by food or values, through eating habits or moral laws; it constructs resistances. 'Effective' history differs from traditional history in being without constants. Nothing in man [sic] — not even his body — is sufficiently stable to serve as the basis for self-recognition or for understanding other men."

Gilles Deleuze sums it up: "Foucault's key historical principle is that any historical formation says all it can say and sees all it can see." So, although I am going to be critiquing 'the civilizing sermon' below I am *in no way claiming that my words and my life are not part* of the civilizing discourse, since if they were outside of that discourse then they would be out of our history and they would be unhearable. My 'opposition' to the civilizing sermon should therefore be viewed as something *inside* the civilizing discourse — since, though my words may say one thing, every bodily action I perform, every 'work' that I do, is in full support of civilization, even these words before your eyes.

> Is reality an hallucination? Or are our hallucinations reality? In a radical thesis arguing just that, a team led by neuroscientist Anil Seth have discovered that there are seven levels of 'reality' and none of them can be accessed by our consciousness, but only on a Wednesday.

You may be thinking that I haven't quite worked out how to put this succinctly... and, if so, you'd be right. I can, however, offer an analogy: the workers movement against capitalism expressed its highest achievement in the formation of Soviet Russia. The Bolsheviks could do nothing else but accelerate the establishment of industrialization in Russia. The worker and peasant movement against capitalism, harnessed by 'revolutionaries,' *was formed by capitalism* — it was part of the discourse — and ended up, unavoidably, creating an industrialization in Russia that remains unequalled in its speed and scope.

The civilizing sermon, the dominant flow of the civilizing discourse — which is one of our modern doxas — can also be referred to as the notion of human progress: 'Thank goodness, dear, that we no longer live in caves.' The immediate and real danger of the civilizing sermon and discourse is that with political leaders such as Narendra Modi and Jair Bolsonaro the eradication of the cultures of tribal peoples (and the 'uncontacted tribes,' see Survival International) is quickened and intensified.

It seems to be a given in our universities and amongst our intellectuals that human society has proceeded through a series of stages to get where we are today. We have gone from 'hunter-gatherer' (a term replaced with 'wild-fooder' in *The Freedom of Things*), to tribes with powerful chiefs, to kingdoms, to empires, to representative democracy. The early anthropologist, Lewis H. Morgan, defined three broad stages of human development. He wrote that we have stepped up from Savagery, to Barbarism, to Civilization.

This precept of stages in human development is so ingrained in our consciousness that academic after academic, historian after historian, social commentator after social commentator, bus driver after bus driver, and so on, continue to submissively and dull-wittedly repeat it. Let's take three examples.

In psychology professor Thomas Suddendorf's, *The Gap: The Science of What Separates Us from Other Animals*, he writes:

> "[The abandonment of] a hunter-gatherer lifestyle in favour of a sedentary agricultural existence... enabled rapid population growth and was a catalyst for development... Those who have continued to pursue a hunter-gatherer lifestyle have increasingly been marginalized."

Listen to the words used here: 'enabled,' 'rapid,' 'catalyst,' 'development' — all these words make the abandonment of a 'hunter-gatherer' lifestyle something positive and necessary for the flourishing of humankind. 'Thank goodness, dear, that we no longer live in the trees.' Maybe Suddendorf did not intend to write such a pejorative analysis of those 'increasingly marginalized' peoples... but he did.

Nihil Evadere

Stephen L. Sass, in *The Substance of Civilization: Materials and Human History from the Stone Age to the Age of Silicon*, expands this narrative in a way that reflects back to us what we really think about 'early humans.' He writes:

> "Early humans faced overwhelming obstacles to survival. They needed food for sustenance, weapons against predators — both animal and human — and shelter from an often brutal environment."

Have a look at that again. Is he putting forward the idea that 'early humans' were kind of 'just like us' — as if *we* were suddenly transported back to the distant past and had no idea how to live properly without our technology? 'Let me tell you, dear, life without a refrigerator is absolute hell, and people in the past had to wait a long time for one to be invented.' He continues:

> "The transition from a nomadic hunter-gatherer lifestyle to a sedentary existence was crucial and first occurred, so far as we know, in the Near East."

Crucial? Crucial for whom? Perhaps the development he indicates was *a misfortune*, similar to the misfortune of animal agriculture for certain animals.

Sass's argument is that "materials guided the course of history":

> "Because materials and their uses have evolved, they lead us back to the foundations of human society, and map the movement from a hunter-gatherer style of life toward a more sedentary existence centered around cities. Dense areas of population develop as the materials that foster them become more sophisticated; the denser the population, the more sophisticated the building blocks. So, too, the higher we go literally (airplanes, skyscrapers) the more complex the substances that take us there."

I do not want to appear mean to Sass here, what I am trying to demonstrate is that he speaks for most of us. He is certainly in good company. The materialist conception of history, as developed by Marx and Engels, provides a similar narrative. They also find that technology and production are the keys to changes in "legal and political superstructures" and the transformation of "social consciousness." Of course, Sass came along long after Marx, and may not consider himself a Marxist, but he is iterating a materialist view of human history. Other writers who have mined the idea that technology is the motor for human 'progress' are the archaeologist Ian Hodder, who argues interestingly that it is our 'entanglements' with *things* — and the fact that these things create problems that need to be solved, usually by the invention of other things — that has driven and continues to drive human history, and historian Yuval Noah Harari.

Harari, in *Sapiens: A Brief History of Humankind*, finds the origin of human flourishing (read: civilization) in something more specific than does Hodder. He argues that people became enslaved to 'wheat' and it was the growing of this crop that enabled the rise of civilization. But these, essentially Marxian theories, were pre-empted by Jean-Jacques Rousseau in 1754 when he wrote:

> "For the poet, it is gold and silver; but for the philosopher it is iron and wheat that have civilized men and sealed the fate of the human race."

With Sass we can see that an aspect of the civilizing sermon is a universalization, or casting back over all history, of the 'modern human' — the civilized creature. This trans-historical universalization has enabled thinkers in the area of evolutionary psychology, such as E.O. Wilson, Steven Pinker, Jane Goodall and Richard Wrangham to validate the notion that humans need a State and civilization to control their violent, 'chimp-like' irrationality and curb the 'eternal' phenomenon of the "demonic male," when, in fact, the State is 'merely' the managerial solution for a too-large population.

The evolutionary psychology view posits humans as essentially, ontologically, 'evil' and in need of civilizing — which is an error in the understanding of what morality is. So, their mistake leads not only to a misunderstanding of morality, but a confusion in regard to the State and civilization that raises both to a mystical level. Gilles Deleuze and Felix Guattari affirmed the incomprehensible godhead of the State when they wrote: "The state appears all at once, and fully armed." If we understand that the State is not some mystic form, but the structure of control, in its various manifestations (chiefdom, totalitarian, democratic, etc), required to manage an over-large population, then the State and civilization is demystified.

> *To be fully clear. The reason we are stuck with a managerial form of society that can be called a State is because for some reason humans in an area became too numerous for the old ways of organizing the social group (which can be glimpsed by looking at the ethnography of 'non-civilized' peoples of today or the past) to continue. Since that misfortune numbers have only risen, and with that so has the development of different types of civilization... until we have what we have today, the first almost truly global economic and social civilization, which has been delivered to us by the*

arrival of the particular wealth generating process known as capitalism. Capitalism is now our society, our social form, our form of reproduction, and we are functionaries of the reproduction of our society (capitalism), just as the social units of any society are functionaries in the reproduction of that society.

However, we are stuck with the huge population, and reducing it would make no difference to our socially constructed perspectives anyway. We would still distribute our pedagogy, our judgementalism, our 'imperialism.' Calls from 'the West' for putting the break on population growth are typically framed within the racist narrative that views 'less developed' parts of the world as backward and ignorant. But any call for a reduction in population, from wherever it emanates, misunderstands why there is a large population and why, although it is what has got us into this mess (by causing the establishment of civilization), **it is not the problem.**

It is important to understand where one sits in the debate on what civilization might be, and what humans are. If we are to seriously imply that 'uncontacted tribes' are stuck hopelessly in an eternal misery of grindingly violent just-post-chimp survivalism and reproductionism... then we had better, if we care about people, liberate them from their plight as soon as possible. This is what Bolsonaro and Modi — to their credit *in terms of honesty* — state explicitly.

Harari, amusingly, goes even further than Sass in his depiction of 'early humans' being just like us modern folk when he writes:

> "On a hike in East Africa 2 million years ago, you might well have encountered a familiar cast of human characters: anxious mothers cuddling their babies and clutches of carefree children playing in the mud; temperamental youths chafing against the dictates of society and weary elders who just wanted to be left in peace; chest-thumping machos trying to impress the local beauty and wise old matriarchs who had already seen it all."

Here is a famous modern historian projecting back through two million years of time the image of a modern family... as if 'history' itself actually means nothing. He urges us to presume that humans behaved and organized themselves in the same way as they do now — but with less knowledge, and less technology — through every different condition of human existence. It is a *Fred Flintstone* narrative of history.

Maybe Harari didn't mean to push a sermon upholding the fantasy of the eternal immutable nature of the human being and the savior values of civilization... but that's what he did. And Pinker would be glad.

Must we continue to listen to the civilizing sermon at almost every intersection of methodology and logic, in all spheres of life, in all discussion?

References and further reading:

Bloom, A. 1991, Prefaces, Notes and Interpretative Essay, in *The Republic of Plato*, Second Edition, Allan Bloom (trans.), Basic Books, New York.

Clastres, P. 2013, *Society Against the State*, Robert Hurley with Abe Stein (trans.), Zone books, New York.

Deleuze, G. 1995, *Negotiations,1972-1990*, Martin Joughin (trans.), Columbia University Press, New York.

Foucault, M. 1969, *The Archaeology of Knowledge*, A.M. Sheridan Smith (trans.), Routledge, 2002.

Foucault, M. 1971, 'Nietzsche, Genealogy, History,' in *The Foucault Reader*, Paul Rabinow (ed.), Pantheon, NY, 1984.

R. Brian Ferguson, *Born to Live*, 2011, and articles online and a forthcoming work.

Foucault, M. 2002, *The Archaeology of Knowledge*, Routledge Classics, London.

Harari, Y. N. 2015, *Sapiens: A Brief History of Humankind*, HarperCollins, New York.

Harrison, P. 2017, *The Freedom of Things: An Ethnology of Control*, TSI Press, Fair Lawn, NJ.

Hodder, I. 2012, *Entangled: An Archaeology of the Relationships between Humans and Things*, Wiley-Blackwell, Chichester.

Marx, K., *A Contribution to the Critique of Political Economy*, and *The 18th Brumaire of Louis Napoleon*.

Rousseau, J-J. 2011, *Jean-Jacques Rousseau: Basic Political Writings, Second Edition*, Donald A. Cress (ed. and trans.), Hackett, Indianapolis.

Sass, S. L. 1998, *The Substance of Civilization: Materials and Human History from the Stone Age to the Age of Silicon*, Arcade Publishing Inc., New York.

Suddendorf, T. 2013, *The Gap: The Science Of What Separates Us From Other Animals*, Basic Books, New York.

Survival International dot org.

8 Adani and The Purpose of Education

Recently [2020], *Survival International*, the organization that campaigns with and for 'tribal peoples,' ran a story about the Indian conglomerate, Adani Group, setting up a Tribal Residential School for children in Bankishole, Baripada, in Mayurbhanj District in Odisha State[1] — a region in Eastern India known for its tribal communities. Adani is best recognized internationally for its mining activities, particularly its recent struggle to get a mine authorized in coal-addicted Australia in the face of massive popular protests.

Tribal Residential Schools have come under scrutiny from Survival International in recent months.[2] As Chairperson for the *Adani Foundation*, Dr Priti Adani said at the opening of the school, which is partnered with the *Kalinga Institute of Social Sciences* (KISS) — an organization that describes itself as 'A Home for 30000 Indigenous Children': "Education is the most powerful tool for social transformation."[3]

It sure is! It creates wage slaves that know their place in society and who are then able to operate as functions in the exploitative hierarchy of capitalism. But, in their short video[4] — which really does have to be seen to be believed and would be an inspiration for Jair Bolsonaro — KISS put their mission much more clearly: "transforming social liabilities into social assets... and converting tax consumers into tax-payers: a unique educational initiative for social transformation and peace."

But, as Survival International report, there are voices of Indigenous resistance.[5] Local Indigenous activist, Soni Sori:

> "We resist this kind of education. Whoever it may come from — Adani or anyone. They give their kind of education because they want our children to

---

[1] "Brazen and shameless:" outrage as controversial Indian mining company opens tribal school, *Survival International*, 12th January 2020.
[2] 'Factory Schools,' *Survival International*.
[3] 'Adani-KISS Inaugurates School,' *The Pioneer* (online Newspaper), 17th January, 2020.
[4] 'KISS Prayer' – on YouTube.
[5] 'Factory Schools: Crimes Against Children,' *Survival International*, Vimeo.

hate jungles. They want our children to hate their own culture. They want to create distance between children and parents."

The story of KISS and Adani is truly disconcerting, but there is a wider issue here too. The truth is that there can be no bridging between the educational systems of modern states and Indigenous ways of raising children. The only outcome of such an alliance is the eventual eradication of Indigenous ways of living.

We live globally within what could be called *a Pedagogical Society*. I would argue that pedagogy stands equally alongside exploitation and hierarchy as a defining characteristic and imperative of 'Western,' modern state, or capitalist society. The notion that 'education' is a good and necessary thing is so pervasive that very few people question it, yet there are signs all around us that education may not quite be what it appears to be.

One could start with its coercive aspect. There are only three sectors of society that are forcibly institutionalized: criminals; the insane (who may be a danger to themselves or others); and children. School is compulsory. Criminals and the insane are put away in order to keep society safe and to be rehabilitated. Children are put away, usually on a day-release scheme... to be 'rehabilitated' *before* they have even done anything 'wrong.'

To get a clearer picture of what education really is it is useful to compare our pedagogical society with non-pedagogical societies. Indigenous societies, if they still have some independence, are not pedagogically oriented. They view learning as a process that must be initiated by the learner and that should proceed at the learner's pace. I am talking broadly here of course but my arguments are derived from, and supported by, the work of anthropologists and educationalists such as Jean-Guy Goulet, Paul Nadasdy, Gustavo Esteva, Peter Gray, Ansgar Allen, Maurice Bloch, and my own involvement with Indigenous Australians.

The most basic expression of the pedagogy at the heart of our global state society is the school. Here the emphasis is — in reality — all on the teaching and the teacher, despite the amount of punishment that might be meted out on the students. This is the reason — since John Dewey at least — that well-intentioned educationalists have recurringly tried to make schooling 'constructive' and based on the learner. In a school situation 'learners' are rounded up and presented with an array of ideological techniques and physical mechanisms that are designed to keep them either engaged or undisruptive. The educationalist, William Glasser, for example, argued that classrooms should be places where students enjoy themselves so much that they do not even realize they are learning. This may sound a worthy endeavor, but there are two immediate problems here. Firstly, as several educationalists have written or implied *affirmatively*, the idea is to 'trick' children into learning. Secondly, as anyone who has seen the waves of educational initiatives wash over school systems year in year out — getting nowhere, even Finland is now falling behind — it is clear that all the work of 'learning' is placed upon the teacher. Students at whatever 'ability level' — it's an open secret — do as little thinking as possible and the teacher does almost all the work. This situation leads to a war of attrition between teacher and student. Only the best and most hardworking teachers are able to maintain a happy atmosphere where grades are acceptable, though they do not usually last too long in the system — while bad and middling teachers carry on unaware of the mediocrity they perpetuate. Teachers could be compared to prison guards: it is better to have respectful and sensitive ones guarding you.

The anthropologist Jean-Guy Goulet in his work with the Dene Tha' of Northern Alberta notes that their society has principles of 'non-interference,' and 'non-intervention' — which means that people will only be given help when they ask for it. To many of us this might seem awful. But what it means is that the autonomy of everyone is respected. In our society we don't have time for such niceties. We will help the old man across the road before he even asks for help because we want the getting across the road to be done quickly. The Dene Tha' might say that in what we perceive as our kindness there is only impatience and disrespect. Correspondingly with learning: children are not rounded up and given instruction. Learning is expected to occur at a time when the learner wants it, through observation. Later, as anthropologist Paul Nadasdy — in *Hunters and Bureaucrats: Power, Knowledge, and Aboriginal-State Relations in the Southwest Yukon* — explains: experts may refine the knowledge gained through observation and mimicry. But only when the learner requests it, through a gentle process of story-telling, correcting mistakes — practically and without a judgmental lecture — and humor.

Every society, naturally, works to reproduce itself, and how children are raised shows how a society views the people who make it up. In Indigenous societies children are trusted to reproduce society. They are given time to work out how things are done. In modern state society children are not trusted to reproduce society... and one wonders why that might be! Parents, education systems, and government are in a continual panic that children need to be trained to cooperate properly in our hierarchical and exploitative society. We don't trust our children. We could ask: What kind of sick society distrusts its children? But it would be better to ask: Why is it necessary for us to distrust our children?[6]

The rise of pedagogy is a reversal of traditional learning and it is a necessary consequence of ensuring that people are trained to work as functions in an exploitative society. It would be no good to let children run around all day in capitalism — they would reject the idea that they should become wage slaves in an inescapable hierarchy. And us adults wouldn't be able to cope with hordes of kids wrecking all the signs and symbols — shops, parks, amenities, workplaces, cars, etc — of our slave condition.

And, to finish, the dissemination of the ethos of exploitation and hierarchy does not stop at the school level. From *The Freedom of Things: An Ethnology of Control*:

> "The University is central to the process. The University sucks in radicality and spits out better ways to manage situations for the benefit of 'progress.' It is never a repository of innocent or objective knowledge. On the contrary, it is an action on the world, a one-way dialogue that disingenuously presents itself as epistemic and objective in the same way that all the aspects of 'Western' existence constitute *a way of life*. In Indigenous tradition there is no university and there is no school because such institutions are the markers and the standard bearers of a different way of living."

Adani and the Kalinga Institute of Social Sciences are right: those Indigenous kids need to be schooled.

[After writing this I was informed of the video *Schooling the World*, from 2010, directed by Carol Black, which asks the question: "If you wanted to change a culture in a generation, how would you do it?"]

---

[6] See footnote 6, in *Misunderstanding Agamben and Camatte*.

9 From Goodall to Pinker to Bolsonaro

(The Grievous Trajectory of Jane Goodall's Theoretical Arrow)

I

We civilized humans seem to think we know everything — except perhaps how to behave decently and rationally *all* the time, as Dr. Jane Goodall noted when comparing Donald Trump to an anthropomorphized image of the 'male' chimpanzee[1] — it is the methodologies and exalted stature of *the sciences*, including history, that have conferred upon us this mantle of knowledge.

As *Sapiens: A Brief History of Humankind* author, Yuval Noah Harari, opines:

> "Today [humanity] stands on the verge of becoming a god, poised to acquire not only eternal youth, but also the divine abilities of creation and destruction."

Long before Harari waxed lyrical about the potential omniscience of humankind the philosopher Ludwig Feuerbach set down a far sounder reason than Harari has for humankind's apparently transcendental consciousness (Schopenhauer and Nietzsche possibly came up with the most useful, by-the-way[2]). Feuerbach's notion was generated from the ways he saw science changing knowledge. Humans, he argued, now had the ability to know everything — not as individuals but as a collective.

To explain with an analogy: people who use buses in a big city know the routes they take, the numbers of the buses, the places they stop. But they don't know all the routes. However, if you brought together all the bus users in the city then any question about how to get from one place to another by bus would be answered. The collective knowledge of the group would, therefore, be a complete knowledge, although individuals could not acquire it as their own personal

---

[1] 'World renowned primatologist likens US President to a chimpanzee,' 2017, *The Independent*.
[2] See: Paul Katsafanas, *The Nietzschean Self*, OUP, 2017. Particularly Chapter 3.

knowledge. In the same way, the only way for bus route planners or coordinators to access this complete knowledge is through documentation, but they cannot, generally speaking, then hold all this knowledge in their individual heads. (Therefore, the usefulness and potential power of computers.)

In a similar way, any scientist has access to all the work of every other scientist and so, theoretically, the totality of scientific research, past and present, amounts to the full knowledge of the world at any particular time. Individual scientists do not know everything but as a group that has recorded its findings... they do. This final frontier of knowledge and science makes the human species, according to Feuerbach, special. Humans have — what amounts to — a collective consciousness (Marx framed it within the term 'general intellect'), and modern science makes that consciousness omniscient. This collective consciousness — stored in libraries of various kinds — allows science to move very quickly in developing new technologies. This then enables what appears to us as an exponential growth in 'progress' over even very short periods of time... a technological 'revolution' every few years.

But this progress is not the progress of humans as humans. The reason many of us, those who are well-intentioned at least, think that humans need to become better, to progress as humans, is because life in civilization is so bad. This is why we have philosophy, and the police; and the impulse to philosophize and police is entirely reasonable, and directly related to the inescapable ethos of progress that is written into our DNA by capital. But the actual progress happening is only the progress of things. Yes, humans change because of the things that are around them, but the 'purpose' of progress is not to develop the human being — to develop enjoyment, leisure, connection and independence — the purpose is to make wealth. Steven Pinker, for example, argues that advances in technology, along with the development of the institutions that govern us, have made us better people — but he warns that most people, and here he consciously echoes Hobbes, are essentially *bad* and if left to their own devices they would revert to all sorts of evil practices. Using this reasoning one can only conclude that the tribespeoples of the Amazon and elsewhere must be living in awful conditions as well as being unspeakably nasty to each other — and so, following Pinker's logic, if we genuinely care about others, we should support the efforts of Brazil's Bolsonaro, and India's Modi, to 'improve' their lives.

II

Eminent thinkers, Richard Wrangham, Dale Petersen, Jane Goodall, Pinker and E. O. Wilson essentially share a common approach in how to interpret and understand what they view as 'human nature.' They share what is, for all intents and purposes, an 'evolutionary psychology' viewpoint. This strand of scientific exploration finds much evidence and justification in the famous studies of chimpanzees — 'our closest living relative' — in Gombe National Park in Tanzania, led by Jane Goodall. There is, I suggest, a direct methodological and theoretical arrow fired, perhaps unwittingly, by Goodall that ends at Pinker… but — *if we keep following the logic* — it becomes apparent that the arrow does not stop at Pinker, it lands at the feet of Jair Bolsonaro and Narendra Modi.

Evolutionary psychology tells us that we can begin to understand what motivates present day civilized humans by looking into how humans of the past reacted psychologically to the environments they lived in. A simple example: humans have a 'fight or flight' response to potential danger because in 'caveman' days humans were always being surprised by saber-toothed tigers that wanted to eat them. Evolutionary psychology also tells us that people can only be relatively free when they are released from the imperatives of survival and reproduction — and such freedom can only be found (of course!) in civilization. This means that all 'primitive peoples' are oppressed by the daily struggle to survive and reproduce. And all other animals are equally fettered. This is why other animals and tribal peoples have no decent art museums or concert halls and no bands like The Rolling Stones[3] — they are too busy staving off hunger all day and trying to have more kids.

It is interesting, by-the-way, that the world's population only exploded after the emergence of 'sedentary agriculture,' which, according to many academics and other apologists for civilization, "enabled rapid population growth."[4] So maybe those 'primitive,' un-enslaved folk weren't even very good at having children…

These well-accepted academic notions about humans 'before' civilization contain some very stupid assumptions. They assume, if you follow the logic properly, that humans prior to civilization were not 'masters' of their environment in the same way that any other animal is 'master' of their

---

[3] See them performing *(I Can't Get No) Satisfaction* in 2019, here.
[4] Thomas Suddendorf, *The Gap: The Science of What Separates Us From Other Animals*, Basic Books, 2013, p270.

environment. It projects back the notion of a modern/civilized human who has not been educated or taught how to dress properly and adds to this the image of a human who is constantly surprised and overwhelmed by the environment they inhabit. These weird fictional 'projected-back people'[5] are only able to become better at living when they have discovered fire; when they have discovered the wheel; when they have learned to trade and to read; when they have discovered the refrigerator...

So, these fictional people of the long-ago past have two important features: they are simultaneously helpless *and* stupid. It is only on the long road to present-day civilization that they become *less* helpless and *less* stupid.

If we think more about how humans 'like us' coped in the wild before television, we discover that we should see all other animals as helpless and stupid too — all of them *only just managing* to survive in their environments. And we must also see all the tribespeoples around the world — who live in the forests, in the hills, and on the plains — as equally helpless and stupid. We are forced to wonder just how these people are surviving *right now* — the misery they must be in! They must be so stressed by their helplessness and the fearful environment they inhabit. Then we are forced to wonder how the 'anatomically-modern' human species survived for the vast majority of its existence — 200,000 years at least — without the benefits of civilization (which began arriving around 7000 years ago), in this continually helpless and surprised state. If they were so helpless and stupid why didn't they die-out long ago, or did civilization save them just in the nick of time? And how is it that all the helpless and stupid animals that inhabit the world seem to carry on surviving? And how come the Yanomami are still here, or the Sentinelese? Questions, questions...

How do/did these groups — modern day tribespeoples; humans who lived between 200,000 and 7000 years ago; and all the animals — manage to persist in such awful circumstances? Their stress levels — due to their stupidity and helplessness — must be, and have been, through the roof. Once again — if we follow the line of the logic — we have no option but to support the humanitarian work of Jair Bolsonaro and Narendra Modi in trying to rescue 'primitive' peoples from their own foolish lifestyles and ignorance. And not only are the tribes of the Amazon and India stupid and helpless, badly dressed, not dressed at all, and lacking in civilized etiquette... they are in the way of making a few dollars. They need to be proletarianized, and if a lot of them die in the process... well, it's no big deal... In this scenario — under the logical big tent erected by Goodall *et al*

---

[5] See the movie *Quest for Fire*, 1981, from which here is a clip.

— Bolsonaro and Modi win twice: firstly, they are doing humanity a favour by bringing civilized behaviour to the savages and, secondly, they are helping their friends make money.

This is the logic required in order to keep faith with the theories and fancies of experts such as Goodall and Pinker. If one uncovers and follows the Enlightenment logic and the civilizing sermon embedded in her research one is drawn to this uncomfortable conclusion, despite her good intentions.

III

It was Marx, interestingly — or alarmingly, depending on the depth of one's investment in Marx — who taught us just how the human species is able to know everything. He went further than Feuerbach, turning Feuerbach's notions of collective human possibility into the science of sociology — the discipline for which he is considered a founder. After Marx, sociological studies were grounded in the empirical collation of factors that amounted to the totality of the economic and social environments that people lived in. If one was to reveal true human motivations it was no longer any use listening to what people said about themselves, one had to investigate their economic and social circumstances. Marx wrote:

> "Whilst in ordinary life every shopkeeper is very well able to distinguish between what somebody professes to be and what he really is, our historians have not yet won even this trivial insight. They take every epoch at its word and believe that everything it says and imagines about itself is true." (*The German Ideology*, 1846)

There is a lot to be said for this approach of course, but the problem with it is that it doesn't always work — in fact, it *never* works in societies without economies, and it works *less well* in societies that have economies that are different to capitalist ones. Money makes liars and deceivers of us all, not always because we are 'bad,' usually because we just want to survive.

Jean Baudrillard pointed out in the early 1970s that the Marxist effort to explain human motivations through the economic environment does not work if the society does not have an economy. Marxists, for their part, have struggled with how to incorporate 'primitive societies' into Marxist methodology, and so have all the other anthropologists who look for the *economic* motor as the key to understanding human societies. The anthropologist Richard Lee, for example, tried his Marxist best to argue that 'primitive society' was a society of economic production with his theory of the 'communal mode of production.' But his argument is ultimately unconvincing. Marshall Sahlins appears more sure-footed: "even to speak of '*the* economy' of a primitive society is an exercise in unreality." Though it is left to Pierre Clastres to state it outright: "there are no production relations [in societies outside of history] because there is no production, for this is the last concern of primitive society."

Marx's sociology works superbly in a capitalist society and so the famous *Annales School* in France decided to study the history of previous epochs — societies with States and classes, not 'primitive societies' — using a form of this Marxist lens. But the broad and compelling histories produced by this school are riven with the same smug, self-congratulatory, vein that runs through the vast bulk of academic work. For them, as with most other historians in fact, it is as if all previous hierarchical and exploitative societies are precursors to an inevitable capitalism. Their approach was to look at societies in the manner of a *Sherlock Holmes* — to place the whole society under their penetrating magnifying glass in order to discover 'the truth.' But like all such endeavors — maybe excepting those of *Holmes* himself — what they really obtained from their studies was only the 'truth' that they already had in their minds.

For example, Fernand Braudel was able to write of (*nine-thousand-year-old*) Çatalhöyük: "But what must be remembered is that the most important source of income for the town was trade." The presumption of 'town,' 'income,' and 'trade' forces upon us a particularly *modern* representation of Çatalhöyük. Braudel encourages us to believe that we could look at what went on there through the eyes of a local *some nine thousand years ago*. But he could 'discover' these things only because *that was all he was looking for*: "[Çatalhöyük and other towns] had made a start, prefiguring the future... At some point these ventures received a mortal blow... [and they] would simply disappear [but] local setbacks notwithstanding, it was here [in the Middle East] that civilization would first spring to life." Braudel was enamored of modern civilization and wanted to uncover its glorious beginnings. Braudel, by-the-way, gave no indication for why these 'early civilizations' disappeared, and he glossed over this fascinating problem — you see, if one is a professional one must ensure that people fail to notice the holes or problems in one's theses, even if they might be apparent to oneself. He was a *Sherlock Holmes* with rose-tinted spectacles, who felt able to pat

Nihil Evadere

what he considered to be a baby civilization on the head for its sterling efforts: 'Well done, Çatalhöyük!'[6]

Braudel's most famous student, Emmanuel Le Roy Ladurie, in 1990, wrote the 'micro-historical' account of a medieval French village titled, *Montaillou*. This was a painstaking investigation that claimed, as he wrote, to have "got down to the basic unit, the unit of the people, the peasants" in order to discover what "made a citizen of Montaillou 'tick' above such basic biological drives as food and sex."

But Le Roy Ladurie should have tried harder — not in his meticulous research but in the effort to be humble or, rather, to intelligently acknowledge that despite all his research he could never see the world *through the eyes* of the people he studied, and so he could never really know them as he claimed.

To explain with an analogy: we can, for example, *understand* when someone tells us that medieval peasants lived by a cyclical calendar derived from agrarian existence but, despite this, we are unable to view time as *a rotation* because we cannot look up from this page and comfortably accept, or throw out the notion, that time is not *linear*. As the historian A. J. Gurevich writes of the transition from feudal to urban capitalist conceptions of time: "The alienation of time from its concrete content raised the possibility of viewing it as a pure categorical form, as duration unburdened by matter."[7] It was the success of the introduction of supply chains, distribution, and factory work, culminating in railway timetables, that led to the abandonment of any sense that time was 'cyclical,' 'seasonal,' or connected to the earth. This linear expression of time is now hard-wired into our brains. (As Baudrillard insists, "it is the object which thinks us... it is the world which thinks us,"[8] so, as he might also have written: the clock thinks us.)

---

[6] Fernand Braudel, *The Mediterranean in the Ancient World* (1969), Siân Reynolds (trans.), Penguin, 2001, Chapter 2, 'The Long March to Civilization.'

[7] A. J. Gurevich, *Categories of Medieval Culture* (1972), G.L. Campbell (trans.), Routledge, 1985, p150.

[8] Jean Baudrillard, *Impossible Exchange* (1999), Chris Turner (trans.), Verso, 2001, p110. I use this quote because I think it is useful 'to think with' in this context. I am, of course, aware that Baudrillard's 'strategy' concerning 'objects' and 'subjects' was *pataphysical,* or as might be said today, 'crypto-communist,' or 'crypto-utopian.' In his last formulations for 'radical change,' he suggests that since objects have taken over all subjectivity 'we' should push this 'post-modern' development to its extreme, in order to see, at least, what might happen; this is the method he indicates by his "Fatal Strategies."

IV

We cannot see through the eyes of a person inhabiting a different mode of living. Our consciousness is determined by the daily life we live, and the principles and values generated by and acting upon this actual daily existence. Once a society is established, then that society becomes an organic whole, a *mode of living* (not necessarily, of course, an 'economy'). A twenty-first century Parisian can as little *decide* to understand time as a cyclical component of the universe as a medieval European peasant could decide to understand time as a separate linear, irreversible, category of the universe.

So, Marx's *Sociology* and the discipline of *Evolutionary Psychology* are the twin methodologies that tell us how humans work in the world — at *any time* and *in any environment and situation*. We are, according to these thinkers, shaped and beset, for all of time, and in any circumstance, by the psychological inheritance of, for example, 'fight or flight,' or 'the demonic male,' and our 'basic need' to *survive*.

In fact, it appears that the whole approach to the study of humans and other animals is based on the tenets of *survivalism*. Apparently, the world is a tough place, full of things that want to eat you or kill you for no reason. The primary task of every animal is therefore to survive these challenges and reproduce themselves, whether it be through surviving in a forest, or creating the technology that enables humans to live in houses and drive cars — and if we think that we have any other real motivations then the historians and sociologists can tell us that these other motivations are secondary, or peripheral, to *survival*, or reproduction. Indeed, this perspective works wonders in explaining the way we live in modern civilization, or capitalism, where money is the meter of the rhythm of our lives: what we recognize as art, philosophy, poetry, and love, are all, in our society simple functions of money, the way we live our lives, and the things we do, are all facilitated by money or its absence. In civilization survival is indeed our imperative, from school to death.

So, is *survivalism* the ethos of 'primitive peoples'? No. They laze about in hammocks, and never work. Their days are full of play and drama. They live a life rich in dreams and connection to their environment, as Davi Kopenawa has explained in *The Falling Sky*.

One of the amusing consequences of the combination of evolutionary psychology with Marxist, or sociological, explanations of how societies apparently operate are these lines, used twice elsewhere in this volume, from Yuval Noah Harari in his book *Sapiens*:

> "On a hike in East Africa 2 million years ago, you might well have encountered a familiar cast of human characters: anxious mothers cuddling their babies and clutches of carefree children playing in the mud; temperamental youths chafing against the dictates of society and weary elders who just wanted to be left in peace; chest-thumping machos trying to impress the local beauty and wise old matriarchs who had already seen it all." (Harari: 4: 2015)

The family group he describes could be any family group from present-day Los Angeles — only *two million* years ago.

But, here, at the close, I want to cut back to *survivalism*. While survivalism is not the logos and ethos of the 'uncontacted tribes,' *it is for us*, and there can be no escaping it. While we can *recognize* that we exist mainly simply to survive and generate wealth for an effectively automated economy it would be foolish and *evil* to use such knowledge to argue that we should fight for the non-survival of the great mass of humanity, or our relatives and friends... as Giorgio Agamben and those on the Christian right, who yearn for the Apocalypse, have done: let Covid rip through the populations, God, or 'life,' will find a way.

10 The Last Humans

(or Why 'Revolutionaries' Should Drop their Millenarianism and support Survival International)

There are two types of 'human being' on the planet, but only one type can truly call itself human.

The 'human beings' who *cannot* truly call themselves human include myself and all the others who are products and functions — not of the earth from which we originate — but of the economy we know as capitalism... whether they reap the benefits of the demented 'wealth' that capitalism generates, or whether they struggle to survive in the depths of the madness that is the flipside of the madness of progress and technological advance. These so-called humans (you and I) are fictions, or creations — or the hollowed-out drones — of an uncontrollable and autonomous economy that has severed all their links — beyond romantic fancies and false claims — to other animals and the earth itself.

The other type is the one that still lives in the forests, in the hills, or on the plains, avoiding the advances of civilization. But their existence is precarious and is becoming more fragile with each passing day. These peoples are the last humans.

Many of us — I used to be one — nurture the dream of a worldwide communist revolution during which capitalism is overthrown and people are suddenly able to live together as equals in a society where there is no systematic hierarchy and no exploitation, where we can decide ourselves what to do and when to do it, where commonality and community is the bond that ties us together instead of money.

These dreams exist on paper, or in digital form, but when they have appeared to come close to realization — for example, in 1649, 1789, and 1917 — they have ended in a totalitarianism even worse than previously experienced. Were these events 'failures' or were they inevitable?

Nihil Evadere

Jean-Jacques Rousseau, whose book, 'The Social Contract,' was used by Robespierre to justify the Terror in the French Revolution, would have opposed both Robespierre and his millenarian leanings. As David Wootton writes in his introduction to Rousseau's 'Basic Political Writings': "Robespierre and the Jacobins admired him greatly, but they misunderstood him profoundly (their Rousseau was invented to serve their own purposes)."[1] But we now *also* know that the French Revolution was the inevitable result of the change in the economy that preceded it. The new entrepreneurs, the industrialists, and the bureaucrats had become the real power prior to 1789 and it was inevitable that that power had to become recognized in the social structure. It was the children[2] of the new economic masters who were the revolutionaries who gave voice to this inevitable institutional change of power — and their promise of democracy and freedom chimed with lower class discontent and anger. The same thing happened in England in 1649 and in Russia in 1917.

After their respective revolutions, things in France and England were dictatorial and messy. The French solved the problem with Napoleon and embarked on an Enlightenment crusade to conquer Europe, this lasted a long time but eventually things got back to some kind of 'normal.' The English got Oliver Cromwell and conquered the Irish, the new regime did not last too long and, after a while, things got back to normal. In Russia the dictatorship lasted a long time and things are still getting back to 'normal.' In Cuba — which may well be, as many people suggest, a better place in which to live than the USA — the transition to 'normal' is still in its early stages.

In each case there was only a change in the ruling class and capitalism won.

In England the change of rulers forever altered the political power structure and paved the way for Industrialization. In France the same thing happened, which is why the French Revolution is identified as a *Bourgeois Revolution*. In Russia capitalism won big time: after 1917 Russia implemented the fastest and most brutal industrialization the world would ever see. In Cuba the economy has not seen the rapid transformation that the nationalist Cuban business leaders who initially supported Fidel Castro had hoped for, and progress has been slow for various reasons, but current leaders are now allowing the concept of private property to enter the political dialogue. In China capitalism also won big. Their Industrial transformation has imitated Russia, and the country

---

[1] D. Wootton, Introduction, *Basic Political Writings*, J-J Rousseau, 2011, Hackett, p ix.
[2] See *Fascism is Not a Pathology*, beginning of Part III.

remains under full dictatorship. North Korea suffers the same kind of economic difficulties and slowness as Cuba... but is not as good a holiday destination as Cuba.

The story of the Garden of Eden is an interesting example of our fate as humans once we allowed hierarchy and exploitation—the State—to rule our lives. But this story, and similar ones from other cultures, insisted that 'the golden age' could not be recreated on earth, it could only be found after death... in heaven. From the time of the first State, when the first Garden of Eden story emerged, everything was about the economy and making the rulers increasingly wealthy... it was all about the treasure, the opulence for some, and the money... and the sinful poor were meant to accept that this was basically all their fault.

The Garden of Eden story is known as the story of the fall from 'grace,' but it is easy to see that the 'grace' is the time before drudgery and exploitation. The religions that told the story were informing the subjects of the new civilizations that things were such — Rousseau said it was because everyone was now dependent on everyone else — that there was no going back to some golden age, they had to get on with toiling for their betters in the name of God, so they could secure a place in heaven. Civilization is a hamster wheel that promises new worlds, but ends where it began, in a cage.

But the image of the Garden of Eden also served those who hated the new conditions as an inspiration to indeed do the apparently impossible and not wait for death but recreate 'the golden age' on earth. Rousseau recognized this impulse in himself and others, but he warned that it should ever only remain an idle fancy.

Civilized people — us hollowed-out drones of the capitalist economy, us non-humans — are stuck in a situation from which there is no way out. Ecofascist types, who want to remove Indigenous peoples from 'nature' in order to preserve it — just like the National Park Service did for native peoples in the US a hundred years or so ago, and Modi is doing in India right now — are as misguided as that other kind of ecofascist who thinks drastically reducing the number of people on the planet will lead to some kind of utopia.

We can't suddenly change who we are. We are slaves to capitalism, who only know how to live a capitalistic life. We would tell people what to do and we would punish those who didn't do what we said — because this is embedded in

Nihil Evadere

our pedagogical culture.[3] This is exactly what happened in the Russian Revolution. The new capitalist visionaries — I mean, of course, the Bolsheviks — took over and did exactly what capitalism 'wanted,' which was not at all what the promise of communism was supposed to be. Despite Lenin's great intellect he never realized that he was *not* the harbinger of 'communism' — he never realized that *he was never anything more* than *a function* of capitalism. As were all the revolutionaries in Russia at that time, as are all the revolutionaries today... as we *all* are, of course.

So, to carry on living in this world, if that is even an option allowed us by the impending ecological catastrophe, we non-humans — *we no-longer-humans, we products and functions of the economy* — have to keep trying to make the best of a bad job.

But there is one single thing we can do that would help to save our 'reputation' in the vast balance-sheet of 'human' history — and that is to completely seal off those areas of the world that contain the tribespeoples and the 'uncontacted tribes' who somehow seem to have always known the evils of civilization, and so have avoided it for millennia.

These peoples are the last humans. They are the revolution that has always been here. They have had no 'fall from grace' in the way we have. They do not live in drudgery and empty despair; they have not had their spirit and humanity hollowed out of them.

But we cannot join with them. We must leave them alone. The revolution has always been with us. We must let it live.

---

[3] See *Adani and the Purpose of Education*.

11 Can We Halt the Complete Colonization of all Humans?

> External obstacles are now only technological, and only internal rivalries remain. A world market extends to the ends of the earth before passing into the galaxy: even the skies become horizontal. This is not a result of the [Ancient] Greek endeavor but a resumption, in another form and with other means, on a scale hitherto unknown, which nonetheless relaunches the combination for which the Greeks took the initiative — democratic imperialism, colonizing democracy.
>
> The European can, therefore, regard himself [sic], as the Greek did, as not one psychosocial type among others but Man par excellence, and with much more expansive force and missionary zeal than the Greek.
> Gilles Deleuze and Félix Guattari, 1991

Western culture — which is effectively global — is a culture of materialism and scientific rationality — grounded, of course, in the capitalism that guides and shapes our daily lives. To be more specific, Western culture is *Spinozian* — for Spinoza successfully concluded that the mind and matter were the same substance, thereby presciently defeating (think neurons and neurotransmitters)[1] the mind/body dualism of Descartes which was the last defense of the 'immortal soul' of organized religion — *and Marxian* — for Marx transformed the philosophic dialectics of Hegel into an empirical sociological system that reflected what was happening in the sciences around him.

Both Spinoza and Marx were expressing the logical, radical endpoints of the Western Enlightenment that was generated by the arrival of capitalism: Spinoza as "the first major figure of the Radical Enlightenment"[2] and Marx as its last.

In 1674 Baruch Spinoza wrote:

---

[1] See, for example, Patricia Churchland, *Braintrust*, 2011, PUP.
[2] Jonathan Israel, *A Revolution of the Mind*, 2010, PUP, p2.

Nihil Evadere

> "Men [sic] are deceived in thinking themselves free, a belief that consists only in this: that they are conscious of their actions and ignorant of the causes by which they are determined.
>
> Therefore, the idea of their freedom is simply the ignorance of the cause of their actions. As to their saying that human actions depend on the will, these are mere words without any corresponding idea. For none of them knows what the will is and how it moves the body, and those who do boast otherwise and make up stories of dwelling places and habitations of the soul provoke either ridicule or disgust." (Take that, Descartes!)

Spinoza believed that true wisdom lay in the aligning of one's intelligence with the immutable truth of the material universe by understanding mathematical proofs. As Israel writes:

> "He gives the example of the earth's rotundity. Only science can prove the earth is round. One may well not believe it is round until shown the proofs. But it is impossible for someone who grasps the proofs to doubt or oppose them sincerely... Hence Spinoza's conception of truth, and the criterion for judging what is true, is 'mathematical logic,' and mathematical rationality universally applied provides, from Spinoza to Marx, the essential link between the Scientific Revolution and the tradition of radical thought."[3]

In his notes for a critique of the philosophy of Ludwig Feuerbach Marx famously wrote: "Philosophers have hitherto only *interpreted* the world in various ways; the point is to *change* it." This line was never a simple urging of philosophers to 'get active' for the good of things, it meant that philosophers had to abandon the world of 'universal absolutes' (think Plato's theory of Forms, or Ideas) and work within the social and environmental processes that were actually in existence. If they did this, Marx believed, they would no longer be 'idle philosophers,' they would be *scientists*.

Echoing Spinoza, Marx writes:

> "In direct contrast to German philosophy [or 'Idealism,' better written as 'Idea-ism,' a development within Plato's theory of Ideas][4] which descends from heaven to earth, here we ascend from earth to heaven. That is to say, we do not set out from what men say, imagine, conceive, nor from men as

---

[3] Israel, J., 2001, *Radical Enlightenment: Philosophy and the Making of Modernity, 1650-1750*, PUP, p244-5.
[4] For an overview see the Wikipedia page: *German idealism*.

narrated, thought of, imagined, conceived, in order to arrive at men in the flesh. We set out from real, active men, and on the basis of their real life-process we demonstrate the development of the ideological reflexes and echoes of this life-process. The phantoms formed in the human brain are also, necessarily, sublimates of their material life-process, which is empirically verifiable and bound to material premises."[5]

Engels further explains how, as Marx put it, 'philosophy as an independent branch of knowledge loses [has, in fact, lost] its medium of existence':

"While natural science up to the end of the last century [1799] was predominantly a *collecting* science, a science of finished things, in our century it is essentially a systematizing science, a science of the processes, of the origin and development of these things and of the interconnection which binds all these natural processes into one great [Spinozian/monist] whole... [so it is with] the Marxist conception of history [which derives its proof] from history itself. This conception, however, puts an end to philosophy in the realm of history, just as the dialectical conception of nature ['a science of *processes*'] makes all natural [traditional] philosophy both unnecessary and impossible. It is no longer a question anywhere of inventing interconnections from out of our brains, but of discovering them in the facts."[6]

Marx's greatest achievement was not to 'predict' or describe communism: it was his thorough and convincing analysis of modern life. The legacy of his insights into how the economy works and how people are apparently constructed in *any* society is now hardwired into all our institutions and social policy. The mirror he held up to his own time, which is still relevant for ours, was powerful because what it revealed was what everyone already knew but hadn't yet expressed. His dialectics only followed what physical and social science was already doing. Westerners had become materialists before he told them that that was what they were — they only realized it, as it were, when he observed it. The rationalism in society that he wished to build on had been generated by the new economic circumstances, it just took his writings to give it a more solid theoretical grounding. But he didn't quite realize the monster he was making even bigger. It could only now be obvious to any enlightened European that — apart from whether private ownership of industry and land is

---

[5] *The German Ideology*, Part 1, Section A, 1845.
[6] Engels, F., *Ludwig Feuerbach and the End of Classical German Philosophy*, Part 4, 1886.

Nihil Evadere

a good or bad thing — they were held back by the persistent irrationality and ignorance[7] of 'the masses'... not only 'at home' but globally.

We can see that Spinoza and Marx thought they were witnessing the advancement — through science — of a rational society, and they wanted to see this promise come into full existence. But there is another important aspect. Both Spinoza and Marx, following science again, were 'monist' — they believed in the 'oneness' of the world and all its workings. So, at the heart of radical thought — as worked out through the Western Enlightenment — is the idea that there is no mind/body dualism, there are no supernatural beings, there are no miracles: everything can be explained by science and rational thinking... that is, *Enlightenment* science, and *Enlightenment* rationality.

> Baruch Spinoza (1632-77) began his career managing the family importing business in Amsterdam, but his passion was creating spectacles. He opened the first ever 'optician's' and his spectacles were worn by many notable contemporaries, such as the philosopher Gottfried Leibniz.

There were, as Jonathan Israel documents, two sides to the Enlightenment — a moderate one (eg, Voltaire, Adam Ferguson) and a radical one (eg, Diderot, Paine). The moderate side was conservative and not so adamant that all falsehoods entertained the world over — by the poor and the foreign — should be actively quashed. Interestingly (you've gotta laugh...), it was the radical side that sought to spread full Enlightenment to all the peoples of the globe.

As Israel notes, the radical *philosophe* Nicolas-Antoine Boulanger argued that "reason, and law founded on reason, should be the only sovereign over mortals."[8] I think that this declaration — on the level of ideas — is the precursor to Marx's 'materialist' declaration that "the veil" of mystification "is not removed" until the reproduction of existence "stands under [the] conscious and planned control" of all. Both are global projects, but Marx's appears to have a more virtuous and more practical strategy attached to it. His plan goes beyond simply stomping around the world saving the poor and 'the savages' from the own ignorance. He thinks they should be an empowered part of the process. (On how 'empowerment' is a double-edged sword now routinely utilized by social agencies the world over, see below.)

---

[7] See, for example, Mikhail Bakunin, *On the Program of the Alliance*, 1871.
[8] Israel, J., *A Revolution of the Mind*, 2010, PUP, p19.

Marx's strategy is more radical than Boulanger's because it is based on the ideal of the attainment of an egalitarian democracy, that is, communism (Frédéric Lordon: "another name for the communist life could be radical democracy")[9]. In this context Boulanger's formula looks like it could simply be an *evangelism* of Western Radical Enlightenment values, whereas Marx's formula appears more 'scientific'. But as it turned out, both systems of enlightenment were *imperialist*. Boulanger and Marx were, of course, conscious of the fact that the rationality they were exporting to the poor and 'the savage' originated in Europe, but they weren't aware that their visions amounted — for the rest of the world — as simply an altering of the European colonial project. Both strategies seek the establishment of *one* rational and harmonious world.

(By-the-way, this interpretation of Spinoza's ideas does not take into account the investigations of Deleuze and Guattari into the notion of 'the One' or 'the plane of immanence,' or the question of whether Marx turned Spinoza's 'immanence' into another 'transcendentalism.' For now, it is enough to touch on how Spinoza's philosophy has come down to us, rather than the possibility of its misinterpretation.)

The notion of the world being one interconnected thing — which is what 'science' tells us it is — and that people are a part of this interconnection rather than a species that somehow exists above the world — connected more to 'God' than to the earth — is indeed a sound one, and one shared by Indigenous peoples. But this message consistently becomes a death knell for Indigenous cultures that resist the 'modern' world — because when two *properly distinct* cultures come to live side by side in one community then one of those cultures always dies.

In countries where there is an ongoing government-funded and Indigenous-supported process of 'reconciliation' between the colonizer culture and the colonized culture there appears not to be some kind of meeting in the middle but a smoothing out of difference in the favour of the colonizing culture. As Eve Tuck and K. Wayne Yang write: "Reconciliation is about rescuing settler normalcy, about rescuing a settler future."[10]

And as Gustavo Esteva and Madhu Suri Prakash write in their critique of 'Development,' 'Human Rights,' and 'The Global Project': "Cultures are

---

[9] Frédéric Lordon, *Willing Slaves of Capital* (2010), Gabriel Ash (trans.), Verso, 2014, p160.
[10] Tuck, E. and Yang, K.W. 2012, 'Decolonization is not a metaphor,' *Indigeneity: Education and Society*, Vol. 1, No. 1, p35.

incommensurable — a condition which seems clearly uncomfortable for those accustomed to extrapolating their own perception of reality on others."[11]

Another work that challenges the 'development' industry is *Participation: The New Tyranny?* in which Heiko Henkel and Roderick Stirrat question the 'participatory' nature of rural development projects around the world — particularly those that go under the aegis of 'Participatory Rural Appraisal' or its offshoots. They write: "the attempt to empower people through the projects envisaged and implemented by the practitioners of the new orthodoxy [reflexive and empowering research methodologies] is always an attempt, however, benevolent, to reshape the personhood of the participants. It is in this sense that we argue that 'empowerment' is tantamount to what Foucault calls subjection."[12]

This is the reality of the situation for Indigenous peoples. The only way out of the (often dishonestly presumed) poverty and helplessness created by the global economic system — according to every entrepreneur, educationalist, or far-left political activist — is to change who they are.

The most perfect expression of the ideals of the Radical Enlightenment is the idea of genuine communism, or anarchism — a world 'government' run by the people (all enlightened) that would be a radical, or direct, as opposed to *representational* democracy. Such an expression is the endpoint of the colonial project of the Western Enlightenment: it is scientific and mathematical rationality for a *global* population that has abandoned 'irrationality' and all 'false consciousness.'

There is more, of course. The Left — all the way to the anarchists — pushes multiculturalism (cultural relativism) and the notion of 'universal human rights.' But these are just two more suffocating and dishonest facets of European colonization. As Esteva and Prakash write: "So it comes to pass, more and more, that under the benign banner of human rights, indigenous and other non-modern communities suffer unprecedented forms of oppression, of suffering and power abuses."[13]

---

[11] Esteva G., and Prakash, M.S., *Grassroots Post-Modernism: Remaking the Soil of Cultures*, Zed Books, 1998, p128.
[12] Henkel, H. and Stirrat, R., 'Participation as Spiritual Duty; Empowerment as Secular Subjection,' (1996), in *Participation: The New Tyranny?* Bill Cooke and Uma Kothari (eds.), Zed Books, 2001, p182, 170-171
[13] Esteva and Prakash, 1998, p114.

Way back in 1998 Esteva and Prakash were exposing the truth behind the slogan, 'Think globally, act locally': "The *universality of human rights*...constitutes *the* moral justification behind "think global." [...] Modernizers and post-modernizers alike assert that global thinking is superior to local thinking. Equally clear, for them, local thinking is limited, parochial and backward."[14]

Truth is a rhombus, in the shape of a curve.

And we should think about what 'multiculturalism' really is without falling into right-wing populist nonsense or the strange and vehemently pro-civilization rantings of Leftist contrarians. Esteva and Prakash write: "Western monoculturalism [is] now cosmeticized and disguised as 'multiculturalism'."[15]

Everyone on the planet has the right to the hollowed-out existence of a Westernized wage-slave... whether they like it or not.

Communism is the logical endpoint of the Radical Enlightenment — the logical arc from Spinoza to Marx — and it relies on all peoples passing through the fire of wage slavery to achieve the necessary consciousness.[16] But communism has never actually been actually realized... maybe the best we can do, as Jean-Jacques Rousseau advised, is to continue to make the best of a bad job. He was not a millenarian who thought that the 'garden of Eden' — or communism — could be returned to or created on earth. He knew he was a slave of society who was unable to break his chains, but he also suggested that we could all persist — as Greta Thunberg, for example, appears to be doing — in trying to keep the bastards honest:

> "As for men like me, whose passions have forever destroyed their original simplicity, who can no longer feed on grass and acorns, nor get by without laws and chiefs [...], they will scrupulously obey the laws and the men who are their authors and ministers; [though they will also] animate the zeal of these worthy chiefs by showing them without fear or flattery the greatness of their task and the rigor of their duty."[17] (One must understand the irony in this passage: Rousseau was trying to get his work published in an

---

[14] Ibid., p10.
[15] Ibid., p28.
[16] See, for example, György Lukács on 'Class Consciousness' (1920), in *History & Class Consciousness*, 1923, at Marxists Internet Archive.
[17] Rousseau, J-J., 'Discourse on Inequality,' (1755), *Jean-Jacques Rousseau: Basic Political Writings, Second Edition*, Donald A. Cress (ed. and trans.), Hackett, 2011, p105.

environment where it was a hanging offence to argue his radical ideas, hence: 'scrupulously obey,' and 'worthy chiefs.')

The striving for the goals of Radical Enlightenment — *the project of the entire Left* — is essentially and effectively a continuation of European colonization.

Western Civilization — and the Left (even unto the anarchists) is a staunch promoter of its fruits — is driven by a unifying and expansionist imperative that is *ethnocidal*. Only ethnocide — the systematic diminishment and eradication of the genuine differences in the cultures of other groups (even under the banner of 'multiculturalism') — can bring global homogeneity. As Tuck and Yang observe above: "Reconciliation is about rescuing settler normalcy, about rescuing a settler future."

Pierre Clastres is an anthropologist who died young in 1977. He had figured out the fearful symmetry of the universalization of European values and he recognized the greater humanity of 'the savages' that he encountered, compared to the hollowed-out, educated Westerners of whom he was one. He pointed out that 'primitive' societies were organized 'centrifugally' in order to maintain their autonomy, as opposed to modern civilization, which is organized 'centripetally': to create a universal homogeneity in service of *the economy* and the European values that support it. These values are daily delivered militarily and, as Esteva and Prakash observe above, through the agendas of human rights and multiculturalism. Anyway, to bring this short foray into the nature of modern leftism/colonialism back to its start point — his writings were in dialogue with Deleuze and Guattari. Clastres wrote: "Savages want the multiplication of the multiple." They want difference, they want 'the Other' — they do not want 'the One,' they do not want the same.

In 1971 Clastres wrote of the Yanomami, and remember that they are still here, still struggling against the ethnocide being brought in on successive waves from Europe:

> "A thousand years of wars, a thousand years of celebrations! That is my wish for the Yanomami. They are the last of the besieged. A mortal shadow is being cast on all sides... And afterwards? Perhaps we will feel better once the final frontier of this ultimate freedom has been broken. Perhaps we will sleep without waking a single time... Someday, then, oil derricks around the

chabunos, diamond mines in the hillsides, police on the paths, boutiques on the riverbanks... Harmony everywhere."[18]

---

[18] Clastres, P., 'The Last Frontier' (1971), in *Archeology of Violence*, Jeanine Herman (trans.), Semiotext(e), 2010, p80.

12 The Tyranny of The Consciousness-Raisers: Leninism, Anarchism, and Jesus.

The bourgeoisie came to power because it was the class of the developing economy. The proletariat will never come to embody power unless it becomes the class of consciousness.

Guy Debord, Society of the Spectacle, 1967.

I am a recovering anarchist, by which I mean: *I am a recovering Leninist*... In my imagination I attend meetings of Leninist's Anonymous, and just like the mantra spoken by each member at the opening of an Alcoholics Anonymous meeting, I must repeat the phrase: *I am a Leninist*.

"What madness," I hear you splutter, "...is this?"

Here is a simple and basic definition of successful Leninism: Leninism is the revolutionary strategy whereby a Party representing the working classes establishes a dictatorship in a region in the name of the proletariat and since they perceive themselves as the genuine voice of the proletarians — whose historic destiny is to abolish capitalism and the state — they allow their government to be referred to simply as a 'dictatorship of the proletariat.' Once their dictatorship is established there are three remaining tasks. The first is to resist the military intervention of hostile powers. The second is to improve the economy so that the extra surplus can be spent on educating the masses and continuing to repel internal and external hostile forces; the third is to raise the consciousness of the masses to the point whereby communism can be properly established. Improving the economy and the education of the masses are the essential components of the 'transitional program' that will inaugurate communism. For Lenin communism could never be established immediately in Russia because of the internal and external pressures on the new State and, *more importantly*, the fact that the workers were not yet sufficiently mature enough to fully understand where their best interests lay and how to obtain them. They needed first to accept the authority of the Bolsheviks and then they had to be educated.[1]

The first difference between anarchists and Leninists is that the anarchists believe that communism can be established at the moment of revolution by creating a region-wide system of direct democracy — whereby all people are involved in all decisions and those tasked with implementing decisions are subject to instant recall/replacement by peoples' councils. Lenin was against the anarchists because he thought that a revolution would be swiftly paralyzed by such a strategy. The second difference is that anarchists do not organize their groups with an official membership hierarchy — they resist the notion of an official leader.

What Leninism and anarchism have in common is the principle that the proletariat needs to raise its consciousness to such a level that it understands not only the fullness of its power but the necessity of ending capitalism. That is, the working class needs to arrive at either a Leninist or an anarchist consciousness. Both persuasions believe that a 'violent' revolution is inevitable – but whereas the anarchists believe that once 'power' is seized it will be redistributed immediately to all, the Leninists believe that power needs to fall into and remain in the hands of the Party until society is ready for communism. While the anarchist tendency believes that the sudden emergence of popular direct democracy will contain, or restrain, the malcontents and oppositionists, and appeal to the doubters, the Leninists are not so confident in people and believe that the revolution will have to be defended with a strong Party leadership in charge of military discipline across society — because, of course, when a revolution happens not every single person is suddenly on the side of the revolution.

The key to communism then, is the raising of the consciousness of the masses to such a level that their natural impulses will be 'communistic.' The anarchists think this will happen prior to the revolution, then during the revolution and soon after by 'organic' means. The Leninists think that while the revolution will both demonstrate the rising consciousness of sections of the working class and

---

[1] Albert Camus put it more succinctly in 1951, when he showed how a story in *The Brothers Karamazov* prefigured the millenarian strategy of the Bolsheviks: "The first step is to conquer and rule. The kingdom of heaven will, in fact appear on earth, but it will be ruled over by men — a mere handful to begin with who will be the Caesars, the ones who were the first to understand — and later, with time, by all men. The unity of creation will be achieved by every possible means, since everything is permitted," *The Rebel*.

express the widespread discontent of the workers in spectacular form that does not mean that they are yet ready – *en masse* – for communism.

In Lenin's text, *What is to be Done?*, 1901, he quotes Karl Kautsky:

> "Thus, socialist consciousness is something introduced into the proletarian class struggle from without and not something that arose within it spontaneously. Accordingly, the old Hainfeld programme quite rightly stated that the task of Social-Democracy [revolutionaries] is to imbue the proletariat (literally: saturate the proletariat) with the *consciousness* of its position and the consciousness of its task. There would be no need for this if consciousness arose of itself from the class struggle."

Lenin explains:

> "This does not mean, of course, that the workers have no part in creating such an ideology. They take part, however, not as workers, but as socialist theoreticians, as Proudhons and Weitlings; in other words, they take part only when they are able, and to the extent that they are able, more or less, to acquire the knowledge of their age and develop that knowledge... Class political consciousness can be brought to the workers *only from without*, that is, only from outside the economic struggle, from outside the sphere of relations between workers and employers... The history of all countries shows that the working class, exclusively by its own effort, *is only able to develop trade union consciousness*, i.e., the conviction that it is necessary to combine in unions, fight the employers, and strive to compel the government to pass necessary labor legislation, etc." (my italics)

So, education is the key – the question is then: how is it to be delivered? The Leninists would say that education is the task of the "professional revolutionaries"[2] — they need to educate enough proletarians to be able to seize power so that they can then educate the rest of society. The anarchists are not so sure about this... They also think that activists should attempt to educate the masses, but when it comes to the revolution — when the revolutionary 'forces' may even still be in a minority — they hope that the message will quickly spread in an organic way, without the need for the iron discipline of a Party leadership.

---

[2] This term is used by Lenin at the beginning of Part IV of *What Is To Be Done?*, and this may be where the phrase entered the English language — for anarchists as a term of derision, of course. See footnote 47 in *Misunderstanding Agamben and Camatte*.

This is why a practical fellow such as Slavoj Žižek has little time for the anarchists and declares, "I am a Leninist. Lenin wasn't afraid to dirty his hands. If you can get power, grab it."[3]

We can also see that Marx is really a Leninist when he argues that the 'veil' of ideology that capitalism generates — which determines that the products of labor have value as commodities and that labor itself is a value and commodity serving the apparently natural processes of capitalism (a notion supported by Christianity/Protestantism) and which leads to all sorts of mystifications — obscures for most people their true social relations and can only be removed when society itself returns the products and direction of labor to the laborers themselves. That is, when all the means of production and all decisions regarding the means of production lie equally in the hands of all the producers.

Marx writes:

> "The veil is not removed from the countenance of the social life-process, i.e., the process of material production, until it becomes production by freely associated men, and stands under their conscious and planned control. This, however, requires that society possess a material foundation, or a series of material conditions of existence, which in their turn are the natural and spontaneous product of a long and tormented historical development."

So, first of all, society needs to arrive at the capitalist stage because only then is the material basis of global communism essentially established; then society needs to get to a point where enough people realize the simultaneous horror and potential of capitalism that a revolution will occur; *then* the economy needs to be modernized and transformed. Lenin in 1920, in a speech to the Russian Young Communist League: "You know that... only after electrification of the entire country, of all branches of industry and agriculture... will you be able to build for yourselves the communist society."[4]

So, for Lenin, it is only *after* the means of production have fallen into the hands of the masses that the masses will be able to learn communism... but until they really know what to do with the means of production it is better for the Party to manage things. So... a strong Party leadership is required for the interim period in which the economy is upgraded and refined and during which the masses will come on board.

---

[3] Slavoj Žižek, 2009, Interview with Jonathan Derbyshire, *New Statesman*, October 29.
[4] Lenin, The Tasks of the Youth Leagues, October 2, 1920.

We know, of course, that there has never been a 'communist/Leninist/Maoist' revolution in a region where capitalism is fully developed — where Marx predicted it *should* appear. Russia was considered by Lenin as industrially 'backward' and this is why he saw his prime task as being to accelerate industrialization there — and he gambled in the meantime (and it was definitely a time saturated in meanness) that he could also accelerate the communist education of the masses.

The anarchists, too, think that everyone needs educating and indeed they were way ahead of Lenin in understanding that workers needed to go beyond 'trade union consciousness.' In his detailed history of that period, Rudolf Rocker,[5] explains how it was the 'anti-statist/anti-party-ist' anarchists associated with Mikhail Bakunin — all expelled from the First International by Marx and his tendency in 1872 – who first came up with the notion of 'workers councils' that are able to move beyond the ideological limitations of the unions.

This council system was elaborated at the 1869 conference of the First International by Eugène Hins, who was part of the anarchist/Bakuninist tendency: "By this double form of organization of local workers' associations and general alliances for each industry, on the one hand the political administration of the committees, and on the other, the general representation of labor, regional, national and international, will be provided for. The councils of the trade and industrial organizations will take the place of the present government, and this representation of labor will do away, once and for ever, with the governments of the past."[6]

But this grassroots-based democratic strategy was considered too risky for Marx, who favored a more direct — or Jacobinist,' as Georges Sorel defined it — seizure of power. Consequently, these anarchist elements were expelled from the International. Ironically for the Marxists, the council idea was reborn in the form of 'soviets' in Russia in 1905 and 1917 – but the Lenin and Trotsky moved quickly, and bloodily, to eliminate the autonomy of the soviets and loyal Bolsheviks were soon put in charge.

But I am straying from the point I am attempting to make here. The point is that the anarchists had clear ideas about how and why the consciousness of the workers needed to be raised. As I mentioned, they pre-empted Kautsky and

---

[5] Rudolf Rocker, *Anarcho-Syndicalism: Theory and Practice*, 1938, Pluto Press, 1989.
[6] Ibid. p72.

Lenin in their assessment that workers on their own could only achieve a 'trade union consciousness.' Bakunin's 'spin' on consciousness-raising was that he emphasized the educative benefits of 'action,' but the action had to be prompted by the revolutionaries: "The great mass of the workers... is unconsciously Socialistic... Our object, therefore, is to make him [sic] conscious of what he [instinctively] wants, to awaken in him a clear idea that corresponds to his instincts."[7]

While Kautsky and Lenin wanted the workers to submit to the wisdom of the revolutionaries, Bakunin wanted the workers to come to their senses through 'action': "*The liberation of the Proletariat must be the work of the Proletariat itself*, says the preface to our general statute (The International). And it is a thousand times true! This is the main foundation of our great association. But the working class is still very ignorant. It lacks completely every theory. There is only one way out therefore, namely — *Proletarian liberation through action*."[8] But, in reality, Bakunin goes nowhere near eradicating the role of the 'professional revolutionary' or the notion of the 'leadership/vanguard of ideas.' Whether socialist consciousness is to be awakened by the work of theorists who encourage education, or theorists who encourage 'action'... it can be clearly seen that Kautsky, Lenin, and Bakunin agreed: "Socialist consciousness is something introduced into the proletarian class struggle from without."

What Bakunin actually disagreed on was the need for a 'dictatorship of the proletariat,' — or a 'transitional period' between revolution and communism — because he saw that phenomenon as a re-creation of the authoritarian State, and he knew that it would be a 'proletarian dictatorship' in name only. But the anarchists were indeed confused and this is why they were swept away in 1918. The confusion lay in the problem of consciousness-raising. How can a radical, egalitarian, democratic nationwide or international system of government be suddenly established if the majority of those subject to the new system are not properly conscious of the benefits of communism and the specific ways communism should be established? No wonder that Žižek still insists: "I am a Leninist, if you can grab power take it."

So, the essence of revolutionary theory is that the vehicle for revolutionary upheaval is the working classes but that they require the correct consciousness to be fully developed in them before communism can be established. The question, then, is whether it is better to raise consciousness to a sufficient level

---

[7] Bakunin, *The Policy of the International*, 1869, Anarchist Archives.
[8] Ibid.

prior to the revolution, or to complete the work after the revolution. The anarchists tend towards the first strategy and so, when it comes to the crunch, and a revolution is successful, the Leninists always win. The only way the anarchists could ever win would be to accept their Leninism — to fully embrace their elitism — and take power *on behalf of* the masses.

> If a great wind passes over one's house, it is the 'weight' of the air inside that pushes the roof upwards. It is the still air in the house that is *guilty* of the roof removal. This is what the poet, John Keats, was referring to when he created the concept of *negative culpability*.

It transpires, of course, that Leninism found out historically that it could never allow communism, as Žižek perhaps unintentionally notes for Mao.[9] And the anarchists, if they had ever been 'successful,' would have found out the same thing — because, in our society, and as every cult leader discovers... when can one ever completely trust one's 'children'?

Raising consciousness is a process that must separate the subject from all wrongness, or 'false consciousness' as Debord would write, and which must be practised in the heart — and only the raisers of consciousness know exactly what the new consciousness is. In the end, of course, a raised consciousness is simply a new loyalty to another ideology and, more importantly, *the proponents* of that ideology. As Jesus said:

> Do not assume that I have come to bring peace to the earth; I have not come to bring peace, but a sword. For I have come to turn a man against his father, a daughter against her mother, a daughter-in-law against her mother-in-law. A man's enemies will be the members of his own household.

> Anyone who loves his father or mother more than Me is not worthy of Me; anyone who loves his son or daughter more than Me is not worthy of Me; and anyone who does not take up his cross and follow Me is not worthy of Me. Whoever finds his life will lose it, and whoever loses his life for My sake will find it.

---

[9] See Slavoj Žižek, 'Lenin Navigating in Uncharted Territories,' *The Philosophical Salon*, May 1, 2017.

13 Fascism is not a Pathology

I

In her recently updated book, *Being Numerous: Essays on a Non-Fascist Life*, 2021, Natasha Lennard expresses dismay that her joyful reaction to the video of alt-right poster-boy Richard Spencer being punched in the face in 2017 was not wholly shared by the liberal establishment. (Let me state at the outset that I shared Lennard's joy and find the video hilarious.)

Her piece on fascism and anti-fascism — which can be found in earlier article-form at the Evergreen Review[1] — explores the apparent motivations for fascism developed by Wilhelm Reich (*The Mass Psychology of Fascism*), Michel Foucault, and Gilles Deleuze and Félix Guattari (henceforth: D&G), all of whom find its roots within the personal traits of people living in capitalism.

Following Reich, Lennard treats fascism as a pathology. My argument below attempts to indicate that fascism is best not considered a pathology, but as a consequence of the inevitable instances of the failure of *Representative Democracy*. Furthermore, we have misunderstood fascism because we have, despite Jean-Jacques Rousseau's early advice, misunderstood the State and Democracy.

The rejection of the notion of political motivations — that we find objectionable — being determined by *pathology* is expressed by Jan-Werner Müller in his treatise, 'What is Populism?' Müller argues that populism is "a permanent shadow of modern representative democracy, and a constant peril" (p11), in which it is always possible "for an actor to speak in the name of the 'real people'" (p101). He contends that it is not "a kind of pathology caused by irrational citizens" (p101), and that if one wants to engage populist voters they should be "understood as free and equal citizens, not as pathological cases of men and women driven by frustration, anger and resentment" (p103). Müller's thesis can be extended to fascism. He argues that the real threat of populism is its anti-pluralism: "Populists are not against the principle of political

---

[1] Lennard, N., *Anti-Fascist Practice and Impossible Non-Violence*, 2018, Evergreen Review, online.

representation; they just insist that only they are legitimate representatives" (p101).[2] So, one can see how fascism begins in populism... but doesn't stay there. What fascism adds to the populist strategy is the eventual closing down of pluralism and Representative Democracy.

When Reich writes: "In its pure form fascism is the sum total of all the *irrational* of the human character... Fascist mentality is the mentality of the 'little man,' who is enslaved and craves authority and is at the same time rebellious" — we can sense at least an inkling here of Reich's feeling of superiority over those not as enlightened as himself. And when he writes: "In our society, love and knowledge still do not have the power at their disposal to regulate human existence" — we can discern that Reich sees himself as central to the task of raising up humanity.

Indeed, his project was not only directed against fascism. He argued that the Russian "masses" of the 1920s and '30s demonstrated that humanity was still too "structurally" immature to escape their cravings for authority because they failed to eradicate capitalism.

Reich locates the root of political fascism in the repressed psyche of ordinary 'little' people. D&G do the same thing, but they would call the root a rhizome. All three effectively demonstrate and encourage — despite D&G's more cautious articulations — an attitude of intellectual, emotional, and rational superiority over 'ordinary' people. Should we follow the course marked out by them? Should we self-appoint ourselves as the only ones who really know what is wrong with the world and how to put it right? Or would putting ourselves on such a lofty shelf just be inviting a long fall?

Reich writes: "Fascism is the basic emotional attitude of the suppressed man of our authoritarian machine civilization." D&G write: "What makes fascism dangerous is its molecular [personal traits] or micropolitical power." This is what they term 'micro-fascism' and, for D&G, it explains why 'the masses' can't help but "desire [their] own repression." It is when these traits link up, they argue, that things become nasty:

> "Fascism is inseparable from a proliferation of molecular focuses in interaction, which skip from point to point, *before* beginning to resonate together in the National Socialist State. Rural fascism and city or neighborhood fascism, youth fascism and war veteran's fascism, fascism of

---

[2] Müller, J-W., *What is Populism?*, UPP, 2016.

the Left and fascism of the Right, fascism of the couple, family, school, and office: every fascism is defined by a micro-black hole that stands on its own and communicates with the others, before resonating in a great, generalized central black hole."[3]

In the preface to D&G's *Anti-Oedipus*, as Lennard notes, Michel Foucault suggests the work is an "Introduction to the Non-Fascist Life," and D&G explain in their follow-up book, *A Thousand Plateaus*: "It's too easy to be antifascist on the molar [citizen] level, and not even see the fascist inside you, the fascist you yourself sustain and nourish and cherish with molecules both personal and collective" (p215).

> *A Thousand Plateaus*, by Deleuze and Guattari, is often incorrectly put in the 'monotreme' section in libraries, due to the word 'plateaus' being mistaken for 'platypus.' Conversely, the book *A Thousand Platypus': A Photographic Record* is often filed under 'philosophy.'

II

It is this struggle with the 'inner fascist' that Lennard is seeking to pursue on a practical and day-to-day level. But while this may be a worthy way to try to behave in one's own interactions with others, it is not certain that people can be changed unless their circumstances change. That is, it is more likely that genuine change happens in people on other levels to that of the human will. We are all social functions of the society we inhabit and everything we do in a capitalist society is used and recuperated by capitalism (our society). Capitalism always benefits from the revolutionaries who claim to oppose it and the charities that claim to put people before profit. An awareness of the stifling absurdity of our social situation in capitalism should not, however, prohibit us from trying to do *kind* things. And one should always place one's kindly or heroic actions within a context of meaninglessness, one that confers upon oneself no nobility, and no sense that what one is doing is right and/or good in *ultimate* terms. The road to hell, as it is said, is paved with good intentions.

When people provide solutions to 'problems' they generally only create new problems. Lennard quotes Paul Virilio: "When you invent the plane, you also invent the plane crash." We could also examine how the various 'solutions' of

---

[3] D&G, 1980, *A Thousand Plateaus: Capitalism and Schizophrenia*, Brian Massumi (trans.), University of Minnesota Press, 1987, p214

people such as Jesus Christ, James Watt, the Jacobins, or the Bolsheviks panned out. And one cannot, for example, cure one's genuine grief by rationalizing it or trying to expunge it by sheer force of will. The 'cure' arrives on different levels: that of time and changed circumstances. We cannot make people 'nice' — and to try to do so would, if one maintains the notion of micro-fascisms, merely be another micro-fascism.

Foucault writes, "The Christian moralists sought out the traces of the flesh lodged deep within the soul. Deleuze and Guattari, for their part pursue the slightest traces of fascism in the body." So, however they put it, the message is that fascism is a corporeal sickness. This is consistent with their philosophical premise that everything in human society is already there in the human being, waiting to be crystallized or enabled.

D&G, I think, got over-excited by their Heideggerian ('always-already') and Reichian (machine civilization/desire) enthusiasms and only managed to invent a new phrasing for a banal morality, one that repeats the insistence that people need to be led away from their stupidities by those who are more enlightened. It is a lot less mystifying — and more practical, *because we cannot make people nice* — to simply treat fascism, following Müller, as an ever-present political threat *in a Representative Democracy*.

III

Earlier I mentioned that the reason we tend to misunderstand fascism is because we misunderstand the State and we misunderstand Democracy. Most narratives concerning the emergence of the State begin with the rise of a chief who bullies people, which leads to a Royal Family, which leads to a retinue that eventually forms a bureaucracy. It is this bureaucracy that then wields the real power. The bureaucracy spreads out over the land and becomes a kind of closed proto-democracy. Eventually there are so many people helping to run the State directly through supervisory — the nascent 'middle class' — and entrepreneurial means that it becomes clear to them that the real power is in their hands and that they should have that power recognized. They begin a movement based on the new circumstances. Oliver Cromwell was landed gentry. Gerrard Winstanley — the leader of the Diggers, the far left of the revolutionists of the 'English Civil War' — was a middle-class businessman. Robespierre was a lawyer. Lenin was famously middle-class. Toussaint L'Ouverture, after being freed from slavery, and before the revolution in Haiti, became a relatively wealthy businessman, owning several properties and his own slaves. Castro was born into a prosperous farming family and studied law at university. Guevara was a doctor. The workers and peasants get behind them because they also like this new 'democratic' idea and because they need some improvement in their lives. There is a revolution (we are not talking about 'revolts' here), sometimes it is bloody. The new leaders realize that the workers and peasants had a slightly different idea about how things should proceed and begin a clampdown. Often the first leaders of the revolution are kicked out, and new people, with a more traditional agenda step in.

The whole of this narrative is fine... except for the very first part. Why, after millennia, did bullying chiefs suddenly appear? If one investigates the anthropology it is clear that peoples prior to the rise of a Chiefdom or State (including present-day 'uncontacted tribes') organized themselves in order to keep group numbers small, and if numbers did start to escalate these groups would 'fission' — they split. Robin Dunbar has famously done work on optimal group sizes and he argues that for humans to operate successfully, collectively, without coercion they must be able to have regular face-to-face interactions — everyone must know everyone else. Once the group becomes too numerous for everyone to know each other it becomes necessary for laws to be laid down.

The key element in the emergence of a new State — Mesopotamia, the Indus, Mesoamerica, etc — was not agriculture or alluvial valleys but the fact there was a rise in the population and for some unknowable reason the group was unable to split (the anthropological term is *fission*).

The classic narrative for the rise of a chiefdom/State is that a rapacious thug organizes a group and takes over the tribe. But the anthropological record suggests that humans were able to resist vainglorious thugs for thousands of years. And how is that there are 'egalitarian' tribes outside of States right now? There must be something else. Many anthropologists and historians suggest that advances in technology — for example, irrigation — led the way for numbers to rise and for people to become enslaved. But how is it that modern 'uncontacted tribes' haven't invented modern farming techniques, increased their numbers and set up a ruthless dictatorship to serve under? Are they just stupid?

The reason powerful Chiefs emerged was because the populace reluctantly agreed that the new circumstances demanded a new way of organizing things. Everyone did not know everyone else anymore and so people could get away with things, cliques could form, 'crimes' could be committed. Laws had to be made and people had to follow them — but the people who didn't like the laws just ignored them. Finally, and this probably happened very quickly, a charismatic person seized the chance for self-aggrandizement... and in the end the populace agreed. A strong leader backed up by thugs would at least keep some peace.

Of course, the power would usually go to the Chief's head and atrocities would be normalized, and if the people weren't totally downtrodden they might support a rival Chief's bid to topple the present one... and so history was written... right up to Representative Democracy.

The State itself is neither evil nor good, it is a managerial solution to the problem of a large population. Imagine the scene: "Yeah, Enki and his gang reckon they can sort out all the problems as long as everyone does what he says and gives him a tribute by sending daughters and sons to work for him, and building him a really good place to sleep in. The whole place will be a lot easier to live in, less chaos, but we'll have to stay where we are and work harder to make sure he gets enough recompense for his trouble. We don't want him to put his thugs on us, but it will be good if he sorts out those lazy thieving bastards who live up by the chickpea bushes..."

IV

The State is often viewed as an obstacle to the ideals of peace and love — and communism — but maybe there is no escaping an authoritarian State, a management structure, when there are so many people jammed together? Perhaps this is one of the many lessons of the Russian Revolution? (If one concludes from this that perhaps the way to peace, love, and communism is therefore to reduce the human population one is — apart from articulating real evil — missing the point that as functions of capitalism such a move would merely be recreating capitalism in a new situation, just as the Bolsheviks did in 1918.)

Jean-Jacques Rousseau opined for the freedom had before the advent of the State and civilization, but he recognized that living in a society where everyone — no matter their place in the hierarchy — was dependent upon everyone else meant that humans could not go back. He decided that we had to make the best of a bad job.

When things in society start to get tough or confusing and political leaders show no real capability or honesty then the opportunity for populism is provided. When people see that things are not being managed well — which becomes evident when politicians all look the same and government appears weak and flabby, or corrupt — then they may tend to favour a populist leader over the pluralism that just offers continued chaos or the same-old-same-old. The Clinton's and Obama (same-old-same-old) paved the way for Trump. But, if populism enables an actual fascist takeover, then the people become trapped and must simply work out a way to survive as enthusiastic or reluctant functions of that dictatorship, or as opponents.

Fascism is not a pathological desire deep within us that only the enlightened can control or dispel with their wise words. And to categorize supporters of fascism — or populism — as being unable to control *an illness* is simply an elitist mystification.

We have all the means to fight populism and fascism if we want to, and without becoming holier-than-thou about our motives. But we may lose, and we may have to endure. We should recognize, however, that the fight against fascism can never be about making a revolution that brings peace, love, and equality to the Earth: because our mass society denies that millenarian delusion. We cannot *win*; and we cannot escape. Rousseau was right: the only way to proceed is to tenaciously attempt to keep the bastards in power, and ourselves, honest.

Despite this, as I am sure Lennard would agree, punching a fascist in the face — for an instant and no more — puts one on the side of the angels.

References and further reading:

Bandy, M. S., 2004, 'Fissioning, Scalar Stress, and Social Evolution in Early Village Societies,' *American Anthropologist*, Vol. 106, Issue 2, pp322-333.

Bandy, M. S. and Fox, J. R., 2010, 'Becoming Villagers: The Evolution of Early Village Societies,' in *Becoming Villagers: Comparing Early Village Societies*, Matthew S. Bandy and Jake R. Fox (eds.), University of Arizona Press, Tucson.

Carneiro, R. L., 1970, 'A Theory of the Origin of the State,' *Science*, New Series, Vol. 169, No. 3947 (Aug. 1970).

Carneiro, R. L. 1987, 'Village Splitting as a Function of Population Size,' in *Themes in Ethnology and Culture, Essays in Honor of David F. Aberle*, Leland Donald (ed.), Archana Publications, Meerut, India.

Dunbar, R., 1993, Coevolution of neocortical size, group size and language in humans, in *Behavioral and Brain Sciences*, (1993) 16, 681-735.

Dunbar, R., 2011, *How Many Friends Does One Person Need? Dunbar's Number and other evolutionary quirks*, Faber and Faber.

Giddens, A., 2010, *The Constitution of Society: Outline of the Theory of Structuration*, Polity Press, Cambridge, pp254-55.

Johnson, G. A. 1982, 'Organizational Structure and Scalar Stress,' in *Theory and Explanation in Archaeology*, Colin Renfrew, Michael Rowlands and Barbara A. Segraves-Whallon (eds.), Academic Press Inc., Waltham, MA.

Lennard, N., *Being Numerous: Essays on a Non-Fascist Life*, Verso, 2021.

Müller, J-W., *What is Populism?* UPP, 2016.

Reich, W., 1933/46, *The Mass Psychology of Fascism*, Orgone Institute Press (1946)/Farrar, Straus and Giroux (1998). Can be found online.

Rousseau, J-J., 2011, *Jean-Jacques Rousseau: Basic Political Writings, Second Edition*, Donald A. Cress (ed. and trans.), Hackett, Indianapolis. (In Rousseau's *Discourse on Inequality*, he lays out his analysis of civilization as a society of centripetal *dependence* from which we cannot escape. Then, in *On The Social Contract*, he outlines how we can try to keep governments as 'accountable' as possible, he was never the bloodthirsty revolutionary Robespierre cast him as. Albert Camus, in *The Rebel*, also, I think, radically misunderstood Rousseau's message.)

Sahlins, M., 1972, *Stone Age Economics*, Aldine-Atherton Inc, Chicago, p98.

14 We Dream the Dreams of Capital

Propositions

All societies are self-reproducing totalities, in this sense all societies are totalitarian.

Modern society is built on a totalitarianism of competing interests.

Much of the critique of society by what might be called the *ultra-left* — a tendency in Western society that still tries to envision the possibility of communism through a Marxian lens (writers such as Debord and Camatte) — elaborates the totalizing nature of capital, yet still insists that members of this totalized society can be 'against themselves' and create a *completely* new society.

We are the products of capital, each of us is an atom of the society of capital, vibrating in tune, we dream the dreams of capital, our horizon is the horizon of capital. Wherever we go, we take capital with us in our socialized 'DNA.'

Eating Habits and Moral Laws

Nietzsche wrote:
> As is simply the age-old practice among philosophers, they all think *essentially* a-historically; of this there is no doubt.

He continues:
> The ineptitude of their moral genealogy is exposed right at the beginning, where it is a matter of determining the origins of the concept and judgment 'good.' (Nietzsche: 10: 1887)

In the *Genealogy of Morality*, from which the above quote is taken, Nietzsche aimed to show that the *morality* of the modern world has a history, it was different in different times, it has changed, and that 'morality' itself is contingent on the specific era or social situation which gives rise to it.

Michel Foucault explains and elaborates, with the focus on historians rather than philosophers as such:

Nihil Evadere

> Historical meaning becomes a dimension of *wirkliche Historie* [real history] to the extent that it places within a process of development everything considered immortal in man [*sic*, and for all other cases, also with 'men' and 'his']. We believe that feelings are immutable, but every sentiment, particularly the noblest and most disinterested, has a history. We believe in the dull constancy of instinctual life and imagine that it continues to exert its force indiscriminately in the present as it did in the past. But a knowledge of history easily disintegrates this unity... We believe, in any event, that the body obeys the exclusive laws of physiology and that it escapes the influence of history, but this too is false. The body is molded by a great many distinct regimes; it is broken down by the rhythms of work, rest, and holidays; it is poisoned by food or values, through eating habits or moral laws... Nothing in man — not even his body — is sufficiently stable to serve as the basis for self-recognition or for understanding other men. (Foucault: 87-8: 1971)

A good example, that I have used previously, of an esteemed modern historian thinking a-historically, thereby appearing to believe that human "feelings are immutable," eternal, and transhistorical, *no matter the social structure and environment*, is offered to us by Yuval Noah Harari in his book *Sapiens*, from 2015. Amazingly, he writes:

> On a hike in East Africa 2 million years ago, you might well have encountered a familiar cast of human characters: anxious mothers cuddling their babies and clutches of carefree children playing in the mud; temperamental youths chafing against the dictates of society and weary elders who just wanted to be left in peace; chest-thumping machos trying to impress the local beauty and wise old matriarchs who had already seen it all (Harari: 4: 2015).

Gilles Deleuze sums up Foucault's argument:

> Foucault's key historical principle is that any historical formation says all it can say and sees all it can see. (Deleuze: 96: 1986)

This means that we are intellectually and emotionally trapped within the society we are born into.[1] It means that all our hopes and dreams, all the things

---

[1] It also means that we tend to view social actions from societies we do not belong to and have no insider knowledge of (for example historical or present-day non-State societies, and also the 'societies' of other animals) in terms of *our own motivations*. We turn, like the makers of Walt Disney's early wildlife shows, every subjectivity we observe into a mirror of our own subjective. It is better, instead, to recognize the limits of what we can

we do to reproduce or alter our society are owned by the *logos* of our society and social environment. We are the products of our society, we cannot choose to be the representatives of another era, another planet, another society. We can delude ourselves that due to our unhappiness, or our rage, or our genius, we are not of this world. We can dress up as Vikings, for example, but there is absolutely no way we can *be* Vikings. We could only be Vikings if we could see the world through their eyes, and to do that one has to be born into a Viking society, or at least live in Viking society from an early age and for so long that one absorbs the entire Viking worldview to the exclusion of one's previous worldview. The case of Narcisse Pelletier is informative here:

> When the fourteen-year-old shipwrecked French cabin boy, Narcisse Pelletier was found by the [uncolonized] Uutaalnganu people on a beach in Northern Australia in 1858 and taken in by them, he had to live a different life and take on a different perspective. After seventeen years, he was an initiated warrior with a family, who had forgotten how to speak French. Pelletier's recapture by an English pearling vessel, which the anthropologist Atholl Chase likens to another episode in the saga of the Australian "stolen generation," was against his will, and he made a number of subsequent attempts to escape. Back in France, Pelletier told some of his story to various interested parties but eventually refused to speak anymore of his time with the Uutaalnganu. Perhaps, as Chase suggests, he grew tired of the fact that people could not understand what he was trying to say. This once-warrior died at the age of fifty, reportedly of *neurasthenia*, a condition symptomatic of "nervous exhaustion or depression," a contemporary diagnosis derived from an analysis of the effects of the disaffections of modern life. (Harrison: 248-9; Anderson: 46-8, 61, 45, 73, 70-2, 68; Merland: 235, 276; Chase: 127, 91, 126)

It is rare to have the experience of living in two completely different societies for enough time to become completely absorbed and imbued by each. What we can learn from the story of Pelletier is that while the entering of a non-civilized, 'primitive' or 'savage,' world led to a full life, the return to civilization led to emptiness and depression. This is the awful experience of colonized peoples.

Our socialization, in whatever society we are born into, is total and totalizing, it is totalitarian. And our life in civilization has, naturally, an overwhelmingly antagonistic and discontented quality to it, which has become perfected in

---

understand. This is explored in greater detail in *The Freedom of Things*, Chapter 7, of particular relevance is the analysis of the Indigenous movie, *Atanarjuat: The Fast Runner* (Zacharias Kunuk, 2001).

capitalism: all our objections to the society of our birth *are generated by society itself*. Our society is the society of competition in everything. This society is *founded* upon competing interests – this is the character of its particular totalitarianism. There is no resentment in 'primitive' societies that do not have exploitation and hierarchy, of which there are many still in existence, their children are not brought up to believe that society needs to be improved and changed, developed and perfected. Neither are they sent to school to learn how to behave and how to survive in *the social world*. The revolutionary of modern times (of all times; there is no revolutionary in societies that have evaded the State) is the product of this competition and the imperative to improve things. There are no revolutionaries in an 'uncontacted tribe' (see *Survival International*), who have a deep desire, or any desire, to overthrow society. They do not live in a society, like ours, that *demands* its own overthrow, its own regular transformation in the name of 'progress;' they do not live in a society that reproduces critics, inventors, and revolutionaries as fundamental elements of its social motor.

There have been two cataclysmic changes in the 'history' of humans. The first was the emergence of civilization, the second was the Industrial Revolution. Prior to these very recent events humans lived on the planet for millennia in small groups that engaged with each other in such ways that they remained at a distance from each other. They never 'joined forces' to create larger groups. They kept their populations low; if ever a population became too large the group would 'fission,' or split. They interacted with the land as part of the land, in the way all animals do (unless they have been domesticated or knocked out of kilter by some environmental phenomenon, such phenomena being regular occurrences since the rise of civilization and its imperative to ruthlessly exploit the land). They had no money and no writing, no history or religion, and their worlds were filled with memory, connection, and story.

While civilization (or at least its earliest form, a hierarchical chiefdom) is caused by an uncontrollable rise in population, it also generates steadily greater rises in human numbers. After the establishment of emergent civilizations there was a generally gradual but significant rise in population numbers right up until the Industrial Revolution, at which point human numbers exploded. As soon as people were trapped into a different way of organizing their society because of their population size people became discontented by the fact that they now lived their lives for others (an apperception that soon also becomes evident in the rulers, and particularly their retinues). They dreamed, if they had the time to, of a simpler and freer life, similar to the one their ancestors were believed to have had, and this discontent, aligned with a feeling of pointlessness and ennui, expressed itself most clearly in what Durkheim observed as the modern affliction of "the suicide of sadness" (Durkheim: 191: 1893).

Hopes and Dreams

Despite the thread of *discontent* that has existed within human emotions since the time of the first civilizations it is unwise to therefore imagine that humans in every epoch since the emergence of the State were essentially the same as we are now, that they shared the same perspectives and morality. The hopes and dreams of, for example, European medieval people were the hopes and dreams of *those* people. The 'interesting' and notable people were reflections of their times, even if they appear as geniuses. Andy Warhol could not exist in medieval Europe, but Thomas Aquinas could. Henry of Lausanne could not exist in Victorian Britain, but Karl Marx could. A 'genius' is a person who ties the relevant known things together to create something that in its 'wholeness' — as a concept, artefact, or system — *appears* new.

Remember, however, that I am comparing two societies that are founded on exploitation and hierarchy here. There are general similarities between these four figures that cannot be made with peoples who lived *before* the rise of civilization, before the establishment of systematically exploitative and hierarchical societies. (Some of these peoples, of course, still live on the planet with us; hopefully we will never engage with them, since that would initialize the active, and irreversible, process of their demise.) There are no geniuses in societies without a State because there is no market for them, in fact because there is no market at all. There is no art or science in societies without a State because these phenomena only exist as a consequence of money and an economy. To consider 'cave-painting' from millennia ago as some kind of nascent art, as if it is the first 'child-like' step on the way to the image of the Mona Lisa that hangs in the Louvre ("Bless them, they *tried*, didn't they?"), is to demonstrate an incalculably patronizing attitude to peoples who have not had the 'fortune' of the Neolithic Revolution, having to build a pyramid, the Renaissance, the Industrial Revolution, the working week, and, perhaps our crowning glory, "the suicide of sadness". It is also, in current terms, or our era, another insidious amplification of the racism established in Europe to support and justify the slave trade that was crucial to the success of the Industrial Revolution.

Our ideas are the ideas of our society and our environment, our dreams are the dreams of our society. We are, like most animals, social beings; it is *the form of our sociality* that generates differences in our lifestyles, habits, and worldviews. A domesticated animal has a different world view — different expectations, different dreams — to an undomesticated one.

It is perfectly natural that a person a thousand years ago might dream, while sleeping, of the endless cycle of rebirth and death, while a person today might dream that an alarm clock was bleeping — and it is quite impossible for either to *genuinely* have the others' dream. It is perfectly natural that uncontacted tribespersons — those peoples who still live in a society without exploitation and hierarchy — do *not* dream of limitless wealth, security, a decent job, a god in heaven, world peace, or communism, while many of *us* do. However, it is also the case that a person a thousand years ago in Europe may have dreamt of a world in common, where everyone was equal, and the wealth of the planet was everyone's to share, in fact they did... just like many of us... because they lived, like us, in a civilization.

Our Lives in Perspective

If all the 'cultural' developments witnessed over the last century in the West have gone to make capital stronger and more far reaching what should the good revolutionary do? Should they oppose anti-fascism, anti-racism, feminism, gender equality, multi-culturalism, and diversity programs, etc., out-right? This is what the revolutionaries Amadeo Bordiga and Jacques Camatte did and they cannot be faulted for their logic. From the 1920s Bordiga was arguing against anti-fascism (and Camatte still cites this position as a key principle):

> We steadfastly maintained that the real enemy and foremost danger was not Fascism, much less Mussolini the man, but rather the anti-fascism that Fascism — with all of its crimes and infamies — would have created. This anti-fascism would breathe life into that great poisonous monster, a great bloc comprising every form of capitalist exploitation, along with all of its beneficiaries: from the great plutocrats down to the laughable ranks of the half-bourgeois, intellectuals and the laity. (Bordiga: Interview 1970)

His famous opponent (though they were always good friends) in the debate on how to fight fascism was Antonio Gramsci. Gramsci argued that one had to make alliances with bourgeois institutions and political tendencies in order to repel fascism, because the likelihood of a revolution occurring under a totalitarian fascist State was much less than under a liberal democratic one. It wasn't that Bordiga thought that a revolution was more or equally likely under a fascist

State, it was simply that he thought a cross-party, or united-front, struggle against fascism would dilute the revolutionary potential of the proletariat and usher in even greater control of the world by capital, and he has, of course, been proven correct, as WWII and its long aftermath of capitalist developments have demonstrated.

But although Bordiga is right on the level of revolutionary theory, and his predictions in this case were correct, is it the 'right thing to do'? Is it *right* to avoid *dirtying one's hands* by collaborating with institutions and political tendencies that have, through a broad combination with various interests, *a chance* of halting a fascist emergence, or overthrowing a fascist regime? Is it 'the right thing to do' to oppose 'race' or gender equality in the workplace, homosexual rights, disability inclusiveness, and all the other movements that aim for the equal rights of everyone in work and society because we know that all these things will just generate new ways for capital to control and exploit us?

Jacques Camatte follows Bordiga's razor-sharp logic, for example, in his opposition (or at least abstention on, which amounts to the same thing) to the movement for homosexual equality (Camatte:1978), which he views as another opportunity for capital's ongoing process of "undifferentiation" which leads inexorably to the "negation of the human species." In this he is right. I agree with him. But do I oppose homosexual equality, or gay marriage? No, I support it. His stand, however, puts him in the same camp — effectively at least (and they publish his writings) — as the extreme right. The movement for homosexual rights, he argues, accelerates the further diminishment of the species through an attack on — or, rather, "emancipation/liberation" *from* — procreation (partly by increasing the prevalence of artificial procedures and surrogacy), as well as the destruction of the 'biological' role of women. Related to these perspectives, and also problematically in my view, Camatte, following Bachofen and Walter Benjamin, perceives "woman" as "the base of the salvation of humanity" (Camatte: 1978).

> Malcolm Lowry, lifelong alcoholic, would probably have never been able to finish his masterpiece, *Under The Volcano*, without the help and support of his last wife, Margerie Bonner. Over the course of their 17-year marriage he only attempted to strangle her twice.

Following the logic of a properly revolutionary *anti*-capitalist opposition, it certainly *is* correct to oppose all movements that aim for equality, because all these equalities do indeed create new ways for money to circulate and the power of capital to consolidate itself, as well as allowing oppositions to 'let off steam' and be re-incorporated. After all, what is this desire for equality? It is a desire to be an equal slave to all other slaves of capital, and in this equalization capital can only be strengthened, through the removal of all 'irrational' or 'traditional' obstacles to its expansion, even if these obstacles were once useful tools for its development. This process by which the *general equivalence* of human life on earth, its *undifferentiation*, becomes completed is not a first step towards revolution, or communism, it is the homogenization of all the humanoid atoms of capital creating one vast social flow of capital that knows no restrictions and no limits.

And the fascinating and unavoidable truth is that this whole process of equivalence and undifferentiation is being pushed forward and constructed, not by some external monster called 'capitalism' (the money economy, hierarchy, exploitation), *but by the people who exist in it* and at its mercy — *by us. Because what else can we do if we want to actively pursue some kind of 'justice'?* How, for example, does one *actively* oppose 'woke capitalism' and not end up on the same side as the extreme right? Put another way, how does one actively oppose populism without *actively* supporting corporations that are sensitive to the moods of their customers? 'Business ethicist' Carl Rhodes demonstrates the foresight of Bordiga and Camatte in his exploration of how capital since the 1950s has incorporated 'progressive' changes in the socio-political climate to enhance their profits, but also recognizes that such corporate endorsements accelerate the 'mood' and therefore change itself. For example, on the question of climate change, or Nike supporting Colin Kaepernick through an advertising campaign (Rhodes: 2021).

So, it might look like the only solution to the intellectual dilemma of whether or not to support 'progressive' capitalism and bourgeois conventions (such as marriage in the form of gay marriage) is to remain absolutely tight-lipped and say nothing, because if one says one is against the Nike ad, or one is against gay marriage then one puts oneself immediately into the camp of the extreme right, even if one's position is justified with the absolutely correct claim that such developments only strengthen capital and increase the circulation of money. But the tight-lipped solution doesn't work either, because if one says absolutely nothing when asked for an opinion, one winds up falling *effectively* into the camp of the extreme right. A principled non-vote, for example, in a referendum on gay marriage — because one doesn't believe in marriage, or voting — equates to a vote *against* gay marriage and a vote *for* homophobia. So, for me, my critique of capital and its relationship to social movements tells me one thing, but there is no way I will allow this critique to affect my actions or the side I take, no matter how messy the politics I am broadly supporting may be.

Baudrillard writes:

> The world thinks us, but it is *we* who think that ... Thought is, in fact, a dual form; it is not the form of an individual subject, it is shared between the world and us: we cannot think the world, because somewhere it is thinking us... I would say that it is the world which thinks us — not discursively, but the wrong way round, against all our efforts to think *it* the right way round. Every one of us could easily find examples of this. (Baudrillard: 54 and 46: 2000)
> [See the PS at the end of *References*]

If 'the world' — by which I mean here, more narrowly than Baudrillard, *society* — thinks us then we cannot think our way out of it, even when we can see some things very clearly within it, because our engagement with the world is always far less at the level of thinking, or critique, and far more, as Foucault and Pierre Bourdieu have informed us, at the level of *our bodies*, and our *habitus* ("The habitus is necessity internalized and converted into a disposition that generates meaningful practices and meaning-giving perceptions," Bourdieu: 200: 1984). Our world is the world of capital (the extraction of relative surplus value, the real 'biopolitics,' see *What is so Special about Relative Surplus Value*), so it is *capital* that thinks us, *it is capital that makes our bodies move*. Whereas the resentment of previous subjects of State life and civilization was something unharnessed, our modern resentment is built into the equation, and feeds into its continual development.

We dream the dreams of capital because *we are capital*. Some of us dream of revolutionary transformation, but this is only because that is one of the organic 'deceptions' of capital. The imperatives of capital are also the imperatives of economy and exploitation, which require *human* stasis. We are witnessing the whole of civilized humanity running in a hamster-wheel *for the sake of the hamster-wheel*, which is capital itself, spinning ever-deeper into its realm of dead eternity. Humans in a State, in civilization, in capital, are unable to create a future through their immersion in, and interaction with, the earth; they exist in a steady-state of exploitation.

> Modern society does not live in the active creation of its future; it lives in the inactive hope of a future, because for the modern world the future is salvation, or its twin: its absence. To live in history, then, is not to live in a forward movement of "dynamic disequilibrium," as the anthropologist Claude Lévi-Strauss put it when illustrating "the machine of the universe" of

peoples who lived, or live, before history (Lévi-Strauss: 63: 1996)... It is to live, no matter how busy we are accumulating for our salvation, in stasis.

If it is disequilibrium that guarantees the creation of a future, it is equilibrium that halts it. As Nietzsche suggested in *On the Genealogy of Morality*, it is to be 'inactive' (Nietzsche: 20) despite the changes in the *character* and degree of inactivity that have been witnessed over the last five thousand years. Dualism and disequilibrium have been replaced by monism or universalism and their equivalence. Activity and independence have been replaced by inactivity and dependence, dynamism by stasis, and time by duration. Returning to Nietzsche's archaeology of morality, we are forced to consider that justice and injustice are elaborations not of injury and vengeance, but constructs of "[a] legal system conceived of as sovereign and universal, not as a means in the battle of power complexes, but rather as a means *against* all battle generally, [in which] every will must accept every other will as equal, [and which becomes] a principle *hostile to life*, a destroyer and dissolver of man, an attempt to kill the future of man, a sign of weariness, a secret pathway to nothingness" (Nietzsche: 50: original emphases). (Harrison: 1-2)

We endure in a society that rests on disaffection and the competition of different interests. We can know this, but we cannot do anything about it, we cannot overthrow it or escape from it, we have to live with it as best as we can, trying to prevent the worst from happening (this is why, for example, it is difficult — not for Bordiga and Camatte, of course, but look where their theories ended up — to not effectively defend pluralism and democracy, even if one is a communist, against fascism). We cannot dream anything other than what our society has given us to dream through the routine moments of our daily lives, whether that be the impossibility of security and safety, or the impossibility of communist revolution. There is no escape from this society apart from its being colonized by aliens or collapsing so completely in an uncontrollable ecological disaster that it wipes out billions of people in horrific circumstances.

We live like slaves on some vast planetary-wide plantation, in which the 'owner' is not a person, but automated capital running through our own veins and the machinery that surrounds us, and from which there is no escape. Imagine this plantation, which has no outside territory, as the dreadful reality described by C.L.R. James in the first few pages of *The Black Jacobins* (James: 6-17) *and* as the glossy depiction created by the TV industry in *Roots*. Think about how the slaves described by James in Haiti and the slaves in *Roots* survived, not in terms of whether one depiction is truer than the other, but in terms of simply what they did to live. Think of yourself as a slave to capital, on this vast planet-wide slave plantation. Imagine falling in love with someone in this world, and maybe even having a child. How are you going to bring up that child? We may *think* one thing, but we *do* another.

References:

Anderson, Stephanie, 2009, The Two Lives of Narcisse Pelletier, in *Pelletier: The Forgotten Castaway of Cape York*, Stephanie Anderson (ed. and trans.), Melbourne Books, Australia.

Baudrillard, J., 2000 (2003), *Passwords*, Chris Turner (trans.), Verso.

Bordiga, A., 1970, 'Against Anti-Fascism: Amadeo Bordiga's Last Interview,' *Overland* website, 24 November 2017.

Bourdieu, P. 1984, *Distinction: A Social Critique of the Judgment of Taste*, Richard Nice (trans.) Harvard College and Routledge Kegan Paul Ltd.

Camatte, J., 1978, 'Amour ou combinatoire sexuelle,' *Revue Invariance*.

Chase, A. 2009, Pama Malngkana: The 'Sandbeach People' of Cape York (and Notes and Commentary), in *Pelletier: The Forgotten Castaway of Cape York*, Stephanie Anderson (ed. and trans.), Melbourne Books.

Debord, Guy, *La société du spectacle*, 1967. My translation.

Deleuze, Gilles, *Negotiations*, 1986 (1990/1995), Martin Joughin (trans.), CUP. See also p105-6.

Durkheim, Emile, 1893 (1997), *The Division of Labour in Society*, W. D. Halls (trans.), The Free Press, New York: "[T]he true suicide, the suicide of sadness, is an endemic state among civilized peoples."

Foucault, M., 1971, *The Foucault Reader* (1984), Paul Rabinow (ed.), Donald F. Bouchard and Sherry Simon (trans. 1977),

Harari, Yuval Noah, N. 2015, *Sapiens: A Brief History of Humankind*, HarperCollins, New York.

Nihil Evadere

Harrison, P., 2017, *The Freedom of Things: An Ethnology of Control (How the Structure of Dependence in Modern Society has Misinformed the Western Mind)*, TSI Press, NJ.

James, C.L.R., 1963 (1989), *The Black Jacobins: Toussaint L'Ouverture and the San Domingo Revolution*, Vintage Books.

Lévi-Strauss, C. 1996, *The Story of Lynx*, Catherine Tihanyi (trans.), University of Chicago Press.

Merland, C. 2009 [1876], Seventeen Years with the Savages. The Adventures of Narcisse Pelletier, in *Pelletier: The Forgotten Castaway of Cape York*, Stephanie Anderson (ed. and trans.), Melbourne Books, Australia.

Nietzsche, F. 1887 (1998), *On the Genealogy of Morality: A Polemic*, Maudemarie Clark and Alan J. Swenson (trans.), Hackett Publishing, Indianapolis.

Rhodes, Carl, forthcoming, November, 2021, *Woke Capitalism: Democracy Under Threat in the Age of Corporate Righteousness*, Bristol University Press.

PS I use quotes from famous established thinkers such as Nietzsche, Foucault, and Baudrillard, not to demonstrate any kind of allegiance to them but simply because they have written something specific that I agree with and which helps articulate my case. I disagree with them all in other areas of their writing, and even in their general intellectual trajectories. It should also be remembered that I am, like them, a product of the era and environment I have been born into, and therefore it is to be expected that I read and use certain thinkers in my own writing, just like everyone else.

15 Threskiornis People, Canis People, Diptera People, Bos People...

The common condition of humans and animals is not animality but humanity.
(Eduardo Viveiros de Castro: 68)

'Human' is a term designating a relation, not a substance.
(Viveiros de Castro: 59: fn19)

The part of the city I live in is frequented by Ibis birds. They are large, mainly white, with a long, curved beak that enables them to dig deep into the softer earth to find food. They look like they might not be able to fly, but they do, and you can often see small flocks of them above, in the sky, pushing themselves through the air. When I observe them, I think: these are the Ibis People, they have their habits and ways and their own lives. I think of them as people because I am now convinced that all living things, however they do it, perceive their world *subjectively*, as *the human*, as *a person*.

The first time this idea — the origin of which I will go into below — struck me with a kind of palpable, tingling force was when I watched our dog. She, too, watched things. She snapped her teeth at flies. She checked where I was. She waited. She came up to me and requested a game or a walk. There is no way, I thought, that she considered herself as 'a dog.' There was no way, I thought, that she felt that I was a category of animal far above her, and that her lot was simply to adjust to us — even though that was what she actually had to do — just like I have to adjust myself to the requirements of the economy and society. She didn't look out at the world as 'a dog' — she viewed things as the human she was.

Dogs, for example, are selves because they think.
(Eduardo Kohn: 73)

The word human comes from the Latin '*Homo sapiens*' and means 'wise or knowing man.' So, our genus is 'man', and the particular species we apparently constitute is the 'wise' species. Of course, such a categorization of 'anatomically modern man' is loaded with pejorative meaning, not least in the promotion of the 'male.' But the term *Homo sapiens* tells us much more about how humans are viewed in 'modern' society. The term sets us above all the 'unwise,' or 'unknowing,' animals, and in the past — and not only the past — the term set 'us' above all the 'unwise' or 'unknowing' other humans that existed around the world: those that could then — and even today — be justifiably treated as livestock, and those that are — even today — considered 'primitive' or 'savage.' Steven Pinker — one of the great intellectuals of our time — would perhaps not even let the poor fully into the modern category of *Homo sapiens*... he argues that "the lower classes" are still not fully availed of civilization because their neighborhoods "form pockets of anarchy in the socioeconomic landscape," and this is a result of their being "deprived of consistent law enforcement" (Pinker: 681). As with the racist image of the Enlightened European in comparison to those from dark and terrifying continents, the poor in our midst form part of the horde of unwise and unknowing that plague polite society. But let's leave Steven Pinker and his friends to their sociobiological Harvard highlife and return to my own small idea.

I have come to develop the habit of viewing other animals as humans, or persons, through my readings of the anthropologies of Paul Nadasdy, Eduardo Viveiros de Castro, Eduardo Kohn, Davi Kopenawa and Bruce Albert, and Claude Lévi-Strauss. Particularly through the book, *Cannibal Metaphysics*, by Viveiros de Castro and the notion of *Amerindian Perspectivism*. Below I present a series of short paragraphs to indicate how I came to my notion.

Lévi-Strauss, describing a myth of the 'Thompson River Indians', the Nlaka'pamux:

Before sending the hero back to his own people, the Goats promise him that he will become a great hunter, capable of crossing the sheerest of cliffs, on the condition that he scrupulously observe certain rules:

"*When you kill goats, treat their bodies respectfully, for they are people. Do not shoot the female goats, for they are your wives and will bear your children. Do not kill kids, for they may be your offspring. Only shoot your brothers-in-law, the male goats. Do not be sorry when you kill them, for they do not die but return home. The flesh and skin (the goat part) remain in your possession; but their real selves (the human part) lives just as before, when it was covered with goat's flesh and skin.*" (From: 'The Mythology of the Thompson Indians,' James A. Teit, 1912, in Lévi-Strauss: 70)

Paul Nadasdy on Kluane First Nation hunting:

A number of authors (e.g., Brightman 1993; Nelson 1983, Tanner 1979) have written extensively on the ritual obligations towards animals that structure relations between human and non-human persons in the Subartic. Adrian Tanner has argued that among the Mistassini Cree, hunting rituals presuppose the real-life existence of animals as they appear in the Cree myth (long-time-ago stories); that is, as persons with whom humans can enter into reciprocal social relations. There is some variation in the nature of these obligations and responsibilities among the different Subarctic hunting peoples of North America, but there are striking similarities across the continent (and indeed throughout the circumpolar world). Hunting peoples across the North believe that human beings incur ritual obligations towards animal people as a direct result of their need to kill and eat them. (Nadasdy: 88)

This is further explained by Agnes Johnson of the Kluane First Nation. Nadasdy writes:

"It's like at potlatch," she said. If someone gives you a gift at potlatch, you must not refuse it, nor do you give it back, complain about it, or find fault with it in any way. It is disrespectful to imply or even think that there is some reason that the giver should not have given it to you (e.g., because it is too expensive and they cannot afford to do so). You just accept the gift and be thankful. To do otherwise – even in your thoughts – shows a lack of respect for the giver. "It is the same with animals," she said. They come to you as a gift... "you never know if you are going to get another such gift, so you must be especially thankful and respectful." [Furthermore,] *to think about the animals' suffering, she said, is to find fault with the gift... and risk giving offence... She told me also that feelings of pride* [in hunting] *were equally inappropriate... since* [one's hunting skills, though important, are] *not in the end what* [causes] *the animal to be caught.* (Nadasdy: 87-8)

Mary Jane Johnson:

When you go out and get an animal, you don't just do it for the hell of it. You don't just do it to play with... You don't go out there and just go, "Well I'm going to go out there and shoot this or shoot that because I want the gall bladder, because I want the horns." You go out there because you have to. You need the food. (Interview with Mary Jane Johnson, Kluane First Nation, 1996, in Nadasdy: 93)

Viveiros de Castro — reversely echoing Pinker above — indicates that our 'modern' (lack of) regard for animals is part of the colonizing project:

The burden of man is to be the universal animal, he for whom there exists a universe, while nonhumans, as we know (but how the devil do we know it?), are just 'poor in the world' (not even a lark...).[1] *As for non-Occidental humans, something quietly leads us to suspect that where the world is concerned, they end up reduced to its smallest part. We and we alone, the Europeans (I include myself among them out of courtesy), would be the realized humans, or, if you prefer, the grandiosely unrealized: the millionaires, accumulators, and configurers of worlds. Western metaphysics is truly the fons et origio of every colonialism.* (Viveiros de Castro: 44)

Peter Skafish, in his introduction to *Cannibal Metaphysics* explains what is termed 'Amerindian Perspectivism':

The basic idea [is] that Amazonian and other Amerindian peoples (from the chuar and the Runa all the way up to the Kwakiutl) who live in intense proximity and interrelatedness with other animal and plant species, see these nonhumans not as other species belonging to nature but as PERSONS, human persons in fact, who are distinct from 'human' humans not from lacking consciousness, language, culture — these they have abundantly — but because their bodies are different, endow them with a specific subjective-'cultural' perspective. In effect, nonhumans regard themselves as humans, and view both 'human' humans and other nonhumans as animals, either predator or prey, since predation is the basic mode of relation. Thus the idea that culture is universal to human beings and distinguishes them from the rest of nature falls apart... (Skafish: Cannibal Metaphysics: 12)

What this means, then, is that our dog, from her subjectively human perspective, viewed me as an animal, not human like her, while I, because I had stumbled across the Amerindian concept of 'perspectivism' could recognize that she saw the world as a human and therefore I can see her as a human.

---

[1] The phrases 'poor in the world' and 'not even a lark,' refer to the writings of Martin Heidegger, whose 'Western metaphysics' were informed by a Christian 'nostalgia' for a kind of 'simple life' without 'technology,' and which he expressed through his support and hopes for the Nazi's. For him non-humans are 'poor in the world' because they can only engage with things as they are presented to them, while the 'human being' (*Dasein*, for Heidegger indicates that the condition of 'being human' is that of *being-there*) can get a sense of what 'more' there might be. This is a specifically Christian procedure for understanding the world, stunningly demonstrated in the films of Terrence Malick, and elaborated in the philosophy of Giorgio Agamben. The quote from Heidegger in full is: "It would never be possible for a stone, any more than for an airplane, to elevate itself toward the sun in jubilation and to stir like the lark, and yet not even the lark sees the open" (Heidegger, *Parmenides*; quoted in Agamben: 58).

For if all existents [in Amerindian perspectivism] are not necessarily de facto *persons, the fundamental point is that there is* de jure *nothing to prevent any species or mode of being from having that status.* (Viveiros de Castro: 57)

This perspectivism, then, enables one to view all beings as having a genuine subjectivity, thereby facilitating an understanding, in us, that other selves, in different form to us, also view themselves as the true 'humans.'

All beings have a genuine subjectivity.

Other selves, in different form to us, view themselves as 'humans' in the same way that we confer this status upon ourselves. Within the many and varied 'envelopes' of outer skin that we see in the living things around us there lies in each… a 'human being.'

But these are complex notions that may not translate well into written language, and so we must make an effort here to relax our hard-and-fast, so-called logic and let images and dreams into our minds. Davi Kopenawa, a Yanomami shaman:

In the beginning of time, there was no game in the forest. Only the yarori *ancestors, who were human beings with animal names, existed. But the forest, which was still very young, and they became other. These animal ancestors began to paint themselves with annatto dye and gradually changed into game. Since then we, humans who came into being after they did, eat them. Yet at first we were all part of the same people. The tapirs, the peccaries, and the macaws that we hunt in the forest were once also humans. This is why we are still the same kind as those to whom we give the name of game. The spider monkeys that we call* paxo *are humans like us. They are spider monkey humans [...] but we arrow them and smoke them when we gather game for our* reahu *feasts. Despite this, in their eyes we are still their fellow creatures. Though we are humans, they give us the same name they give themselves. This is why I think our inner part is identical to that of game and that we only attribute to ourselves the name of human beings by pretending to be so. Animals consider us their fellow creatures who live in houses while they are people of the forest. This is why they say, "humans are the game that live in houses."* (Kopenawa: 386-7)

I will kill flies that invade my personal space, if I first can't shoo them away, but I know the fly is a person, one of the Fly People, and so it appears to me that I am still wrestling with these ideas. I think respectful Indigenous hunting should continue, and the 'uncontacted tribes' should be left to their own devices. I no longer eat or use animals that have been killed for money. Of course, our civilized lives make our survival dependent on money, but we can draw *some* lines in the sand. I am now genuinely horrified by industrialized animal agriculture and the torturous harvesting of cow milk. The other day we were in the car at an intersection on a blissful summer's day when a large truck passed in front of us packed with young cattle, their glistening noses pressed up against the gaps in the container frame... on their way to the slaughterhouse.

> Sound-proofing of industrial slaughterhouses is a costly business. Pigs are particularly notorious for excessive squealing when being lined up to die. But a company in Spain has developed a mute golden retriever that can produce all kinds of ham without any of the noise.

References and further reading:

Agamben, G., 2002, *The Open: Man and Animal*, Kevin Atell (trans.), SUP, 2004.

Kohn, E. 2013, *How Forests Think: Toward an Anthropology Beyond the Human*, University of California Press.

Kopenawa, D. and Albert, B. 2013, *The Falling Sky: Words of a Yanomami Shaman*, Nicholas Elliot and Alison Dundy (trans.), Harvard University Press.

Lévi-Strauss, C. 1996, *The Story of Lynx*, Catherine Tihanyi (trans.), University of Chicago Press.

Nadasdy, P. 2003, *Hunters and Bureaucrats: Power, Knowledge, and Aboriginal-State Relations in the Southwest Yukon*, University of British Columbia Press, Vancouver.

Pinker, S. 2012, *The Better Angels of Our Nature: The Decline of Violence in History and its Causes*, Penguin Books.

Viveiros de Castro, E. 2014, *Cannibal Metaphysics*, Peter Skafish (ed. and trans.), Univocal Publishing.

16 Ultra-Left, Post-Left, Anti-Left Marxists... A Twitter Appendix

In June 2021 I decided to embark on a short excursion into the realm of Twitter, firstly to give my article, 'Misunderstanding Agamben and Camatte,' a wider readership. The article is far too long for any journal to publish and, anyway, I have no academic connection. This article sought to correct the notion that Giorgio Agamben's work promotes violence toward 'things as they are,' and that Jacques Camatte's work promotes any active opposition to the state or current society. But the article begins and ends, most importantly, with the problematic suggestion that the work of both these thinkers has flowed seamlessly into a far-right and traditionalist discourse. This 'afterthought' constituted the second part of the Twitter excursion: an exploration of the heritage of Martin Heidegger in Western philosophical and communist discourse (see various translations concerning Agamben and Heidegger under the name *Nihil Evadere/Contrahistorical*, on the *Medium* website).

Eventually (the third and final part), I saw that there has emerged a whole 'post-left,' or 'anti-Marxist left' in the last few years and that this has its roots in an 'anti-politics' milieu that developed out of the ultra-leftism that slowly emerged after WWII, particularly through the tendency represented by *Socialisme ou Barbarie* (and going on through Gilles Dauvé, *Théorie Communiste*, *Endnotes*, *Tiqqun*, *Nihilist Communism*, etc). This new set of thinkers, the post-left, anti-left, etc., hate 'the left' as much as the far-right do, but instead of attempting to change the course of 'the left' they have endeavored to abandon the left, thereby, amusingly or not, they have effectively completely lost their way, or sunk into the arms of the far-right. Many, such as those around *Frère Dupont/Monsieur Dupont* include 'anti-vaxxers' and appear immersed in right-wing Christianity.

So, for example, the lauded Marxist, Elena Lange (her recent book is published by *Historical Materialism*, whose Editorial Board includes Marcel van der Linden and David Broder), promotes anti-vax protests worldwide and attended one in Switzerland, writing on Twitter (18/9/21): "Not kidding, the revolution will be Swiss [picture of Swiss flag]. So happy to be a part of this. These are good times, actually. The apathy is gone!"

In Lange's 'Substack' she writes of the composition of the demonstration (September 18th, 2021, near Zurich) in glowing terms and waxes lyrical on the apparent myriad of different types of people (a trope of the far-right for describing these events) there and their cries for 'liberty': "And with this biggest grassroots democratic protest in the history of the Swiss Confederation in the last decades, people seem to be just short of toppling the government."

Yet Lange also proclaims to be a communist ("If you want to understand how the dictatorship of capital works in this present world of ours, it sure helps to be a communist"), and writes at the end of one of her Substack articles: "We must make an end to this. The sooner, the better. Against the dictatorship of the Covid regime, against the left and its PMC [Professional-Managerial Class] lackeys, for the dictatorship of the proletariat."

If only Lange had attended the demonstration holding a placard with the words, "For the Dictatorship of the Proletariat!" and argued her case with the other demonstrators. One wonders just what kind of reception Lange might have got. Either Lange is quite dramatically confused about things in general, or she is a witting or unwitting 'lackey' (to use her phrase) of 'red-brown confusionism.'

Lange also writes: "My job is to destroy the left." Lange states that she doesn't look at leftist sites, indeed she only appears to retweet from the far-right (see below) and sites such as *Noncopyriot*, which produce anti-left and pro-Agamben texts, and appear to share her perspective. Other Twitter presences in this style are *BCryptofash*, Aimee Terese, Geoff Shullenberger, and *SAL*.

Elsewhere Lange approvingly retweets from *Unherd*, *The Spectator*, *The Bellows*, *The American Conservative*, etc. And claims, like the conservative, Josiah Lippincott, who invented the term 'biomedical security state,' that, "Agamben is the theorist of our political time."

And *Frère Dupont* (*Monsieur Dupont*), who also retweets reactionary propaganda (*A Certain Plume*), states for his text, *I Am Not Chuang*, 2020, that, "I am making a work of neo-reaction available in the interest of communism." *Dupont* writes that 'neo-reaction' has all the best "texts" and "techno," such as the recourse to the idea of 'freedom,' and that communists 'must seize them and make them their own.' (*Dupont* appears to use terminology from Nick Land in this text, and certainly Land has been an inspiration for *Frère Dupont* in the past.)

But *Dupont* mistakes the solidarity and mutual aid that is the core of what is good about the 'socialist' impulse *at the ground level* for the way 'leftism' has developed at the governmental level, *Dupont* writes: "What is leftism but corporations anticipating potential equal rights litigation?"

What *Dupont* misses is that to be 'on the left' (at whatever level) is to be in constant dialogue and antagonism *with* 'the left' and with one's own impulse to do good in the world. To be 'outside of the left,' as Camatte and Agamben have proved, is to open space for the reaction through whatever variety of *red-brown confusionism*. (For what it's worth, 'the left' should always endeavor to protect *pluralism* at all levels.)

Agamben, Lange, and *Dupont*'s interventions also facilitate the bourgeois individualist selfishness that is expressed in the act of not wearing a mask, or not getting vaccinated: because they encourage readers to value their own personal freedom over the health of others (despite the dubious and hilarious claim of making a heroic stand against 'biomedical despotism').

Anyway, both Lange and *Dupont*, like others, have approvingly retweeted the misleading 'news' stories that have been put out by the far-right and the anti-vaxxers to demonstrate the apparent imposition of tyranny and the apparent resistance to it, and they have gone along wholeheartedly with the falsehoods contained therein.

Dupont's lacuna on the question of solidarity and mutual aid and the continual challenges these phenomena pose to democracy, life in civilization, *and leftism itself*, is perhaps revealed by what appears to be a capitulation to the reactionary discourse on 'freedom' as 'the right of the individual': "The beneficial element of neo-reaction is articulated precisely in its *exercise* of freely speaking, causing offence and transgressing against institutionalized value sets." Such a (desperate/confusing/confused) sentiment appears to align itself more with someone like Jordan Peterson and Avi Yemeni than anyone else... but maybe, following the path of negative theology — the *via negativa* — as *Dupont* does, this is intentional?

> Apophatic or negative theology - the *via negativa* - is the dominant strategy today for the last true communists hoping to attain communism, which is, for them, synonymous with God. As Walter Benjamin wrote: "The way to the messianic is through the back door."

Nihil Evadere

Moreover, in a tweet, *Dupont* writes: "Instead of ceding the idea of freedom to the right as the left wing of capital demands, it is necessary to contest its meaning, and so seize it back." This sentence a) presumes that 'freedom' is some kind of transhistorical concept in regard to the biology of the human (a social being); b) indicates nothing about what the 'contestation' is founded upon; and c) fails to recognize that the calling for solidarity has not only come from medical professionals: it has come, far more massively, from those 'ordinary' people (the vast majority worldwide) who want to keep their loved ones and the people around them safe.

This is the strange and interesting situation someone like *Frère Dupont* is unable to grasp, because he needs to find 'the enemy' in the same specific place as always: the mythical, personified, evil State (the question of whether the State is 'evil' or not is addressed elsewhere in this volume). What has in fact happened is that notions of socialist solidarity and mutual aid (not infecting others) have aligned with the medical profession's concern to treat and contain the virus. Not only this, 'socialistic solidarity' has also aligned with those governments that have followed, or felt forced to follow, the medical advice. This is certainly an interesting phenomenon, and Roberto Esposito, a philosopher very close to Agamben, has wondered, *instead*, if this alignment could create a space for something new and beneficial in terms of social solidarity. Personally, my own pessimism tells me that it won't, but it is still early days, and shifts in thinking on a societal level happen prior to our being aware of them. Certainly, the backlash against the neo-fascist trojan horse which is the anti-vax movement is a good thing.

The covidskeptics, like *Frère Dupont*, however, and because they have swallowed too much of Giorgio Agamben's Heideggerian nonsense, see only 'biomedical tyranny' and the kind of literal cataclysm that it now feels like they must have been secretly hoping for all along. As *Dupont* writes, following Agamben closely, and without a hint of irony: "the function of the mask at an interpersonal level is equivalent to the enclosure of common land in the Seventeenth Century" (*I Am Not Chuang*).

This 'movement' also includes the crude conspiracists at *Winter Oak Press*, Paul Cudenac, *Nevermore Media*, *The Invisible Committee/Tiqqun* (with their 2022 text, *Manifeste Conspirationniste*), *Lundi matin*, *Endnotes*, and *Ill Will Editions*. All these phenomena appear to be a kind of anarchist or 'ultra-left' version of QAnon. The *Manifeste Conspirationniste* (by the *Invisible Committee/Tiqqun*) demonstrates a clear continuation of the *Situationist International* narrative of the *conspiracy of advertising* (who would have thought that advertising might be unscrupulous or deceitful?), as well as a distinctly 'cool young man' orientation (despite their probable advancing years). They write: "There is a designer behind every innocent object we use, behind each detail of the *pissoir* where we urinate, behind each light in every display we approach."

How it has come to this hilariously mad and hyperbolic state of affairs is not, however, incomprehensible. It has come about through the osmotic mushrooming of the work of Heidegger, Agamben, Camatte (and Bordiga)... *and all the ultra-left*, who have put their money on a millenarian moment that they admit is not even visible on the 'horizon,' rather than assiduously seeking more justice in a society from which, like any society, there is no escape (as Camatte told us, but not even he appears able to listen to himself).

Long ago I had my very small part in all this, of course, which is why I have called for everyone to put their copies of *Nihilist Communism* (by *Monsieur Dupont*) in the bin. Up until mid-2021 I used to think, despite having developed a disagreement with the millenarian core of the book, that, 'at least it says some good things.' But since it most definitely exists as part of the trajectory of 'left anti-leftism,' as well as directly (yes, weird but true, through one of the editors of *Athwart* magazine) participating the consolidation of a neo-conservative Christianity in the US, it stands as just another minor monument to a particular kind of stupidity. This stupidity — my own previous stupidity — I have discovered has two origins, the first being the millenarian one, and the other being the one that extends back at least to *Socialisme ou Barbarie* (and, differently, to Bordiga in the late 1920s), and the emergence of the 'ultra-left.'

Anyway, here they are....

Carl Schmitt and Hannah Arendt

"Europe stumbled into WWI without real enmity. Real enmity was engendered by the war itself. It began as a conventional state war of European international law and ended as an international civil war of revolutionary class enmity" (C. Schmitt, *Theory of the Partisan*, 1963).

"The magnitude of the violence let loose in the First World War might indeed have been enough to cause revolutions in its aftermath even without any revolutionary tradition and even if no revolution had ever occurred before" (Arendt, 1963, *On Revolution*).

"A Europe, as I would like it to be, can only exist when the actually existing 'Europe' has collapsed" (Giorgio Agamben, 2015, *Die Zeit*).

So, for the 'global civil war' (*Tiqqun*) to eventuate, we must first agitate for 'a conventional state war of international law.'

Negri on Agamben

"[Agamben] was never involved in political struggles, and he very much regrets not having had such experiences. He is quite limited when it comes to understanding politics" (A. Negri, 2004, from *In Praise of the Common*, 2008).

Agamben and Cayley

The reason Agamben and [David] Cayley fall in with the far right on the pandemic is because they view the State's response as planned/conspiratorial. But the responses of govt., in this new situation, are made on the fly, forged from competing social forces and authorities.

Agamben and Cayley's narrative 'forgets' that what they argue has already been argued by Trump, Johnson, Modi, Bolsonaro, and others. They should be holding these figures up as the first heroic front line against the 'technical-medical despotism.'

Agamben and Cayley's analysis — of the ever-combining, hegemonic, automatic social forces that make up the competitive society of capital — is weak, binary, and unhistorical, which is why it fits so well with the view of society expressed by the 'hard-done-by' populists.

Agamben and Cayley desire the return to a 'natural life,' but this is impossible once civilization is established on a global scale. Agamben and Cayley's solution, in more ways than one, is Heideggerian.

Agamben, Heidegger, Fusaro, Camatte, Vitalism

Giorgio Agamben claims his interventions on the pandemic separate 'the vaccine' from the 'political use' of the vaccine. Is this to distance himself from the far-right who are now able to claim him as one of their own? ...

It is important to note that Agamben used the analogy of the yellow star *after* it had been already been used by the far-right and anti-vaxxers in Europe. One might think, if he had been unaware of this, he would have been embarrassed and apologetic... instead he writes:

... "only a fool could equate the two phenomena [yellow star/green pass]," indicating that when he made the comparison he wasn't really, and that those who thought he was making a comparison are simple fools. Even though he wrote:

"The 'green card' establishes that those who do not have it are the bearers of a virtual yellow star."

This 'distancing' comes too late and has no weight. Agamben's entire philosophical journey — a traditionalist critique of modernity — has taken him on a trajectory that could never escape the gravitational pull of Carl Schmitt and Martin Heidegger...

'The state of exception' has become mythical among anglophone readers of Giorgio Agamben. To bring it down to earth it can be read as 'state of emergency.' Indeed, they are one and the same:

Agamben 2014: "power today has no form of legitimation other than emergency. It [endlessly] refers to it and... secretly works to produce it ([obviously] a system that can now only function on the basis of an emergency is also interested in maintaining it at any price?)."

Agamben 2021: "It is not necessary to have a great legal education to appreciate that, from the point of view of the suspension of constitutional guarantees, [...] the only relevant one, there is no difference between the two states [state of exception and state of emergency]."

Why have communist revolutionaries been so enamored of the 'state of exception'? It implicitly indicates that we had freedom — or a freedom worth defending — under state rule (civilization) in some previous exploitative and hierarchical era of social organization...

... or even just a year and a half ago — even if Agamben does not state this explicitly. For communist revolutionaries to use the state of exception as a plank in their theory is therefore illogical (captain).

But the most interesting aspect of the concept is that the pandemic starkly reveals how easily it folds into a far-right critique of the left-liberal establishment. Agamben's treatment of the concepts of Schmitt and Heidegger, via a Foucauldian detour...

... have brought his philosophy right back to the reactionary morass from where it began. His conceptualizations have slipped seamlessly into the traditionalism and anti-modernity of far-right and populist discourse.

Agamben's pandemic claims are interesting because they offer a way into an understanding of how his philosophy can be so easily taken up by the far-right. Since the 1960's he has, along with others on the left, helped facilitate Heidegger's long march through the institutions.

The traditionalism that is core to his theses – the complaint against 'technology' (Heidegger), the 'dispositif' (Foucault), the 'apparatus' (Agamben) – is beautifully, if ultimately poisonously, expressed in the movies of another Heidegger student, Terrence Malick:

This video from 'Like Stories of Old' shows how seductive Heidegger can be:
Transcending Heidegger – Understanding Terrence Malick

Heidegger blamed the Jewish people for their own industrialized slaughter because they had, he claimed, facilitated the rise of an anti-human modernity contiguous with technology. The Shoah/Holocaust, for him, was a way of reconnecting with pure being. (Black Notebooks.)

But this issue of traditionalism is not only to do with the Heidegger/Foucault/Agamben arc. Jacques Camatte, for eg, holds effectively traditionalist views (the main reason the far-right in Italy is attracted to him) in regard to biology and the role of 'women.' It's a big mess.

Another example. Diego Fusaro's twitter self-description: "Independent student of Hegel and Marx. Beyond the right and the left, against turbocapitalism." What is the implication of 'turbocapitalism'? What traditionalist, anti-modernist, historicity is promoted here?

It seems that any abandoning of the left – termed as 'neither left nor right' – only feeds into reactionary politics, Camatte, for example, following his mentor Bordiga, still considers anti-fascism to fuel something worse than fascism itself (see 'Dialogue with Bordiga').

Perhaps it is worth thinking seriously about why anti-vaxxers, Fusaro, Agamben, Camatte, and those within what might be termed the Vitalist Left, currently occupy the same broad cultural space. A space that is always ultimately, finally, dominated by the reactionary right.

Where Are We Now? (Agamben and Heidegger)

While Giorgio Agamben insists the 'pandemic' is not entirely 'real' and the political use of it is deleterious to society, it would also seem that the current predicament offers some revolutionary hope, he writes: "What is certain is that new forms of resistance...

...will be necessary, and those who can still envision a politics to come should be unhesitatingly committed to them. The politics to come will not have the obsolete shape of bourgeois democracy, nor the form of the technological-sanitationist despotism that is replacing it."

The above is from "Where Are We Now? The Epidemic as Politics." Agamben urges us to not worry about death from Covid-19, because 'fear' allows tyranny. He (mis)uses a quote from Michel de Montaigne in the same way as the far-right antivaxxers use quotes about 'freedom':

"Knowing how to die frees us from all subjection and from all constraints."
The title, 'Where Are We Now,' may be inspired by one of Heidegger's last poems:
But where are we
When we try
To re-enact Rilke's call:
"Keep ahead of all parting..."?
Are we dwelling in death?

Agamben is (famously?) associated with the post-Situ group, *Tiqqun*, the title of whose text 'Call' is probably also inspired by Heidegger, who wrote of the 'call to conscience' and the 'call to Being.' Agamben and *Tiqqun* also developed 'Bloom theory'...

...which refers to Arendt's depiction of the 'banality' of Eichmann's 'evil,' which could not have been formulated by Arendt without taking on board Heidegger's formulation of the "averageness" of "*the they*" (Das Man): "*the they is everywhere...*" (B&T § 27).

(An intelligent exegesis, from 1999, of *Tiqqun*'s relationship to Heidegger and avant-gardism, which will never be published by the Agambenistan Heidegerrians at *Ill Will Editions*: https://theanarchistlibrary.org/library/d-caboret-p-garrone-avant-garde-and-mission...)

Agamben, like Heidegger, has a revolutionary vision of a simpler, more 'traditional' world: "We are not expecting a new god or a new man — rather we seek here and now, among the ruins that surround us, for a humble, simpler form of life" (Nov 2020).

(In conversation with Karl Jaspers in 1933 Heidegger said of Hitler: "Education does not matter. You should just see his wonderful hands!" Beware of those who seek 'the authentic life' in huts in the woods...)

Agamben has gone beyond Heidegger's formulation that we can only be saved in our expectation of a god, who may remain absent — "only a god can still save us" — and focused on simple 'use,' the 'being-there' on its own; the abandonment of the apparatus/technology.

Heidegger: "The power of the root-unfolding of technology, the destruction of language, and the disintegration of Europe define the destiny to which we are exposed and which calls for a corresponding reflection."

(Agamben constructs his indications of a 'coming community' or a 'coming politics' in exactly the same way as Heidegger: "for destituent potential it is necessary to think entirely different strategies, whose definition is the task of the coming politics," 2014.)

Heidegger continues, quoting Burckhardt: ""I am convinced that the day of decline begins with democracy in [ancient] Greece. Thereafter, things began to fall apart...""

Heidegger adds, "Our Europe is disintegrating under the influence of a democracy that comes from below against the many above." Wiegand explains this comment on democracy: "He is not alone in holding "democracy from below against the many people above"...

...responsible for this decline [of Europe]. This view of democracy grasps not only at the frequently renewed and always destroyed dream of a world democracy, but also equally at the instability and powerlessness of those 'above'."

Agamben too, notes the instability/potential: "It is possible, however, that the war on the virus, which seemed an ideal device, which governments can measure and direct according to their needs much more easily than a real war, ends up, like any war, getting out of hand."

War is potential, as Schmitt and Arendt confirmed in 1963 — 'Theory of the Partisan' and 'On Revolution.' — which Agamben and Tiqqun remembered for their theses on 'civil war.' Shouldn't the revolutionaries support the draconian measures for the potential they offer?

...Perhaps *Ill Will Editions* do: "We are entering a phase of struggles [the "Covid-19 crisis"] that do not fit easily into familiar matrices of left and right wing thought. Learning how to move [in these] complex spaces... is the order of the day." (If so, then God help us...)

Agamben's fantastic and cloistered journey should be a lesson for the revolutionary left. Marx and Heidegger share the desire for 'authentic' human community and 'being' (*species-being* = *being-with*) and they both believed humans could escape...

...the self-alienation at the heart of modernity. It is the non-acceptance of the inescapable nature of our society that fuels both the dictatorship of revolutionaries and the continuing appeal of fascism.

Whenever it is imagined that 'modernity' can be halted, or abandoned, 'traditionalism' emerges. We saw this in Russia, in Germany, and later in Iran, and now, again, in Afghanistan.

On Heidegger and Iran, this:
Re-working the Philosophy of Martin Heidegger: Iran's Revolution of 1979 and its Quest for Cultural...

And this:
<u>Heidegger's Ghosts - The American Interest</u>

Bourdieu on Heidegger

Pierre Bourdieu: "It is perhaps because he never realized what he was saying that Heidegger was able to say what he did without really having to say it. And it is perhaps for the same reason that he refused to the very end to discuss his Nazi involvement:

to do it properly would have been to admit (to himself as well as to others) that his 'essentialist thought' had never consciously formulated its essence, that is, the social unconscious which spoke through its forms, and the crudely 'anthropological' basis of its extreme blindness,

which could only be sustained by the illusion of the omnipotence of thought [cf. Agamben]."

<u>https://monoskop.org/images/c/ce/Bourdieu_Pierre_The_Political_Ontology_of_Martin_Heidegger_1991.pdf</u>

Pierre Bourdieu's 1975 book on Heidegger was largely ignored, he re-organized it and retitled it for his 1988 book. Bourdieu explains the premise of the first book: "It was a reading of [Heidegger's] work itself, with its dual meanings and covert undertones, that revealed some of

the most unexpected political implications of Heidegger's philosophy, at a time when they were not recognized by historians: its condemnation of the Welfare State, hidden deep inside a theory of temporality [cf. Agamben's condemnation of 'medical tyranny']; its antisemitism,

sublimated as a condemnation of rootlessness ('errance' [cf. Camatte]); its refusal to disavow the commitment to Nazism, evident in the torturous allusions which punctuate Heidegger's dialogue with Jünger [influencer of Heidegger and star in Agamben's reactionary pantheon];

its ultra-revolutionary conservatism, which inspired not only philosophical strategies of radical overcoming but also, as Hugo Ott has shown, the disappointed philosopher's break with the Hitler regime, when it failed to reward his revolutionary aspirations to the vocation of philosophical Führer.

All of this was there in the text, waiting to be read, but it was rejected by the guardians of orthodox interpretation [eg Marcuse, Lefebvre; Derrida, Deleuze, etc],

who have felt their privileges threatened by the unruly progress of the new sciences,

and so have clung like fallen aristocrats to a philosophy of philosophy, whose exemplary expression was provided by Heidegger, erecting a sacred barrier between ontology and anthropology.

But the best that the orthodox can hope for is to scrutinize the blindness of the professionals of insight, which Heidegger manifested more clearly than any other philosopher, and which they continue to reduplicate and consecrate through their willful ignorance

and disdainful silence." [Bourdieu, 1988]
Agamben, 2016:
"These controversies [over Heidegger] rest on a misunderstanding of the definition of 'anti-Semitism' and its use. The way it is used today, this word designates something that has to do with the persecution and the extermination of the Jews.

One does not have to use this word in order to describe someone that, even if his opinions about Jews are erroneous, has opinions that have nothing to do with these phenomena." (Agamben on Heidegger 2016: http://jcrt.org/religioustheory/2017/02/06/philosophy-as-interdisciplinary-intensity-an-interview-with-giorgio-agamben-antonio-gnolioido-govrin/)

Heidegger, Beaufret, and Char vs Beckett

How did Heidegger, unrepentant Nazi, become the sweetheart of 'Continental Philosophy,' friend of poet René Char, the theme of Beckett's *Malone Dies*, and the idol of the Italian philosopher of destituent politics, Giorgio Agamben?

"Essentially, [French philosopher, Jean] Beaufret was the first intellectual to defend Heidegger [after WWII]. [Anthony] Cronin records that Beaufret had, "rather unusually for a Frenchman of that era, become acquainted with the work of Wittgenstein and the Viennese...

and he was to become, in Geert Lernout's words 'Heidegger's most important French advocate and teacher of a whole generation of French Heideggerians.'" (RS)

"Beaufret was a legendary professor of philosophy, having trained generations of students and future professors," (P&R) though he never taught a specific course on Heidegger, writing: "one cannot *summarize* Heidegger's thought. One cannot even *present* it." (PJ)

"Char indisputably read most of Heidegger's work through the prism of Beaufret's admiration (and Beaufret was a friend as well as a mentor for Char)." (MW) "Char and Heidegger became friends in 1955... Through the agencies of the philosopher Jean Beaufret...

they met in Provence for the now famous '[seminars] at Le Thor (1955, 1966, 1968, and 1969), and remained friends until Heidegger's death [1976]" (MW). Agamben, of course, attended the last two, and dedicated his *Stanzas* to Heidegger in 1977.

From the 1970s Heidegger's legacy was in trouble, "culminating in the furore caused by the publication in the late 1980s of studies by Bourdieu and Victor Farias on the 'fascistic' nature of Heidegger's use of language and the extent of his collaboration with the Nazis.'

Char died [1988] just before these studies were published, but his last months were undoubtedly disturbed, even haunted, by the virulent attacks on Beaufret's position as an apologist for Heidegger and for Heideggerian thinking." (MW)

Just over a month before Char died an article appeared in *Le Monde* concerning two letters by Beaufret to his ex-student, Robert Faurisson (a famous Holocaust denier), expressing support for his work and his own doubts concerning "the existence of the Nazi gas chambers." (MW)

Samuel Beckett and Beaufret were friends in the 1930s, Beckett nicknamed him 'the Bowsprit.' They both were part of the avant-garde intellectual life of Paris. But maybe the book *Malone Dies* (1951) articulates a break from Beaufret, and, therefore also, Heidegger?

Malone Dies was written after Heidegger's *Letter on Humanism* (1947), a reply to 12 questions sent by Beaufret. RS argues that Malone Dies is a parody of

Heidegger and Beaufret. In Malone Dies, the 12 questions become 21 (eg "Why has my soup been stopped?").

In 1946, Heidegger, Roudinesco writes, "'had just come out of the Schloss Haus Baden, the sanatorium where he had been undergoing treatment for the psychosomatic disorders that followed his expulsion from the university." (RS)

'Similarly, in *Malone Dies*, Malone finds himself in some sort of institution, and his character Macmann is incarcerated in "a kind of asylum."' (RS)

There is also a reflection of Heidegger's paean to peasant life, but in reverse, "Think of the price of manure, said his mother." There is an Aryan theme, the story ends with murder and 'blood and soil' imagery and perhaps an allusion to the modern 'das Man' ('the *they*')

used by Heidegger and *Tiqqun* (*Bloom Theory*): "Going to meet him Lemeul killed him in his turn, in the same ways as the other. It merely took a little longer. Two decent, quiet, harmless men, brothers-in-law into the bargain, there are billions of such brutes."

René Char went one way, falling for Heidegger and his call "to be a poet in a destitute time," (later also attracting Agamben, and *Tiqqun*, who wrote "what critique needs now is poets and theologians"), despite the knowledge of Heidegger's Nazi commitments,

while Samuel Beckett, in his refusal of Pauline, messianic, time, and 'philosophy' itself, went the other. Beckett jokes: "Do you believe in the life to come?" asks Clov, "Mine was always that," replies Hamm.

It's as if Beckett is making fun of Agamben a decade before Agamben met Heidegger (and discovered Benjamin). Heidegger's 'insightful moment' never enters like a 'shard' into the endless waiting that constitutes Beckett's universe:
"What time is it?"
"The same as usual."

(PJ) Pierre Jacerme, essay in D. Pettigrew and F. Raffoul (eds), *French Interpretations of Heidegger: An Exceptional Reception*, SUNY 2008 (P&R).
(RS) Rodney Sharkey "Beaufret, Beckett, and Heidegger: The Question(s) of Influence," in *Samuel Beckett Today*, Brill, 2010.
(MW) Michael Worton, *Between Poetry and Philosophy: René Char and Martin Heidegger*, 1996.

Byung-Chul Han and Agamben

Byung-Chul Han (a Heideggerian), Oct 20, 2021, on Agamben (a fellow Heideggerian): his views are "simply stupid," and, "I have a feeling that Agamben doesn't know what democracy is.":

https://www.askanews.it/video/2021/10/20/byung-chul-han-agamben-non-mi-incontra-perch%c3%a9-non-ha-green-pass-20211020_video_11184644/

Byung-Chul Han:
"I invited Agamben to a meeting at Villa Massimo [Rome]. The Goethe Institut also invited him. Agamben replied to me and to the director of the Goethe Institut that he was afraid he could not accept the invitation because the event would require a Green Pass.

"He does not have a Green Pass. After I received this email I lost a lot of respect for Agamben. What he is doing is a political abuse of a friendly personal invitation. He uses the friendly invitation to stubbornly manifest his problematic position.

"Agamben in his old age refuses to be vaccinated, because he sees in the vaccination a scheme of the state to extend political domination or because, like many anti-vaxxers, he fears that vaccination will render him helpless; it is simply stupid.

"I myself don't agree with the Green Pass for the workplace, and particularly the threat that you can be suspended if you don't comply. But the theory of the "state of exception" does not help us...

"I would just like to ask him if this measure conforms to democracy and the constitution. Democracy is not something that is given once and for all, but something that you always have to fight for. I have a feeling that Agamben doesn't know what democracy is." B-C Han.

For those of you who continue to not read Camatte

For those of you who continue to not read Jacques Camatte (who claims to be beyond any form of enmity), here is his view of Gilles Dauvé, which he wrote in 1983 and put on his site, Revue Invariance, in 2001:

"It is magnificent that Dauvé/Barrot has entitled his magazine 'La Banquise' [Pack Ice], which corresponds very well to what he and his companions are: the living dead. It also corresponds to the fact that his pupils called him an undertaker!

[Translators note: *La Banquise* ceased in 1986. Dauvé started a new journal with a more positive title, *Le Brise-glace*, or Icebreaker, in 1986. His current magazine, on the Internet, is *Troploin* which may indicate that his pessimism has returned.]

"Obviously the living-dead cannot 'create' another dynamic of life. But there is more, by reproaching me for 'my optimism' they resign from their position as representatives, as they conceive of themselves, of a class that must be revolutionary.

"Indeed, what are leaders who cry out for defeat, for asphyxiation, worth? It is certain that blissful optimism is ridiculous, but optimism determined by a certain prediction is an assurance of strength for a struggle or for staying alive." (*La Mort Potentielle du Capital*)

What is this 'certain prediction'? It is the prediction of the emergence of true human community, which takes time, and will only be possible if civilized humans survive the imminent ecological disaster. Camatte describes his strategy:

"I just want to show that we are in a dynamic of destruction which poses the necessity of another dynamic which must be TOTAL and, therefore, I posit myself directly as a totality, centralized in myself, and thus I am my goal and my movement.

"If I am right to propose that I cannot merely be 'individuality' but must at the same time be Gemeinwesen [community], my position is valid for millions of beings. For it is not I who creates ex-nihilo, rather it is through me that a certain humanity establishes itself.

"I want to bear witness to this. I am, if you want, like a prophet. In order to bear witness, one must also denounce, bring to light, commend, and sensitize women and men, but I do not proselytize in any way... Our journey must be a call to others..."

The above text is from: *Extrait de lettre*, 1978 (included on the website in 2001), in the appendix to 'Origine et fonction de la forme parti,' on the site Revue Invariance.

The Point of Departure

Jacques Camatte, *Point de Départ*:
"From then on, an historical-theoretical investigation of the human phenomenon became necessary to situate the wandering of the species, to understand how the separation from nature and the dynamics that followed from it had come about.

"It was necessary to grasp how the development of the dynamic of value, then capital was set in motion, first in the West, and then elsewhere. At the same time, it was necessary to make an inventory of the contributions of other geosocial areas to the species' future.

"This led to an investigation into the various traumas of the species across different areas. From all this, the emergence of *Homo gemeinwesen* — the species that will succeed *Homo sapiens* — could be revealed.

"The new species will be in continuity with nature and the cosmos. Its consciousness will not possess a function for justifying its existence — the species will operate solely within the activities of enjoyment.

"Initially we operated in a dynamic of struggle and opposition, which aimed at the negation of this world and its replacement with a society that affirmed the true *Gemeinwesen* of humanity (K. Marx).

"We abandoned the struggle and the opposition because it was ineffective, and we sought another dynamic of life. This led us to locating the starting point, the origin of Homo sapiens, and then to detecting the emergence of another species." Camatte 2003.

[I am sure that many who read the above thread simply nodded their heads and muttered, "Yeah, cool..."]

Bachofen, Benjamin, Jesi, Illich, and Camatte

Judith Butler has observed that Terfs have found themselves aligned with the far-right. In the same way, Jacques Camatte finds himself on the same side as the far-right because of his fear that 'the human species' is being 'fragmented' and made 'artificial.'

Camatte, like Walter Benjamin and Furio Jesi before him, share the view of 'woman' put forth by the 'male supremacist' Jakob Bachofen (*Das Mutterrecht*) and writes: "At the base of the salvation of humanity there is woman." Benjamin, btw, literally adored Bachofen...

Of an image of Bachofen, Benjamin writes: "An almost maternal largesse, spreading over the whole physiognomy, gives it a perfect harmony," and he considered Bachofen's greatness to have emerged from "his veneration of the matriarchal spirit."

But Camatte's 'ennobling' of 'woman' ultimately serves the same function as it did Bachofen: "If *Das Mutterrecht* is 'a paean to the marvel of women,' as one of Bachofen's later reviewers claim, it is also a slap in the face" (Cynthia Eller, *Gentlemen and Amazons*, 2011).

Camatte argues that in the 'hunter-gatherer' phase (his view of 'primitive peoples' is that they are/were 'fearful' and 'cave-man' like) the sexes became segregated, but "with the invention of agriculture woman regains an essential importance."

This importance was diminished, however, by a later segregation that was built around "the invention of the kitchen."

The influence of the revolution of agriculture, for Camatte, is directly from Bachofen. Eller writes: "agriculture [for Bachofen] stands for the type of procreation that matriarchy initiates: no longer randomly sowing his seed in the swamp of communally owned women, ...

... man now [Bachofen writes:] 'opens the woman's womb, lays his seed for the purpose of generation... [and harvests] the child from the maternal garden'... woman as earth, man as seed... The earth gives birth, and women give birth" (Eller reiterates).

Similarly, David Cayley quotes Ivan Illich's epiphany: "On the icebox door two pictures were pasted. One was the blue planet and one was the fertilized egg. ...

... Two circles of roughly the same size, one bluish, the other one pink. One of the students said to me, 'These are our doorways to the understanding of life'."

For Bachofen Amazonism was initially a positive response to male lust, but it descended into producing "man-hating, man-killing, war-like virgins" so it was good they were defeated and succumbed again to male charms and superiority, thereby restoring the correct balance.

Camatte views the possible trajectory of feminism in the same way: "With feminism we see another manifestation of *the Amazons*," which further presages the "risk of fragmentation" of 'the species' (*Amour ou combinatoire sexuelle*).

But, for Camatte, the most serious danger to 'the species'/humanity is not diversity or segregation of the sexes in different cultural, or modern, situations, it is "the danger of the destruction of the species through homogenization, that is, by the loss of all diversity."

For Camatte, the diversification of sexual modes (an aspect of 'wandering') is immediately recuperated by capital and used as another tool of homogenization, or undifferentiation. He writes: "Sexes and modes of use, with their multiple variations, ...

... are available to women and men at the hypermarket of love that capital establishes. The buyer only has to configure his or her combinatorial."

The making of the possibility of any sexual combination, for Camatte, is not only a disaster for the species in terms of further distancing it from 'nature,' it becomes another way for capital to reduce humans to a single undifferentiated function of capital itself.

If one reads *Amour ou combinatoire sexuelle* it becomes clear that, for Camatte, it is OK for women to love women and men to love men, but this should not be referred to as 'sexual,' because activities that do not produce children are not sexual.

The problem, for Camatte, is that the gaining of 'homosexual' rights ("It follows that I think that capital may very well come to accept homosexuality," 1978) has helped the emergence of phenomena he regards as deleterious for both children and the future of the species...

... that is, the ability to produce children via medical intervention/assistance and surrogacy.

So, to resist the further artificialization of humanity one should oppose proposals to establish rights for others to live in the same way as 'normal heterosexual' couples, that is, getting married, or having children... just like the extreme right-wing traditionalists do...

[Addendum: Donald Trump on gay marriage: "I have so many fabulous friends who happen to be gay, but I am a traditionalist," *NYT* interview, May 2011.]

So, if there was a vote on, for example, 'gay marriage,' one would either vote against it or not vote at all. But abstaining would amount to a vote against...

...and so one would find oneself in the camp of the reactionaries, just as Camatte has done. In the same way, the Terfs, by their similar abstinence, as Butler notes, have found themselves in the camp of those on the right and extreme right who push their anti-gender ideology.

Other Tweets and Threads

"*Theory* wanders around universities worldwide... extracted from authors who are combined in a generic radical posture (Agamben, Benjamin, etc). *Theory* is cutting-edge... [users can find prêt-à-porter ideas that fill university papers quickly and superficially" (Barbara Carnevali, 2016).

'Destituent politics' (politics for a destitute time) reflects Heidegger's yearning for 'the simple peasant life' unencumbered by (Jewish) 'modernity,' and a life without 'why' (a fascist dream of course). This fascist impulse is articulated positively in the article *Without Why: The Existential A Priori of Destituent Action*, 2021, at the site *Ill Will Editions*.

> Søren Kierkegaard, friend of the Danish King, opponent of democracy, particularly the vote for women, is often referred to as *The Father of Existentialism*. But others claim that title for Heidegger (Nazi) or Sartre (Stalinist). Wittgenstein wrote: "Kierkegaard was a saint."

A tweet in response to a Frère Duponter who described his 'organizing efforts' at his work (whether the claim of 'organizing' is genuine or not is another matter) as being "much less concerned [as to] whether someone voted for Trump, despises masks and the vaccine, or has backwards views about gender, than whether they show an inkling of nerve to challenge the company":

In my (large, heavily unionized) workplace the anti-mask/lockdown folk are anti-union, anti-left, viewers of Fox News, conspiracy theorists, and admirers of Putin! Hard for me to spend much time with them. You must have far thicker skin than I.

See link for useful genealogy of *Tiqqun/The Invisible Committee*, written in 1999/2002.
"It is within the eccentric reality of 'bullshitting college kids with underdeveloped literary ambitions that *Tiqqun* has found its audience."
https://theanarchistlibrary.org/library/d-caboret-p-garrone-avant-garde-and-mission

The Legacy of the 1990s

There must be many people (orig, from 'the left,' but later Agamben-ized, having already been Deleuzed) who didn't get their kids vaxxed 20 or so years ago because of theories the vaccine caused autism. Perhaps, in the current moment, they have, to fend off embarrassment, ...

... 'dug their heels in.' In this way they have forged a concrete alliance with the individualist libertarians of the far-right (eg., retweeting far-right 'news' or covidskeptic 'science.' They are no longer walking on Heidegger's supposedly transcendent water, they have sunk, ...

... along with their anti-leftism, into 'the holy' (or Van Morrison's 'mystic') without trace.
PS And is Giorgio Agamben a kind of Chauncey Gardiner of the University/the Academy?

Social Reproduction

Anyone who thinks modern society is 'dysfunctional' or 'breaking down' must also think that there was a time in 'modernity' when things were OK, or that society can be 'fixed' – but our society (modern civilization) is founded upon exploitation and hierarchy, and the motors...

... for this society are competition, the rise and fall of ideologies and entrepreneurs: breakdown, discontent, and renewal. It is civilization that runs on revolutionary premises, 'the revolutionary communists' are merely another factor in the reproduction of civilization...

... and whose own lifeworld is also subject to the dynamics of 'rise and fall,' independent of their own activity. Modern civilization is faced with only one decisive possibility: an ecological catastrophe impossible to control. All other apparent possibilities...

... are within the remit of society and therefore only a factor in the reproduction of our society.

Agamben and Camatte again

Agamben and Camatte have shown that to be against the Left is to fall into the arms of reaction. So it might be useful to think how one might engage with politics inside the Left, rather than simply abandoning the Left (and falling into the arms of reaction).

There is no escape. We have to make the best of things. We cannot create another world, because we are the world. If we tried, we would only recreate ourselves, but in an 'accelerated' or worse version. History has already taught us this lesson, many times.

Family Life vs Revolution

The first millenarian that history knows is Zoroaster.

Millenarians believe, like Jesus, that 'heaven' can be established, or re-established, on Earth if people break with their old traditions, their old family-life, and join the prophets of the new future.

Millenarians announce the purging of 'sin' and 'the sinful' and the establishment of peace and harmony. They believe that we can pass from the condition of enslavement in civilization to a world without evil.

Some of us become millenarian ideologues in young adulthood. If later we have our own family, the dogma is imperiled. Family life pushes visionary principles toward the window. But a pious *taliban* (student of the faith) shuts tight the windows.

This is why all radical communist theory wants to disband the family. For communists and the most religious (cf. the life of the monk), it poses the deepest danger to vision and praxis.

So, if one cannot make the revolution, one must endure one's days with its worst enemy: one's own partner and one's own children.

For example, *Endnotes Journal #5*:
https://endnotes.org.uk/file_hosting/EN5_To_Abolish_the_Family.pdf

(In civilization we are stuck with 'the family' as an organizational unit, it is not possible to dispense with it without introducing something worse, invariably something more intensely patriarchal.)

The family is always the enemy of communism. All instances of trying to enact communism have worked against the family. The family, for communism, is not love, but universal love denied. And 'universal love' is just another poison from the cabinet of utopian medicine.

What is society?

Are we the avant-garde of capital? (With a Q and A at the end.)

If the working class is an aspect of capital — in the same way the middle class or ruling class is — then all subsections of our social form are also aspects of capital.

Artists and rebels — and their 'works' — must, therefore, also be aspects of capital. If so, then the concept of 'recuperation' (from Guy Debord and the *Situationist International*) is meaningless. Rebellion itself is an aspect of capital, because capital is the particular social form that is built upon the constant revolutionizing of its exploitative processes. Therefore, any of us who 'work' for communism, the revolution, world peace, social justice, totalitarian dictatorship, fascism, technological change... or anything to 'make things better'...

...constitute the, more or less radical, avant-garde of capital.

Q: "This is a hefty *if* — is Marxism just a sociological functionalism with 'society' scribbled out and replaced with 'capital'?"

A: Yes, our society is the society of capital.

All (different) societies are different (eg feudal society vs capitalist society). Once established (capital was established well before the Ind. Rev.) they are 'organic' wholes/social forms. But these 'different' societies have a common basis

— they are civilizations (hierarchy and exploitation as the inevitable function of management, itself the function of large population). The only 'really' different society (that we know of) is the non-State society, the societies of the 'uncontacted tribes.'

Marxism is the millenarian impulse reconfigured under science (which began prior to the English Revolution). The millenarian impulse is the most radical response to the dissatisfaction of living in a State. It tells us we can remake the Garden of Eden in a new form. It began...

as far as we know, with Zoroaster. All these most radical responses to the State have become religions (historically, religion follows politics, not vice versa) — so Marxism became the latest Abrahamic religion. But, to go back to that element of your question... yes...

... Marxism is another function of society/capital — another avant-garde of capital (though a particularly powerful one). Marxism, as we know, has only helped to develop capitalism, it has only acted in the interests of our society (which is a society founded upon management,

... exploitation, and hierarchy). See, for example:

Q: "You've knit yourself a conceptual straight-jacket so thorough and deterministic, that I cannot see how it leaves you room for any normativity —

any means of justifying a choice between this or that tendril of capital, between, say, your 'right' or 'left'."

A: Before I answer properly, I need to know exactly what you mean by 'normativity'?
Q: "Clarified after the em dash!"

A: OK, I wasn't sure (and here is a definition: "Normativity is the phenomenon in human societies of designating some actions or outcomes as good or desirable or permissible and others as bad or undesirable or impermissible").
So, you are right that my conceptualization raises

the philosophical problem of whether any choice is good or right, since they all serve society. However, on a practical level, the good and right choices are (fairly) clear. Those choices being ones of kindness and 'toward justice' in a situation we cannot escape from.

Therefore, my conceptualization frees us from the dream of escape, and forces us to consider how to live in the (inescapable) here and now. So (although/because I argue there can be no willed escape from our society), in casting off my revolutionary/millenarian notions

I have slipped out of a particularly debilitating and mystificatory straitjacket. I am free now to keep rolling the rock up the hill... instead of remaining in my room, poring over sacred texts, and worrying...

Q: "It seems to me that they [choices] are not very clear at all, nor are kindness and justice at all unambiguous."
A: No, of course they are not unambiguous — which is why I wrote 'toward justice' in scare quotes, and also the word 'fairly.' But if we can't decide

what is a 'more correct' (or 'more virtuous') way of dealing with things and events as they transpire, then we end up doing nothing and where does 'doing nothing' lead us? Like Camatte, into the arms of the traditionalist far-right, and, like Monsieur Dupont, into the arms of

anti-vax far-right 'freedom fighters.'
(It all begins with the refusal to vote as a principled anarchist stand, which, held as a 'transhistorical' principle only serves to apparently endow the holder of the principle with some kind of sacred, but wholly delusional, purity.)

Q: "I think all of the interesting questions begin when you must ask how to live rightly in the 'here and now.' But these are the perennial questions of ethics, and of political philosophy, and — well, I suppose, I am interested in where your answering of them will lead you."

I think, since I have pretty-well laid-out where my thinking has led me to across this twitter account, the more pertinent question to ask (because this is the subject of my entire twitter intervention) is: Where has your philosophizing led *you?*

We Became the Tools of the Right

Maybe, instead of doing what the right wanted us to do 40 years ago, which was to abandon the left parties and the unions, we should have stuck harder with them?

[It is possible, of course, to make the case that the beginning of all this 'letting the right get away with it' lies in the millenarianism of all communist/anarchist revolutionaries, those who, like the Decembrists of the 1820s, prefer "a fine death."]

How do we engage with 'the left' when so much of what it does is betrayal? I think that we need to kind of go back to 19th century positions and work assiduously to bring about more 'social justice.' We need to get involved in unions and political parties.

Perhaps the 'failure' of the left and the unions has been due, more than a little, to our being 'taken-in' by the right (by Thatcher and Reagan), and believing they were useless because they failed and were destroyed?

Of course, we (the milieu I was part of — which has now, in its worst iteration, become the 'post-left') wanted communism — in a kind of 'all or nothing' way. 'More of the same' was not appealing to us, so much so that we became against 'the left' on principle.

I grew up under Thatcher and if I look at how my thought developed in a kind of counter-intuitive way, I can see that I was not an antagonistic response to Thatcher but a 'child' of Thatcher.

Nihil Evadere

Before I got involved in anything I already distrusted the left and the unions. When I did get involved I went straight to anarchism. But I moved ideologically quite quickly, soon becoming essentially 'ultra-leftist.'

Throughout I was involved somewhat in unions and various strikes etc. However, I also 'knew' it was all a lost cause; the miners were defeated, the print workers were defeated.

Although the unions were never going to make a revolution, their disappearance made the possibility of a revolution an ever-fading fantasy. So I was 'outside and against' the unions, [while still being an active union member, so I wasn't really 'outside'] while still participating in 'discontent.'

My developing anti-politics was exactly what Thatcher 'wanted' for the far-left. We all, across the whole spectrum of the left, essentially and effectively, gave up.

So, 'anti-politics' was a product of things like Thatcherism and Reaganism, and it suited their purposes. It was never really an anti-politics it was just a coma. And now the waking up from the coma has proven to be a drift to the crazy-right and Christianity.

It is still, of course, an expression of defeat, but defeat is so eloquently written about in theological texts, and so theology has become the new means by which to express the uncertainty and doubt, the 'weakness,' 'sin,' 'destitution,' and 'destituent potential.'

Atheism is good. Anyway, people involved in church stopped believing decades ago — because none of us, apart from those who follow Agamben, can now believe in God (unless one does it like Spinoza, but that's atheism). These days only the anti-political believe in God.

The influence of Salvador Dalí is testament to the enduring charm of the 'apolitical' attitude. Dalí 'withdrew' from politics as splits within the Surrealists intensified and instead became a fan of Hitler, Franco, and later, the noösphere.

The most effective voices now for the return of the church are people like Agamben and the whole of this 'anti-politics,' or 'post-left' milieu. So, there is need of atheism now more than ever.

It could begin with the debunking of Walter Benjamin, and the whole 'messianic' discourse. If one starts with Benjamin, and the influences on him, then Heidegger and Agamben might suddenly disappear like crossed-out cartoon characters.

What, at least, we can know is that the 'anti-left' and their hangers-on, and Agamben and the Heideggerians, are still doing the work of Thatcher and Reagan all these years later.

Anti-politics, communization theory, nihilist communism, etc., have become 'post-left' and anti-left, and a new kind of 'anti-woke' conservative Christianity — Thatcher and Reagan must be smiling with deep satisfaction.

The Biomedical Security State

An article on the origins of the term, 'biomedical security state,' coined by Josiah Lippincott, who writes:
"Ordinary citizens must fight back against this biomedical security state." And...

"Our leaders, like Ron DeSantis, are right to lead the charge." Lippincott asserts that "Agamben is a prophet of our time."
https://www.theamericanconservative.com/articles/seeing-the-biomedical-security-state/

[*The American Conservative*, Sept. 2021]

[Elena Lange agrees: "Agamben is the theorist of our political time."]

Should we all go Pentecostal now, Father?

Frère Dupont ('Nihilist Communism') and his associated milieu tend toward a right-wing, individualist, Christianity.

Certainly their religiosity/theology does *not* tend toward the kind of Christianity that seeks social justice, or that which is often concerned with the plight of the poor or dispossessed. They prefer monks who live in the woods and agonize over 'grace' and what it is to 'be.'

Nihil Evadere

At least two long time 'brothers' (they use this term for each other) are 'pro-life' and anti-abortionist [they have, for example, positively retweeted 'pro-life' texts], and (probably) against gay marriage (as is Jacques Camatte, of course — who is against gay marriage for traditionalist reasons rather than via a specifically Christian conservatism).

There are direct connections with magazines such as *The American Conservative, Athwart, New Atlantis, First Things,* and others.

They are also, by varying degrees, 'covidskeptic' and 'traditionalist,' and they promote right-wing propaganda on the virus. They associate online with pro-Republicans and 'grifters' like Aimee Terese.

They are anti-left and anti-strike, though they endorse the demonstrations of the anti-vaxxers who have a well-known far-right pedigree.

They regard these anti-vax demos — which are dominated by media personalities (emergent and established) *who are monetizing the phenomenon* (following the Trump model) — as "a fragment of the real."

To grasp the trajectory of FD — from ultra-left to effectively far-right — one must recognize the Heideggerian influence, particularly via Agamben. This influence is, ofc, riven thru current scholarly, 'revolutionary,' and religious discourse. FD is part of the bandwagon.

One doesn't have to have read much Agamben to have absorbed him. He is quoted and praised profusely in academic and 'radical' literature. Like Heidegger, his great mentor, he writes 'inscrutably.' Agamben is the 'Chauncey Gardiner' of the Academy.

It is amusing that, mainly via the influence of Agamben (and his use of Heidegger, Benjamin, and St. Paul) those who might once have become atheist anarchists are now joining seminaries.

In the work *I am not Chuang, Frère Dupont* outlines a strategy for increasing the appeal of communism by using the stylistic tools and methods of the new right, the 'neo-reaction.' To this end he pushes far-right propaganda.

How many are on board with this strategy? It's certainly not a pretty strategy, since it means reading the words and thoughts of far-right figures, and then promoting them. It is perhaps a strategy of 'reverse cryptofascism,' or maybe it could be termed *cryptocommunism*?

I am not Chuang by FD is an exercise in narcissism. He writes elsewhere on twitter, in regard to his writing: "It often strikes me that I try to do the work of the world." [More recently his kitsch hubris is expressed in these terms: "I see myself as an underground man, a sexton beetle, nothing but an agent of mechanical decomposition."]

Jesus and FD carry the same burden upon their shoulders, this gives them the right to be aggrieved: "*Eloi, Eloi, lama sabachthani?*" (The Cry of Dereliction).

The above observations are drawn from past knowledge of (which I've only recently been able to process), and recent engagements with, the FD milieu.

It is useful to see how the intellectual genealogy of the FD milieu — *particularly because we all share much of it* — has led them, and others, into such an abhorrent ideological mess.

It's The Dialectic, My Dear

A thread touching on why 'communist/anarchist revolutionaries' of the anti-left persuasion (ie, for example, all the 'once and future' ultra-leftists) are, necessarily, a bit weak and confused:

Dialectics are a phenomenon of philosophy, logic, and argument: a framework for attempting to establish knowledge, or a truth, between contradictory perceptions or opinions. (The dialectic, as Deleuze and Guattari noted, leads to "interminable discussion.")

Marx, via Hegel, transferred this idea to history and created a way of narrating history that showed how opposing social and economic forces created new conditions.

The novelty of this approach (towards how history is made) lay in the objection to the traditional idea that it was powerful individuals who made history rather than the social and economic forces that created those powerful figures.

The consideration of the two conflicting approaches to how history is made — the traditional and the Marxist — have sparked much intellectual debate of course. If Hitler had not been born would another person have fulfilled his role?...

'Men make history,' Marx wrote, 'but not of their own choosing.'

Philosophy is fun... meanwhile...

But Marx's 'materialist conception of history,' being equipped with the lens of the dialectic, had an extra power: it was predictive. And at that point Marx departed from his science and donned a holy robe.

Marx could now see the endpoint of history. Capitalism would give birth to communism.

But it didn't.

('History,' of course and in fact, can only be understood, or rather, interpreted, with differing levels of 'weight' or plausibility — depending upon the era in which the interpretation is presented — from the vantage point of the future.)

And there is no scientist of Marx's caliber around now to convince us that he wasn't wrong and it's just taking longer than expected. So we are left with the last seminarian (taliban) defenders of Marx, descended from *Socialisme ou Barbarie*, Debord, Dauvé, etc...

For example, *Cured Quail* write:

"the proletariat, state and capital all share a common interest: life in its inverted form. To abolish one was always to abolish them all."

But what evidence is there for this (sacred?) formulation? Is it not a statement of faith similar to a belief in 'the afterlife' or the return of Jesus?

(But maybe I am wrong to take them at their word. Perhaps nothing *Cured Quail* and the anti-left milieu write is actually serious, riven, as it is, with a knowing 'weariness' — one must remain, of course, 'cool' and disdainful.)

We are socially constructed beings; we are formed by our society (a society of proletarians, a State, and capital). Therefore, how we are created is how we create...

Marx taught us this, but then he effectively denied it, and it is his denial of his own method that the last students of Marx grasp hold of.

But let's play along with *Cured Quail* a little here, if they are using the Marxian dialectic here, how are they using it?

Perhaps they mean that these things that are 'us' (proletarian, State, capital) will be abolished by social and economic forces beyond our conscious will? But it doesn't sound like it, since they have consciously stated 'what must be,' as if, like Marx, they already know it.

So, the dialectic, if they are using it, is a matter of faith. And if they're not consciously using it here, then they are repeating the last mantras of a faith that once seemed 'revolutionary' but has proven otherwise, except for the pious, who refuse to abandon their church.

Cured Quail's anti-left prognoses regarding society are weak and confused (though monetizable by the Academy) because they are holding onto the shirttails of Marx's big millenarian and Idealist mistake.

But it is important to remember that Marx's way of viewing society (minus the prediction of communism) is fundamental to us. Isaiah Berlin noted that his methodology forms "part of the permanent background of civilized thought."

(Indeed, it could be said that we are now all 'marxists,' even the fascists, perhaps especially the fascists — or at least the anti-pluralist totalitarian-ists of every shade, which, of course, includes the anti-leftists.)

But whether Marx was a genius individual without whom history would have been different, or whether he was the product of his times, and another would have filled his shoes, is also up for fun intellectual and academic debate.

Cured Quail and the others form the last limping prophets of proletarian revolution; they speak of 'revolution' as mystical immanence which is apparently understood by their mostly academic flock, but which cannot ever be revealed in concrete, non-mystical, terms.

The 'science of revolution' (the Marxian dialectic) that Marx elaborated has been shown to be quite unscientific, and now, after the 20th century, all that is left to the true believers is a retreat into Marxian ecclesiology, communicant gibberish, and a quietist hope.

Nihil Evadere

These anti-left Holy Joe's, or alternative Jehovah's Witnesses, still insist that their (evidence-less) faith is truth, while also insisting, like the left-communists they are descended from, that communism has never happened:

Endnotes (Jasper Bernes):
"In the successful revolution...";

Frere Dupont ('I am not Chuang')
"Communism [is the] human community at its fullest amplitude";

Théorie Communiste (quoted by *Cured Quail*):
"After the communist revolution there is no more society."

In previous times over the last two hundred years such contradictory matters of faith (eg the contradiction between knowing what a revolution is despite never having seen one, or even having read about one) led many theorists to an early and mad grave.

But maybe the current anti-left communists are too cynical and witty for such an inglorious end.

The sooner that this millenarianism (of Marx; anarchism; and the destituent or 'coming' politics of Heidegger, Agamben, and Tiqqun; and Talibanism, etc) is revealed as what it is and then abandoned completely, the better. We've other, less crazy and more useful, things we should be doing.

> The second issue of *Skewered Snail*, a journal exploring "the potential of potentiality with particular regard for the illegibility of language and the failure of art to establish communism" is due in 2034. It will feature a cover composed of feathers and coffee beans, set in resin.

Mystifying Folk

Joshua Clover writes:

"It [the State] is not the source of our unfreedom, just the manager thereof."

Our notion of 'freedom' is an Enlightenment myth. The possibility of — the confused misnomer of — 'true freedom' in *any* kind of life is a communist, or radical democratic, myth.

The idea that we are 'willing slaves' of 'authority', the State, or Capital is founded upon a disdain for 'the unenlightened' mixed with confusion about why we have the State/civilization. The State is indeed the manager of us, but not in the way Joshua Clover thinks it is.

It cannot be removed, transcended, or dissolved because the reason it exists is not due to 'power' but demography (which one cannot or, rather, must not, attempt to alter — for example, by nutjob revolutionary eco-fascist decree).

Capital-ism

Despite an apparent 'rationality' global industrial society is suffused with myth. Eg, the myth of 'race,' 'nationalism,' 'God,' of 'work,' of 'identity,' etc. There is also the myth of 'Capital.'

Of course, in all these myths there is an element of reality or, at least, all these myths have an effect on 'reality' (whatever one deems 'reality' to be, ofc).

The myth of capital, as derived from Marx, is a cultural phenomenon of the State. We socially reproduce our society in a State form, we have no choice in this: a State is the only way to manage a large population. The myth of capital, like other myths, obscures a simpler reality.

Those academic communists who insist on engaging in lengthy Marxian hermeneutics on the subject of 'capital' only serve to distance their readers even further from the reality of our daily lives.

But even Marx let himself be carried away with the dynamics of his own myth after stumbling upon the 'essence' of what 'capital-ism' is. But he should have stayed at his beginning point and mined that initial observation.

In 'Capital,' Marx defined two ways of creating a surplus from the labor of others. The first is the extraction of *'absolute surplus value'* (asv). Extracting asv means profiting from the labor of others by making them work longer or harder or getting more of them to work.

Nihil Evadere

This economic model comes up against predictable limits: people die from overwork; you can't get enough of them; they cost too much to keep healthy; and so on. The second way of creating a profit is to make improvements in the organization of their tasks,

and to introduce machinery to allow labor time to be more productive. This second way is called the extraction of *'relative surplus value'* (rsv) — and it is the prime motor of capital-ism. The profits available from this second way of doing things are dependent not upon absolutes

like the number of workers, or the availability of a resource, but upon the entrepreneurs' ability to innovate production, supply, and distribution methods so that profits increase *relative* to other factors that remain constant or that might even be reduced.

New methods or machinery, for example, and as we all know, may mean less workers are needed.

But capital-ism did not always exist, something specific brought it into existence, and we can sense that capital-ism is different to all previous economic forms

because of the remarkable phenomenon of the Industrial Revolution. Suddenly three hundred years ago the scene was set for going from handloom to power-loom weaving... then to trains, cars, to splitting atoms, to computers, smart phones, etc.

The Industrial Revolution was not the natural culmination of five thousand years of the rise and fall of civilizations since Mesopotamia, it was not the result of a growing intelligence in humanity that enabled individuals to master what we call science and technology:

it was the coming together of the weaving industry, dominated by work-ethic oriented Protestants; gold from the Americas; and the Atlantic Slave Trade.

The key factor in this revolution of human and planetary existence was the profit-making strategy developed by the weaving entrepreneurs of Northern and Western Europe.

These merchants set up efficient supply and distribution networks around the core productive unit of the woollen weaver who worked at home, and crucially they ensured their weavers had efficient handlooms to enable higher productivity.

The gold and the slavery, and the Protestantism, only helped support the new economic method and ensure that it had the space and time to spread to other ventures and become universally successful.

The new economic method was the extraction of rsv, as Marx termed it. The method fitted in perfectly with the emergent work ethic of the Protestant movement in Europe — and the gold and the slavery buoyed up the new environment until it was fully established.

But it was the extraction of rsv — in a word, *capital*-ism — that ultimately and essentially triggered the Industrial Revolution.

Whether workers are slaves or peasants or hired labor is not the issue for defining a capital-ist enterprise — it is the fact that profits are used to generate even greater profits by investing in improved production methods, *and that money is not left idle.*

In capital-ism people became a special type of resource — one that can be eternally adapted to work at different rhythms, in new situations, with new machinery and processes — entrepreneurs realized that humans were adaptable and could learn new skills.

The Industrial Revolution was the culmination of various chance forces combining rather than the expression of a triumph of concerted human will.

The social organization and astonishing technology we see in the world around us is less the invention of bright people who have been well-educated and more the product of the imperative to increase rsv, the capital-ist way of increasing profits.

The appearance of the steam engine owes more to the strategy or, rather, social imperative of acquiring rsv than it does to the acclaimed genius of James Watt.

And the consequences of the emergence of the systematic acquisition of rsv were increased monetary wealth for *a whole class* — who, crucially, now knew that to stay rich they had to keep innovating and investing. The emergence of the 'science' we have today was, also, not the culmination of eons of human ingenuity — it was the result of this same particular method of pursuing wealth, as it still is.

It was only during "the great watershed of the sixteenth century" that it became apparent that capital-ist production had become the dominant economic mode in western Europe. It is only in a fully capital-ist mode of production that the whole of society is geared towards,

as well as determined by, the raising of the relative productivity of each worker. This is the motive for technological innovation. It is why today, when capital-ism has become part of our very DNA, we witness a proliferation of James Watts'.

So, the enormous technological 'achievements' during and after the Industrial Revolution are not some magical culmination of human history...

they are the specific result of a society that emerged by organizing itself on the principle of being able to extract an infinite sum of profit from the ever-adaptable resource of the human being.

Absolute Tyranny

Within the big tent of 'left' millenarianism (which is subsumed within the bigger tent of 'millenarianism of all shades') there are many tendencies, often more opposed to each other than articulate about what they think they want. So the earnestness of someone such as

Mark Fisher is different to the pro-Situ aesthetic of *Tiqqun/The Invisible Committee*. But today 'left' millenarianism is a wholly literary and academic event, it is only the 'right' millenarianism of Dugin or the Taliban, for eg, that exists as a more authentic 'praxis.'

Of course, all millenarianisms quickly lead to the demolition of 'pluralism' and the establishment of absolute tyranny, even in their 'micro,' or 'emergent' cult form, as Jonestown, or Debord and Bernstein's adventures with the Letterists and the SI, proved.

> Although many believe that toilet paper is made from the melancholy of fallen angels it is, in reality, composed from the dust left behind by butterfly wings.

Mickey Moosenhauer

17 Just One More Thing...

The notion that one can collectively or individually will one's emancipation from one's society is a fundamental error. One cannot escape the society that defines one and, because it is society that defines us, we cannot redefine society in any meaningfully different way.

The only reason that some of us entertain the possibility that we can emancipate ourselves by some revolutionary or total turnaround is because the logos of our society is built on constant change and renewal, transmitted ideologically to us through the narrative that we are 'free' (in the right circumstances) to change ourselves and to change the world around us.

Hermits, for example, may appear to have escaped society, but they have only taken it with them, inside of them. They have only made themselves unsocial. All social revolutionary transformations of society, since history began, have been unable to dispense with hierarchy, exploitation, and tyranny. They have been unable to redefine society properly because the revolutionaries are defined by their society. There is no way out of the loop.

The only peoples, in recent times, who have 'escaped' their society have 'escaped' it against their wishes — *one cannot choose to abandon who one is* — because they were colonized.

INDEX

Aarons, Kieran, 10, 79, 83-4, 84 n. 16, 85-7, 88-9, 92 n. 25, 97-9, 102, 105, 108, 112
Agamben, Giorgio 9ff., 77ff., 122, 133 n. 42, 135 n. 45, 161, 166ff., 191, 235 n. 1, 238ff.
Allen, Ansgar, 77, 168, 180
Althusser, Louis, 47-8
Anabaptists, 24-5, 130-1
Anderson, Stephanie, 156, 222, 230
'anti-vaxxers' 10-1, 239ff.
Arendt, Hannah, 106-7, 242-3, 247, 248

Bachofen, Jakob, 10, 121, 226, 256-8
Bacon, Francis, 20
Badiou, Alain, 61ff., 67-8, 71, 87
Bakunin, Mikhail, 43-4, 54, 56, 63 n. 91, 68, 70-1, 74, 199 n. 7, 209-10
Banaji, Jairus, 31, 154, 155
Bartleby, 90 n. 23, 105 n. 45, 112
Baudrillard, Jean, 12, 91-2, 106 n. 46, 164-5, 166, 168, 187, 189, 228, 231
Beaufret, Jean, 250ff.
Beckett, Samuel, 250ff.
Benjamin, Walter 10, 80ff., 98ff., 107-9, 226, 240, 252, 256-8, 266-7
Berardi, Franco 'Bifo,' 78, 82, 164
Berlin, Isaiah, 37, 71, 270
Bernes, Jasper, 135 n. 45, 271
Bernstein, Eduard, 44
Bernstein, Michèle, 49, 276
'biomedical security state,' 266
Black, Carol, 182
'Bloom Theory,' 94, 104, 109, 112, 167, 247, 252
Bockelson, Jan, 25, 46
Boehm, Christopher, 147 n. 64
Bonacci, Valeria, 102

Bookchin, Murray, 24 n. 20
Bordiga, Amadeo, 57ff., 63, 66, 68, 78, 82 n. 14, 87, 110-1, 120, 121, 225-7, 229, 242, 246
Bosteels, Bruno, 65-6, 69 n. 106
Boulanger, Nicolas-Antoine, 199-200
Bourdieu, Pierre, 228, 249ff.,
Boyle, Robert, 20, 39
Brahe, Tycho, 20
Braudel, Fernand, 188-9
Britt, Brian, 87-8
Broder, David, 238

Camatte, J., 10, 17 n. 6, 59-60, 63-4, 67 n. 102, 68, 77ff., 120ff., 161-2, 170, 182 n. 6, 220, 225-7, 229, 238, 240, 242, 245-6, 249, 254ff., 260, 263, 267
  Camatte on Heidegger, 12 n. 4
  as 'prophet,' 17 n. 6, 78-9, 140, 255
Camus, Albert, 13, 44 n. 46, 71 n. 109, 76-7, 106 n. 47, 112 130, 145, 148, 206 n. 1, 219
Capp, Bernard, 21-3, 31 n. 35
Carnevali, Barbara, 88 n. 21, 258
Castoriadis, Cornelius, 50-1, 55-6, 74
Castro, Fidel, 193, 216
Cayley, David, 243, 257
Cesarano, Giorgio, 168, 170
Cesari, Donatella Di, 114
Char, René, 250ff.
Chase, Atholl, 222, 230
Cimino, Antonio, 81, 88-9
Cioran, Emil, 125-6, 135 n. 34, 142
Clastres, Pierre, 19-20, 69, 129, 141, 188, 20-4
Clover, Joshua, 272
Cohen, G. A., 40ff., 65
Cohen, Margaret, 92 n. 26
Cohn, Norman, 23ff.

278

Collu, G., 162, 170
Comunione e Liberazione, 120-1
CounterPunch, 9
Coupat, Julien, 92 n. 25, 93 n. 28, 95 n. 33
Covid, 80, 114, 139, 191, 239ff.
Cromwell, Oliver, 31, 143, 193, 215
Cultural Revolution (Shanghai Commune) 61-2
Cured Quail, 56, 269ff.

Dali, Salvador, 265
Dauvé, Gilles, 51, 52-3, 55, 56, 59, 65, 66ff., 83, 97 n. 34, 133 n. 40, 238, 254, 269
Debord, Guy, 12, 49-50, 55 n. 73, 93-4, 121 n. 2, 161-2, 205, 211, 220, 261, 269, 276
Deleuze, G. and Guattari, F., 61 n. 85, 64, 122, 164-5, 173, 176, 178, 196, 200, 203, 212ff., 221, 250, 268
    D&G's Heideggerianism, 215
    'Deleuzed,' 259
destituency:
    as 'potential/power/politics' 9, 10, 80-1, 89, 95, 104, 108, 247, 250, 258, 265, 271
    'destituent partisanship' (Aarons) 97-8
    'destituent times' (Heidegger) 10
    'destituent violence' (Agamben) 98-9
    destituent vs constituent power 97
    'insurrectionary destitution' (Aarons) 102
    'messianic destituency' 79
Deutscher, Isaac, 45-6

Einstein, Albert, 39-40, 43, 54
Eller, Cynthia, 121 n. 3, 256

Endnotes, 53 n. 68, 56, 63 n. 91, 66ff., 71, 95 n. 33, 97 n. 34, 122, 131-2, 135, 238, 241, 261, 271
Engels, Friedrich, 37 n. 35, 38, 40, 42-3, 48, 132 n. 38, 198
Esteva, Gustav, 180, 200-3

Ferguson, R. Brian, 178
Feuerbach, Ludwig, 37, 123, 183-4, 187, 197
Foucault, Michel, 12, 51, 111 n. 49, 113, 162, 164, 172-3, 210, 212, 214, 215, 220-1, 228, 231, 245
Frankfurt School, 12, 51 n. 60, 59 n. 78
Fusaro, Diego, 121, 244, 245-6

Galileo, 20
Goldman, Emma, 159, 168, 170
Goodall, Jane, 176, 183ff.
Gorky, Maxim, 146 n. 62
Goulet, Jean-Guy, 180, 181
Gramsci, Antonio, 57, 225
Grossman, Vasily, 25 n. 23, 145-6
Gurevich, A.J., 137, 189

Hamacher, Werner, 99-100
Han, Byung-Chul, 253
Harari, Yuval Noah, 176-8, 183, 191, 221
Hardt, Michael, see *Negri*
Harvey, David, 37-8
Heidegger, M., 9ff., 108, 115, 122, 125 n. 18, 235 n. 1, 238, 241, 241, 243-5, 246ff., 258-9, 259, 266, 267, 271
    Heideggerian communists/leftists, 165
Henkel, Heiko, 201
Hill, Christopher, 20ff., 129
Hins, Eugène, 209
Historical Materialism, 238
Hodder, Ian, 175-6, 178

human consciousness as "superficial and falsifying," 73, 183

Ill Will Editions, 9ff., 56, 71, 72 n. 110, 241, 247, 248, 258
Illich, Ivan, 257
Israel, Jonathan, 36 n. 33, 196, 199,

James, brother of Jesus, 84
James, C.L.R., 229-230, 231
Jaspers, Karl, 17, 26ff., 32, 36, 130, 247
Jesi, Furio, 256
Jesus, 15-16, 18, 84-5, 113, 211, 215, 260, 268, 269
Johnson, Agnes, 234
Johnson, Mary Jane, 234

Kafka, Franz, 82, 83, 106, 167
Kalinga Institute of Social Sciences, 179ff.
Katsafanas, Paul, 73 n. 113, 183 n. 2
Kautsky, Karl, 96, 207, 209-10
Kepler, Johannes, 20
Kierkegaard, Søren, 258-9
Kohn, Eduardo, 232, 233, 237
Kopenawa, Davi, 15, 15 n. 4, 190, 233, 236
Kotsko, A, 11 n. 1
Krader, Lawrence, 158, 170
Kropotkin, Peter, 159, 170
Kunuk, Zacharias, (*Atanarjuat: The Fast Runner*), 222 n. 1

Lange, Elena Louisa, 121, 238-40, 266
Le Roy Ladurie, Emmanuel, 189
Lefebvre, Henri, 55 n. 72, 250
Lenin, 25, 25 n. 23, 40 n. 38, 44 n. 46, 47-8, 48 n. 53, 52, 69-70, 94, 96ff., 99, 106, 106 n. 47, 110, 143, 146, 195, 205ff.
anarchism as a subcategory of Leninism: 210-1
definition of Leninism: 205
precursor: 25
Lennard, Natasha, 212ff.
Leibniz, G.W., 79 n. 10, 199
Lévi-Strauss, Claude, 73-4, 229, 233
L'Ouverture, Toussaint, 215, 231
Lowry, Malcolm, 226
Lukács, György, 202 n. 16
Luxemburg, Rosa, 40 n. 38, 44-5, 57

Machiavelli, 45-6
MacIntyre, Alasdair, 160, 170-1
Malick, Terrence, 235 n. 1, 245
Mallarmé, Stéphane, 108
Mandel, Ernest, 29 n. 28, 40 n. 38, 68, 138
Mao, 93 n. 27
Marx, Karl,
    As prophet 36ff.
    As scientist 37ff.
Mathews, Shailer, 84
Matthys, Jan, 24ff.
Mattis, Léon de, 97 n. 34
Mbembe, Achille, 163-4, 171
Melville, Herman, 90 n. 23, 105 n. 45, 112 n. 50
Merleau-Ponty, Maurice, 74
millenarianism (definition) 129-130
Monsieur Dupont/Frère Dupont, 133, 135, 166, 238ff., 259, 263, 266-8, 271
    'I am not Chuang,' 267-8, 271, 133 n. 42, 239, 241
Müller, Jan Werner, 212, 215
Müntzer, Thomas, 24

Nadsady, Paul, 233-4, 237, 180
Nancy, Jean-Luc, 115
Napier, John, 21, 71
Negri, Antonio, 61, 62, 69

Negri on Agamben's
'Heideggerism,' 112-3, 243
Newton, Isaac, 20-1, 71
Nietzsche, Frederick, 10, 73, 88 n. 21, 122 n. 4, 172-3, 183, 220, 229, 231
Nihilist Communism, 6, 9ff., 166, 238, 242, 266
Not Bored!, 49 n. 57, 50 n. 59, 53 n. 65, 92 n. 25, 93 n. 28

Oates, Joyce Carol, 90 n. 23

Pannekoek, Anton, 40 n. 38, 47
parametric determinism, 138
pedagogical society, 177, 180, 182, 195
Pelletier, Narcisse, 222
Petersen, Dale, 185
Pinker, Steven, 32, 233-4, 153, 176, 178, 183ff.
politics and religion:
  chronological relationship, 15
Pomeranz, Kenneth, 28
Prakash, Madhu Suri, 200-3
Preliminary Materials for a Theory of the Young-Girl (Tiqqun), 97-8

Rasmussen, Mikkel Bolt, 93-4, 105, 112
Red Brigades, 120-1
Reich, Wilhelm, 212ff.
Rexroth, Kenneth, 24 n. 20
Rhodes, Carl, 227
Rocker, Rudolf, 209
Ross, Alison, 99, 100-2, 104, 108, 164
Rousseau, J-J, 13, 144-5, 158, 176, 193-4, 202-3, 212, 217, 218, 219
Rühle, Otto, 110, 165-6

Sartre, Jean-Paul, 259
Sass, Stephen L., 175-8

Schmitt, Carl, 80, 88, 94, 95-6, 106, 242-3 244, 245, 248
Seth, Anil, 173
Situationism/Situationist/*Situationist International*, 48-50, 51, 53, 69, 92 n. 25, 93-4, 105, 132 n. 37, 133 n. 40, 241, 262
Slezkine, Yuri, 16 n. 5, 17-8, 129-131
Skafish, Peter, 235
Smith, Linda Tuhiwai, 159-60
Socialisme ou Barbarie, 12, 50, 53, 59, 63, 122, 238, 242, 269
Sorel, Georges, 99ff., 104 n. 43, 209, 98
Sori, Soni, 179-80
Spinoza, Baruch, 36, 141, 196-7, 199-200, 202, 265
Stalin, 25, 59, 106 n. 47, 145
  precursor: 25
State, emergence of, 142-5
Stirrat, Roderick, 201
Suddendorf, Thomas, 73 n.111, 174, 185
'suicide of sadness' (Emile Durkheim), 153, 224, 230
survivalism, 177, 190-1

Tarì, Marcello, 86 n.19, 101,
Théorie communiste (TC, or Roland Simon), 52ff., 65, 66ff., 71, 72, 97 n. 34, 146 n. 62, 238, 271
Thompson, E.P., 155, 156
Tiqqun (*The Invisible Committee*)/*Imaginary Party*, 9ff., 51-2, 76ff., 160, 166-8, 238ff.;
  Manifeste conspirationiste (2022), 241-2
  tiqqun/tikkun name derived from Walter Benjamin, 92 n. 26
time, 137, 189
Tkachev, Pyotr, 94

Tönnies, Ferdinand, 10
traditionalism, 10ff., 120-2, 165, 238ff.
Tronti, Mario, 110, 119
Trotsky, 40 n. 38, 44, 45-6, 69, 209
　Trotskyism, 40 n. 38, 68
Tuck, Eve, and K. Wayne Yang, 200, 203

Van der Linden, Marcel, 238
Vaneigem, Raoul, 49, 53, 87 n. 19
Vico, Giambattista, 94 n. 30
Virilio, Paul, 214-5
vitalism, left vitalism, 244, 246, 244
Viveiros de Castro, Eduardo, 15 n. 4, 232ff.
Voltaire, 111, 138, 140, 199

Weber, Max, 32ff.
Williams, Evan Calder, 97 n. 34
Wilson, E.O., 176, 185
Winstanley, Gerrard, 21, 22, 143, 215
Wittgenstein, Ludwig, 115
Wood, Ellen Meiksins, 28ff., 159
Woolf, Virginia, 73 n. 113
Wootton, David, 145, 193
Wrangham, Richard, 176, 185
writing as a phenomenon emerging from 'accountancy,' 73
Wu, Yiching, 62

Zartaloudis, Thanos, 101-2
Žižek, Slavoj, 62, 87, 99, 100, 208, 210, 211
Zombie ant fungus, 161
Zoroaster, 9, 17-8, 130, 260, 262
Zwickau Prophets, 24

Reviews of
The Freedom of Things: An Ethnology of Control,
Peter Harrison, TSI Press, 2017:

"There is a root honest politeness in Harrison's handling of scholarly literature, where he frequently fairly summarizes a work's argument, then admits that this conclusion is indeed a logical one, and yet offers a counter one of his own while salvaging data or portions of arguments that support his work.

 The Freedom of Things is the most interesting anthropological work I've read in years, with some stunning passages that strike me as Sahlinsian. Some portions require serious work to navigate, but this is a work worthy of the effort."

David H. Price, *Journal of the Royal Anthropological Institute*,
Volume 25, Issue 4, December 2019

"Harrison's ethnographic focus provides a wealth of insight that should provide fertile ground for debate over issues of principle, not just practice, within radical politics, the importance of posing problems which are themselves forms of theoretical anti-production, and through which one might offer not just more solutions, but perceive the solutions on offer through a more critical lens."

Jared McGeough, *Anarchist Studies*,
Volume 27, Issue1, January 2019

"He's very well-read, and catholic in his range, drawing on up-to-date popular writing [...] as well as hard-headed academic work. [...] But he's blessedly lacking in obscurantism, and allows his passion for communication to steer his style between jargon and excessive abstraction on the one hand, and dumbing-down or patronizing on the other."

Gyrus, *Dreamflesh* Website,
October 2017.

Printed in Great Britain
by Amazon